# New Managerialism in Education

*Also by Kathleen Lynch*

THE HIDDEN CURRICULUM

EQUALITY IN EDUCATION

SCHOOLS AND SOCIETY IN IRELAND

EQUALITY AND POWER IN SCHOOLS: *Redistribution, Recognition and Representation*

INSIDE CLASSROOMS: *The Teaching and Learning of Mathematics in Social Context*

EQUALITY: *From Theory to Action*

AFFECTIVE EQUALITY: *Love, Care and Injustice*

*Also by Dympna Devine*

IMMIGRATION AND SCHOOLING IN THE REPUBLIC OF IRELAND

CHILDREN POWER AND SCHOOLING: *How Childhood is Structured in the Primary School*

# New Managerialism in Education

## Commercialization, Carelessness and Gender

Kathleen Lynch
*University College Dublin, Ireland*

Bernie Grummell
*National University of Ireland, Maynooth*

and

Dymphna Devine
*University College Dublin, Ireland*

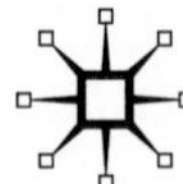



First published 2012 by
PALGRAVE MACMILLAN

Palgrave Macmillan in the UK is an imprint of Macmillan Publishers Limited, registered in England, company number 785998, of Houndmills, Basingstoke, Hampshire RG21 6XS.

Palgrave Macmillan in the US is a division of St Martin's Press LLC, 175 Fifth Avenue, New York, NY 10010.

Palgrave Macmillan is the global academic imprint of the above companies and has companies and representatives throughout the world.

Palgrave® and Macmillan® are registered trademarks in the United States, the United Kingdom, Europe and other countries.

ISBN 978–0–230–27511–9

This book is printed on paper suitable for recycling and made from fully managed and sustained forest sources. Logging, pulping and manufacturing processes are expected to conform to the environmental regulations of the country of origin.

A catalogue record for this book is available from the British Library.

Library of Congress Cataloging-in-Publication Data
Lynch, Kathleen, 1951–
New managerialism in education: commercialization, carelessness, and gender / Kathleen Lynch, Bernie Grummell, Dympna Devine.
p. cm.
ISBN 978–0–230–27511–9 (hardback)
1. Education—Economic aspects—Ireland. 2. Education and state—Ireland. 3. School management and organization—Ireland. 4. Sex differences in education—Ireland. 5. Neoliberalism—Ireland. I. Grummell, Bernie, 1972– II. Devine, Dympna. III. Title.
LC67.I73L96 2012
338.4'73709417—dc23 2012011162

10 9 8 7 6 5 4 3 2 1
21 20 19 18 17 16 15 14 13 12

Printed and bound in Great Britain by
CPI Antony Rowe, Chippenham and Eastbourne

# Contents

# List of Figures and Tables

## Figures



## Tables

# Acknowledgements

Research for this book was funded by the Department of Education and Science, Gender Equality Unit. We gratefully acknowledge their support and particularly the assistance given by Rhona McSweeney with whom we liaised directly.

All books are a collective effort, as is *New Managerialism in Education*. It would not have been possible to complete the work without the help of many people. We would like to express our appreciation to all our colleagues in the Equality Studies Centre in the UCD School of Social Justice for their support and encouragement throughout the project. We are especially grateful to our first research assistant on the project, Siobhán Fleming-Underwood who assisted so ably in compiling data in the early stages of the project. Maureen Lyons and Margaret Crean worked tirelessly in helping to prepare the final text for submission; we thank them for their generous academic and personal support at this final stage; and Maureen for her work throughout the project. We also wish to thank our colleagues in the School of Education in UCD and those in both the Department of Education and the Department of Adult and Community Education in the National University of Ireland, NUI Maynooth. They facilitated Dympna and Bernie by giving them the time and space to help them complete work on the book.

There were many people who gave advice and guidance in planning the research, enabling us to enter into dialogue with educational leaders across the various sectors of education. We would like to express our appreciation to all of these, and in particular to those who served on the Advisory Board for the duration of the study. We are especially grateful to those in leadership positions in Irish education, at primary, second level and higher education, and in the Department of Education and Science, including management bodies, teacher unions, professional associations and a range of other stake holders in education. Without their assistance, the project could not have been successfully completed.

Principals of schools and those who hold senior posts in colleges of further and higher education are extremely busy people; they are frequently overworked. We wish to thank them sincerely for giving of their time so generously at interview. We also greatly appreciated the help of the various education journalists whom we interviewed for their insights on Irish education. We hope that this book will be of benefit to all of the people who contributed to it and that it will stimulate both a national and international debate about the impact of new managerialism on education.

Many thanks to our publishers, Palgrave Macmillan, for their support in completing the work, especially to Philippa Grand and Andrew James for nudging us along to completion.

Finally, we would like to thank our families and friends for their love and support, for giving us the 'freedom from necessity to write and to think'. As Pierre Bourdieu observed, it is a great privilege to have such freedom and we hope we have honoured it in this book. *Go raibh míle maith agaibh go léir.*

Some parts of this book are developed from articles that we have co-authored and published previously. An earlier version of Chapter 4 was published in the journal *Educational Administration and Leadership (2009)* while Chapter 7 is an updated version of a paper published in *Gender, Work and Organization (2010).* We are grateful to the publishers of these journals to allow us use material from these articles.

# Part I
# Governance in Irish Education

# 1
# New Managerialism as a Political Project: The Irish Case

The Irish government embraced new public service (NPS) management as a mode of governance to promote neo-liberal economic and social policies from the 1990s onwards (Collins, 2007). The project was framed as one of 'modernization', but the practices were not just 'modernist'; the technical processes involved in new managerialism were distinctly political.

This chapter opens with a brief overview of some of the core tenets of the new managerialism project and its alignment to neo-liberalism. It then proceeds to outline the historical and cultural context that facilitated the enactment of the new managerial and neo-liberal project[1] in Irish education in which this study is contextualized. The chapter explores how neo-liberalism became the reigning policy discourse in Ireland and, in particular,how it came to increasingly dictate educational discourses and practices, especially in higher education through a new managerial code. But the new managerial project has not had a free reign in Irish education. The chapter also explores the ways in which it was contested especially in primary and second level education.

## New managerialism

New managerialism is not a neutral management strategy, it is a political project, borne out of a radical change in the 'spirit of capitalism'.[2] It heralds a new mode of governance that provides a unique type of moral education for businesses and organizations modeled on business. It represents not only a change in management but a new form of capitalism:

> Management literature during the 1990s offered ideals, propositions for the organisation of people, and modes for structuring objects and

> forms of security – all of which were so different in nature from that which had been on offer during the 1960s that it is difficult not to conclude that capitalism has broadly changed its spirit in the past 30 years.
>
> (Boltanksi and Chiapello, 2005a: 166)

What was sought were

> lean companies that work in networks involving a wide range of actors; team-based or project-oriented work organisations, geared towards customer satisfaction; and workers' overall enthusiasm thanks to the vision of their leaders. Lean, 'light' and 'fat-free' firms … subcontract everything that is not part of their core business.
>
> (Boltanksi and Chiapello, 2005a: 181)

From the 1990s onwards, market-led models of control and regulation became the prototype for work organizations both inside and outside capitalism. New managerialism was not just about management, it was about establishing new set of values and practices embedded in a complex series of social, political and economic organizational changes (Clarke et al., 2000: 7). It focused on outputs over inputs, measured in terms of performance indicators; it proposed to break down large-scale organizations into smaller units; it emphasized the language of choice, competition and service users and it promoted the decentralization of budgetary and personal authority to line managers as well as project-led contractual employment arrangements (Chandler et al., 2002: 1054; Clarke and Newman, 1997; Clarke et al., 2000: 6; Court, 2004; Docking, 2000; Jennings and Lomas, 2003). What was significant about new managerialism is that it was not only exported through the veins of neo-liberalism between countries (Boltanksi and Chiapello, 2005b; Harvey, 2005), it was also exported systematically from the private to the public sector as a mode of governance. When applied to the public sector, it involved the inculcation of market values and practices into the regulation and organization of that sector (Farrell and Morris, 2003).

Within education, new managerialism redefined what counts as knowledge, who are the bearers of such knowledge and who is empowered to act – all within a legitimate framework of public choice and market accountability (Olssen and Peters, 2005). At the organizational level, Deem (2004) typifies new managerialism as comprising three overlapping elements consisting of a narrative of strategic change (persuading others towards new understanding and actions), a distinctive organizational form (as noted above) and, finally, a practical control technology that challenges established practices among professionals, not least of which is professional autonomy.

One of the purposes of new managerial reforms is to curb the power of professionals in public sector organizations (Farrell and Morris, 2003).[3] The enactment of performance indicators and the availability of surveillance mechanisms, instituted through new information technologies, made the task of managing and controlling professionals much more feasible than it had been hitherto. But while professionals needed to be controlled, their assistance was vital for the successful implementation of managerial reforms. Management complicity was vital for realizing the new managerial project, and for this reason the role of the senior manager or leader had to be reconstructed (Gleeson and Shain, 2003). The project of reconstructing educational leaders to enact new managerial reforms became a core part of public sector reforms in many European countries, including Ireland from the early 1990s (Houtsonen et al., 2010).[4]

## The historical context of the neo-liberal project in Ireland

Ireland operates within the Anglo-American zone of influence for reasons of history, culture, language, colonization and trade. It is not surprising therefore that it also displays many of the features of its powerful neo-liberal neighbours in terms of its social, health and education policies (Esping-Andersen, 1990; Houtsonen et al., 2010; Korpi and Palme, 1998; McDonnell and O'Donovan, 2009). While the tone and pace of neo-liberalism was accentuated in the Celtic Tiger era, Ireland was not a newcomer to pro-market politics in the 1990s. Ireland never had a socialist government or even a labour-led government that could successfully institute public control and ownership of key services, including education (Allen, 1997). Organized labour was not a powerful player in a state consumed by nationalism after the partitioning of the country in 1922. In post-independent Ireland, socialist, communist, and even social democratic labour politics were demonized as dangerous especially in the 1930s (Lee, 1989: 184). The Catholic Church played a key role in resisting anything that smacked of socialism. This became most evident in the late 1940s and 1950s when the Minister for Health Dr Noel Browne's attempt to introduce basic free public health care for mothers and young children was defeated by the power of the Catholic Church, augmented by the medical profession protecting their interests in private medicine (Lee, 1989: 313–22).

On the economic front, post-independent Ireland initially pursued a policy of free trade followed by a policy of protectionism which culminated in massive emigration, poverty and economic decline up to the 1950s: 'Ireland's overall growth performance in the 1950s was one of the worst in Europe, emigration reached record levels for this century, and confidence about the viability of the economy reached an all-time low' (Kennedy, Giblin and McHugh, 1988: 55) The lack of infrastructural investment in agriculture and in industrial research and development meant that Ireland was poorly placed to compete in European markets after accession to the EU in the 1970s (Lee, 1989). While it did develop large successful state-owned industries in key service areas, notably in energy and transport, and pursued some successful social projects, including a big public housing programme and rural electrification (Tony Fahey, 1999; Kennedy et al., 1988), it relied heavily on multinational capital in the form of foreign direct investment to revive the economy from the 1970s onwards (O'Hearn, 2003). Not only did Ireland become beholden to transnational capitalism, it was beholden to it through lack of regulation and low taxation.

> [S]ince the southern Irish state correctly realised that the main incentive to attract transnational corporations (TNCs) was low corporate taxes, it pursued a neo-liberal growth model that matched low taxes and fiscal restraint with minimal government interference in business.
>
> (O'Hearn, 2003: 35)

Moreover, it allowed inequality to rise through providing tax concessions to the wealthy at the expense of the poor and welfare dependent.

> [F]or several reasons, including a spurious association of fiscal restraint with economic success, the state abjectly failed to mobilise the fiscal resources that were created by rapid growth in order to reduce inequality and improve social welfare. Instead, it turned these resources back, through tax reductions that favoured the wealthier members of Irish society.
>
> (O'Hearn, 2003: 35)

As Ireland failed to develop economically after independence, it also failed to develop socially. It did not develop a strong welfare state comparable to those in Northern and Western Europe in the post-World War II era. There was a socially disengaged (and social justice indifferent) nationalism at the heart of official public thinking; this was coupled with minimal investment in academic scholarship and research in any social scientific field with the exception of neoclassical economics (Lee, 1989: 563–77). Although none of the major political parties in Ireland openly endorsed neo-liberal politics of Thatcherism in the late 1970s or 1980s, rising indebtedness[5] led to neo-liberalism being adopted through political pragmatism and opportunism rather than explicit ideology. The language of social democracy remained intact but the policy and practice belied the rhetoric. Ireland weakened its fragile welfare state by greatly reducing the means to fund it through taxation. After 1987, there was agreement on the three core principles of neo-liberalism, that (1) public spending had to be cut back, (2) tax cutting was the key to encouraging enterprise by individuals and companies and (3) wage costs had to be reduced and union power curbed through legislation (Allen, 2000: 14–15). The benefits and burdens of these policy decisions were not shared equally:

> In 1987, the top rate of tax on companies that were not exporting manufactured goods stood at fifty per cent. By 2002, the rate had dropped to 12.5% – the lowest in Europe. Capital gains tax was cut from forty per cent to twenty per cent. The social security contribution of employers at current prices had dropped from 3.2 per cent of GDP in 1988 to 2.7 per cent in 1996, the second lowest in the EU.
>
> (Allen, 2003: 69)

Social partnership was the guiding framework for policymaking (involving employers, trade unions, farmers and civil society organizations) from its inception in 1987 to its collapse with the economic crisis in 2008. Social partnership provided a forum for policymaking particularly in regulating wages; over time however, it became a cloak behind which deep inequalities were ritualistically named and then largely ignored (Allen, 2000; Meade, 2005).

While there were challenges to the neo-liberal orthodoxies from a variety of sources, including challenges from within the machinery of the State through the work of the Combat Poverty Agency (CPA) from 1986 to its closure in July 2009,[6] the research evidence the CPA provided was often only given token recognition at policy level. Disparities in wealth, wages and welfare continued to rise over the social partnership era (Cantillon, 2008). The work of civil society organizations promoting social justice, including religious bodies such as Conference of Religious in Ireland (CORI) Justice Group and the Community Workers'

Co-Operative was also given more rhetorical than policy recognition. By the end of the Celtic Tiger era there was a widespread feeling that people had been deceived and that the social partnership system had greatly advantaged a small elite at the expense of the majority, especially at the expense of those with low incomes and those on welfare (Allen, 2007; Murphy and Kirby, 2011).

Given its history of nationalism, sustained patterns of emigration of the young (and of the young and well-educated in the 1980s), and a deep-seated anti-intellectualism in the socio-political sphere (Chubb, 1982: 22), Ireland was a fertile ground in which to breed neo-liberal policies in the 1990s (Phelan, 2007). While there were dissenting voices in the academy challenging neo-liberal politics (Allen, 2000, 2007; Baker et al., 2004; Coulter and Coleman, 2003; Kirby, 2002; Lynch, 2006; Murphy, 2002; Meade, 2005), these were politically and intellectually subsumed under the weight of neo-liberal rhetoric promulgated within the machinery of the state (McSharry and White, 2000; Forfás, 2009).[7] Moreover, most academics were party to the national consensus that growth was good for Ireland even if inequalities persisted. There were voices of dissent but also of acquiescence (O'Connor, 2006). Not all of those who did focus on the growth of inequality that followed from neo-liberal policies thought that it was a major problem; they claimed that the levels and depths of deprivation in Ireland were a good deal more modest than suggested by radical critics of the Celtic Tiger (Fahey et al., 2007: 67–103).

Challenges to the Celtic Tiger ideology in the media from prominent journalists (O'Toole, 2009), were individualized events, construed by politicians and commercial interests as the 'axe grinding' of individual commentators. At a corporate level, the print and televisual media remained highly consensual, accepting the inevitability of poverty and inequality (Devereux, 1998; Titley, 2010).

In the global arena, the oil crisis in the 1970s heralded the beginning of the challenge to state-intervention policies in the economic field. The Keynesian social democracy principles guiding Western capitalist states, including Ireland, were systematically undermined. They were replaced with neo-liberal policies that involved offloading the cost of the welfare state from capital to labour through marketization, deregulation[8] and privatization of what were once public services. Competition in the market place took precedence over economic and social development guided by the state. Redistribution was treated as a subsidiary goal, and capital accumulation through 'growth' was and is the guiding principle of public policy (Harvey, 2005).

The success of the neo-liberal project in terms of increasing returns to capital was visible in a short time in Ireland. European Commission data showed declining returns to wages across Europe from 1990 onwards. The decline was especially evident in Ireland where 'data on the adjusted wage of the total economy ... indicates that the share distributed to wages declined [from 71.2% to 54%] and was faster in Ireland than in the original European Union 15' (Allen, 2010).[9]

The neo-liberal project had many dimensions, and one significant dimension was the belief that the market was the ideal mechanism for providing public services on a fee-for-service basis. This idea was promoted by a host of powerful financial and capital interests working through multilateral agencies such as the Organisation for Economic Co-Operation and Development (OECD) and the World Bank (Pollitt, 2003). It was a deliberate and planned response to the declining returns to capital identified in the 1970s (Harvey, 2005). While it impacted on all Western countries over the following 20 years (gaining pace after the breakup of Soviet-controlled Communist bloc of Eastern European states in the early 1990s), it was instituted to best effect in countries within the Anglo-American zone of influence, notably Britain, Australia, New Zealand, the United States and Ireland.

Although the engagement with neo-liberalism and new managerialism in Ireland can be understood in the context of Ireland's heavy cultural reliance on Anglophone countries, there were also other historical factors at play especially in education. Ireland experienced massive emigration and economic decline throughout the 1950s (Lee, 1989). Education was held to be largely accountable as it had failed to deliver the technologically skilled work force that was deemed essential in an industrialized era. Under the guidance of the OECD, a review of education was initiated in 1962 and the *Investment in Education Report* was published in 1965. This report strongly endorsed human capital theory as a guiding principle in education policy (O'Sullivan, 1992). Modernization discourses from the 1960s onwards resulted in the 'older emphasis on education as a means of personal development [being] challenged if not replaced by a new emphasis on shaping the educational system to meet the ... demands of the labour market' (Clancy, 1996, cited in Farrell, 1998: x). Over the next three decades, educating students for employment, especially in science, engineering and technology became the primary focus of government policy. The overly classical and humanist orientation of Irish education, deeply embedded in what O'Sullivan (2006) terms a 'theocratic' approach, was deemed to be unsustainable economically and replaced with a market-led system.

While participation rates in education at primary and second level improved significantly with the expansion of second-level education that the modernization and 'scientization' drive facilitated, the Irish economy continued to struggle and patterns of emigration of the young (and increasingly educated) continued into the 1980s. This was allied with a continued conservative nationalism and anti-intellectualism in the socio-political sphere, whereby Ireland lacked a critical analysis of public policy over an extended period of time. Garvin claims that 'religious and socioeconomic organizations such as trade unions, business, parts of the bureaucracy and the churches defended their turf in ways that effectively preserved a status quo' (Garvin, 2004: 3). The sense of disempowerment and stasis instilled by the dominant power holders provided a fertile ground in which to breed neo-liberal policies in the 1990s (Lee, 1989; Phelan, 2007) not only with respect to economic policy but regarding public services generally and education in particular. There was little education research in Ireland in the post-independent years; no books were published examining the wider relationship of education to society between 1922 and 1962 (Mulcahy, 1981: 1). A deep-rooted consensualism, aligned with a new meritocratic individualism, and an essentialist view of human intelligence underpinned much of educational research in Ireland in the 1970s and 1980s (Lynch, 1987).

While human capital theory provided the framework for Irish education from the 1960s onwards, other more distinctly neo-liberal principles came in to play in the 1990s. Accountability was one of the key principles informing policy development in the *Education White Paper* in 1995. This paper called for more appropriate 'performance indicators' for measuring educational outcomes. The Department of Education and Science began to use the language of the market from that time in its key strategy documents beginning with *Implementing the Agenda for Change* in 1996. Strategy statements from the DES retained this orientation into the new millennium where the market language of 'customers and clients' replaced that of students and learners (Gleeson and O'Donnabháin, 2009: 30). The EU has also helped promote a market ideology in education not least by the ways in which it has tied the purposes of education so closely with that of the economy in the Lisbon Agreement. The Department of Education in Ireland followed the UK direction as it mutated over 15 years from being a Department of Education, to being a Department of Education *and Science* to being a Department of Education *and Skills*, with a 'Customer' (our emphasis) Charter and a Customer Action Plan in 2010 (DES, 2009). It strongly emphasizes skill development for employment in its strategy statements.

Strategic planning and legislation emanating outside the education sector impacted directly on it. The Strategic Management Initiative (SMI) adopted by the government in 1994 was designed to 'reform' the civil service along new managerial lines. The SMI led to the *Delivering Better Government Report* (1996) by the Secretary Generals of the Civil Service. Both the SMI and the 1996 report culminated in The Public Service Management Act (1997) which was designed to 'modernize' the entire public service. All these developments led eventually to a national Performance Management and Development System (PMDS) being developed in 2000. The new legislation, and its related accountability systems, instituted a technicist approach to change that was strongly driven by business rhetoric:

> Advocates of 'running the government like a business' and practitioners of the NPM [New Public Service Management] approach to the reform of the public sector have sought, at least in part, to have the public service operate according to 'market-like models'. NPM is based on an economic understanding of governance in which the market – or approximations to it – is regarded as the ideal mechanism for the allocation and delivery of public services. Central to this approach is the perception of the citizens as customers.
>
> (Collins, 2007: 31)

Whereas in other countries politicians wrote the reforms, often in the face of deep opposition from public servants, one powerful segment of the Irish public service was a willing ally in realizing new managerial practices, namely, senior civil servants (Gleeson and O'Donnabháin, 2009: 29). The SMI that heralded change in the Irish civil and public service 'was neither imposed nor forced. It emerged from the concerns of senior civil servants about the current performance of the system over which they presided and its ability to meet the challenges of supporting an effective State for the twenty-first century' (Collins, 2007: 36–7 citing John Murray, 2001).

The ways in which senior civil servants aligned themselves with new managerialism is not surprising for a number of reasons. New managerialism demanded a bifurcation of power that allowed control to remain centralized while responsibilities were decentralized.[10] Senior public service managers in the new managerial regime were also in a position to make financial gains when market principles were applied to the evaluation of their own positions. The negotiation of performance-related-pay and the benchmarking of private and public sector salaries led to substantial awards to higher civil servants (Cradden, 2007: 176–7).[11] Senior policymakers in the public service were also potentially advantaged by new managerial practices, as they were potential corporate players in a market-oriented economy. Senior state managers can and do migrate from serving the public interest to serving capitalist interests in a relatively simple manner, especially when there is no sanction or control on such movement (Sklair, 2001: 17–18). The various tribunals and reports that have been published since the Irish banking crisis show how senior civil servants often moved from serving public interest bodies to being expert advisers to financial (and other) commercial institutions (TASC, 2010). Under new managerialism senior public servants were encouraged to define their role as leaders and innovators, people who were marketable both inside and outside the public service. Their role as public servants was no longer their defining identity; they were professional managerial elite and their public service experience (and the insider knowledge it offered, especially in taxation and revenue) was a resource for work in the corporate sector.[12]

While teachers and school principals were not in a position to exploit their experience in schools in the same way that senior civil servants could, some did move to the private sector and established successful for-profit colleges. The Institute of Education was founded by a teacher as was Hibernia, the on-line teacher education college. Moreover, the culture of education and management changed even for those who stayed within the public sector. The concept of the principal as a chief executive officer (CEO) gained considerable ground in the 1990s and 2000s. Both primary and second-level principals formed their own management networks (the Irish Primary Principals' Network (IPPN) and the National Association of Principals and Deputy Principals (NAPD)). Numerous conferences and meetings were held and the concept of the principal-chief-executive was a frequent subject for debate, even if not endorsed. And principals felt under pressure to conform to new managerial principles even if they did not endorse them (see Chapters 6, 7 and 8 in this book).

## Neo-liberalism and marketization

The pressure to make education and other public services (especially health) into marketable services is a specific goal of the General Agreement on Trade and Services (GATS), the purpose of which is to liberalize all services in all sectors of the economy globally (Robertson et al., 2002). The move to marketize sectors of education is an objective that Ireland has endorsed in higher education in particular. It has facilitated the private for-profit sectors of education in expanding even in sensitive areas such as upper second-level schooling and teacher education. The call for higher education institutions to service the 'Smart Economy' and to 'strike a balance between the demands of the market and their academic mission' (Department of Education and Skills, 2011: 92) strongly suggests that higher education is to be more market-oriented in the future. The reasons for wanting to make education a tradeable service are not only to reduce the cost to capital of taxation for public services, but also because of the profit potential of the more sought-after and/or exclusive areas of education. In the year 2000, UNESCO estimated that education was a $2 trillion global 'industry' and it has multiplied in value since that time (UNESCO, 2007). There is a profitable return to be made if education can be traded, especially among those sectors of the global society that can afford it.[13] The private for-profit colleges in Ireland recruit globally and in many of their programmes, students from outside the EU would constitute a significant proportion of their students (Department of Education and Skills, 2010). Public higher education institutions in Ireland are also actively promoting student recruitment overseas (outside of Europe especially) to balance their budgets.

The success of neo-liberal marketization is also evident in the way education is now a major sector within the global economy, even outside the 'for-profit' sector. It operates 'both as a basis for national economic competitiveness, particularly in the race to develop "high skills" labour, and as a traded good' (Ball, Dworkin and Yryonides, 2010: 523). The UK earned £28 billion in 2003–4 from the education services industry alone, compared with £19 billion from the financial services sector and £20 billion from the motor industry (ibid.). The rising returns to education has been accompanied by an expansion of private, for-profit service providers in the UK in particular (Ball, 2007). In Ireland, the sale of education and ancillary services contributed approximately €900 million to the economy in 2010 (Department of Education and Science, 2010: 31). Selling education as a commodity is now a key component of the services economy.

## Implications of commodifying education

The move to make education into a marketable commodity has implications for learning in terms of what is taught (and not taught), who is taught and what types of subjectivities are developed in schools and colleges (Rose, 1989; Olssen and Peters, 2005). In a market-led system, the student is defined as an economic maximizer, governed by self-interest. There is a glorification of the 'consumer citizen' construed as willing, resourced and capable of making market-led choices. Education becomes just another consumption good (not a human right) paralleling other goods and the individual is held responsible for her or his own 'choices' within it. The state's role is one of facilitator and enabler of the consumer and market-led citizen (Rutherford, 2005). Neo-liberalism embeds not only a unique concept of the learner in education, it also maps on a new set of goals to education that do not sit easily with education's purpose as a key institution in protecting people's human rights.[14]

There is also a strong incentive within the neo-liberal framework to weaken the power of the teaching profession and to casualize labour in education to reduce costs. While national data on the casualization of teaching in education is not available in Ireland at the time of writing, the signs are that casualization is being normalized. At the Annual Congress of the Irish National Teachers' Organisation (INTO) in April 2011, the president of the union claimed that the unemployment of young teachers was the biggest single threat to the profession. The introduction of the Employment Control Framework (ECF) by the government in 2011(as a condition for receiving IMF and ECB loans) meant that public service staffing was drastically reduced. This paved the way for casualization in education (and other public services) for a considerable time as most contracts under the ECF are for a defined period with no guarantee of permanency as would have been standard practice hitherto.

Even prior to the ECB and IMF requirements, primary and second-level teaching had already been increasingly de-regulated as there is declining control over the number of people who qualify in teaching nationally. The opening up of a for-profit teacher education college (Hibernia) in the early 2000s has been the most significant development in this regard. Hibernia is now the biggest single provider of primary teachers in Ireland.[15] While second-level teachers have traditionally qualified through postgraduate teacher education programmes in the universities, and numbers qualifying in different subjects have been limited by state regulatory bodies, from 2011 Hibernia will also be educating second-level teachers. As Hibernia has all its courses approved by the Irish Teaching Council, and as it is recognized by HETAC (the Higher Education Training and Awards Council), it can offer courses to anyone who can pay the fee (€9,000 per annum); in this context the oversupply of teachers and casualization of teachers is likely to continue.

As education becomes marketed, and especially when it is designed for-profit, it does exact a price: the US Government Accountability Office (GAO, 2010) found that the courses in for-profit colleges cost several multiples of what they cost in comparator public colleges. Moreover, there are very few core full-time faculty members in for-profit colleges: an estimated 95 per cent of academics are part-time in the University of Phoenix compared with an average of 47 per cent nationally in the US. The casualization of the academic and teaching staff is a close correlate of market-led education and clearly facilitates profit (Hill, 2005).

## Change and resistance to change by teachers

Despite all the changes occurring through the endorsement of neo-liberal principles at management levels, evidence from schools suggests that not much may have changed at the classroom level. Gleeson and O'Donnabháin's (2009: 34–6) analysis of how performance indicators (outlined in the 2005–7 Strategy Statement – the High Level Goals – (HLGs)) for second-level schools operate shows that they were (and are) not measured primarily at the individual (student) or school level in assessing the outcomes of education. Only a very small number of the performance criteria were based on assessing student learning.[16] The work of individual teachers was not assessed in any detail. Most of the focus remained on policy implementation at a general (rather than individual) level. Staffing, teacher supply, the timely delivery of reports, training days delivered, management structure and the pace of implementation for syllabi changes are all monitored but not the work or practices of teachers in classrooms.

> One of the great paradoxes of Ireland education is that, while the official discourse is replete with references to change and reform, much of the available evidence suggests that little change has occurred in teachers' beliefs and values.
>
> (Gleeson and O'Donnabháin, 2009: 37)

Unlike senior civil servants, teachers are not contenders for the transnational capitalist class. Business models of management do not sit easily with teachers' professional training, their day-to-day work, or their socialization for senior posts which were centred in Education Departments rather than Business schools. Moreover, teachers were and are highly unionized with almost all teachers being members of one of three unions that work co-operatively through a loose federal arrangement. The unions were strongly resistant to new managerial norms and values and were powerful enough to resist many key demands in ways that were not true in other countries. The power of the teacher unions is something that the Chairperson of the Labour Court (himself a former teacher) recognized as early as 1985:

> The teachers' unions collectively, between them, had become the most powerful group in Congress – notwithstanding the industrial power of the ITGWU and the FWUI [now SIPTU]. As a professional body, when they moved politically they were akin to the IFA [The Irish Farmers' Association]. They had that solid institutional political clout, insofar as they permeated every parish in Ireland, every political party in Ireland, every cultural, sporting and recreational body.
> (Kieran Mulvey, Interview, Cunningham, 2009: 217)

While teacher unions have varied in their response to new managerialism, with secondary teachers being more open in their opposition than primary teachers (particularly the ASTI in the early 2000s), there was generally no support for the ideal of linking pay in a linear manner to performance, a key dimension of the new managerial order (Cunningham, 2009: 266–300).[17] School league tables, such as those introduced in the UK, were not introduced in Ireland, largely due to the power of teacher unions, but with the support of parents and religious bodies that owned the majority of schools at both primary and second level. Teachers' fears of invidious comparisons between schools and teachers were shared by religious bodies and were aligned with parental fears that such league tables would place too much pressure on children, and possibly make individual children's educational achievements visible in small village and town communities. Moreover, as there are no public assessments or examinations at the end of primary education, there was little scope to have league tables at this level. The net outcome was the introduction of a system of 'Whole School Evaluation', whereby evaluations of schools take place on a partnership basis between the school, the management body, the parents and the inspectorate of the Department of Education and Science. The work of individual teachers is not assessed in the reports.[18] However, while school-level examination results are not published as league tables, newspapers have created a type of league-table system by using Freedom of Information requests to identify the percentage of children from different schools that go on to higher education. While this practice has been strongly critiqued by a variety of groups, it has had parental support, especially middle-class parents who can afford to choose schools. The newspapers have created a type of league-table system by default.

The power of the media to create agendas in education is increasingly evident in Ireland as elsewhere (see Chapter 10). Although the media are not identified as major players in educational policymaking, they are increasingly powerful in setting agendas which school managers must heed, in a media-driven age. In an increasingly competitive and diverse society, reputational criteria and entry to what is perceived as the 'best' school becomes even more pronounced (Devine, 2011; Lynch and Moran 2006). Principals become ever more conscious of how 'their' school is positioned in the competitive stakes.

Media challenges to teachers are not new however. Teachers have been strongly criticized in the media and in politics for what is perceived as protectionism of considerable privileges for many years (Ní Murchú, 1995). But they have maintained a relatively united front on industrial issues (Cunningham, 2009: 307). They have also strategically tapped into parental anger against cutbacks in education at different times, including those arising from the banking crisis. The latter culminated in a highly successful march organized by the three Teacher Unions that brought 50,000 people on to the streets (including parents and students) to defend education from cutbacks on 6 December 2008, at the height of the banking crisis.

Another factor that has militated institutionally against new managerialism is that primary schools (especially), but also second-level schools are deeply integrated into the fabric of local communities, towns and villages. Teachers are not a distant professional elite. There are over 3,000 primary schools and 740 second-level schools in a small country of 4.5 million; schools tend to be small by international standards. Their size alone militates against a managerial model. Moreover, the principal is also a teacher in most of the small primary schools and in some smaller second-level schools. The online-manager and worker divide that is assumed within the new managerial frame does not apply.

## The role of teacher trade unions in negotiating educational policy

Ireland has had a long history of teacher unionization, beginning in 1868 with the founding of the Irish National Teachers' Organisation (INTO) and of the Association of Secondary Teachers, Ireland (ASTI), in 1909 (Coolahan, 1981: 31, 70). The teachers' trade unions have traditionally had, and continue to retain, a powerful position in the negotiation and implementation of Irish educational policy and practice (Coolahan, 1981; Cunningham, 2009). Their powerful position is related to the numerical strength of the Irish teacher unions. The INTO alone had 32,215 members in 2010 (INTO Central Executive Committee Report 2009/10) with virtually all full-time teachers being union members.[19] In Ireland, teachers' willingness to work collectively to protect their members' conditions and their consultative relationship with state and other statutory groups (Drudy and Lynch, 1993; Allen, 2007) places them in an influential position in educational policymaking relative to teachers in other countries.

Moreover, teachers are key figures in all main Irish political parties. They are major players in Irish political party life. In 2011, teachers represented the largest single profession among new deputies who were elected to the Dáil (The National Parliament). *The Irish Times* reported after the General Election that '[o]f new deputies, whose pre-politics occupations can be identified, twelve are teachers, five worked as lawyers, four are farmers, three are postmasters and three are former bank officials .... Three of the new deputies qualified as chemists. Only seven of the new deputies could be classified as small businesspeople, while the one with most practical experience as an employer is probably Mick Wallace' (*Irish Times,* Saturday, 5 March 2011). Moreover, both the new Taoiseach (Prime Minister) and the Tánaiste (Deputy Prime Minister) who were elected in 2011 were teachers. A blog profiling all deputies in the Dáil (National Parliament) up to 2011 also showed that teachers were the largest single professional group in all the major parties[20] and the *Irish Independent* (1 March 2011) claimed that teachers were still the dominant group in the new Dáil 2011.[21] While there has been no in-depth analysis of how teachers influence political parties in Ireland, there is no doubt that their strategic location in parties across the political spectrum contributes significantly to their influence.

In recent decades the power of the unions has to be contextualized in terms of the working relationship they have built with successive governments. Teachers' unions are formally represented in all major decision-making bodies that design and implement educational policy, including the Teaching Council (which is dominated by teachers), the NCCA, HETAC, FETAC, the External Monitoring Group for Senior Cycle, the Post Primary Advisory Group on In-service and the Registration Council. They are represented at every level of educational policymaking. They have been very prominent in exercising their rights of representation and consultation under the Education Act (1998).

Allen (2007: 112) argues that 'the Irish state has taken an active interest in restructuring the union movement itself so that it fits in with the needs of Irish capitalism. The state strategy has been to incorporate the union leaders so that they come to share the same general objectives as the employers and state officials'. This has occurred within the context of social partnership agreements negotiated between state, employers, unions and community groups across Irish society during the 1990s (Ó Riain, 2006). Teachers have been party to this partnership process and have managed it to good effect in terms of their pay and conditions over many years. (Their salaries are among the highest in the OECD, according to *Irish Times*, Tuesday, 14 September 2011). However, the power of the teachers' unions to drive the education agenda is now being tested in the wake of the collapse of the social partnership arrangement between government and mediator groups and the ongoing economic crisis (Cunningham, 2009).

Teacher resistance to new managerialism has been very significant in Ireland. While the government adopted the rhetoric of new mangerialism at official levels and some of the practices by having performance indicators, measures of accountability, strategic plans (High Level Goals) for schools, etc., the available evidence would suggest implementation of the reforms are less honoured in practice than in theory at both primary and second-level education. The strategic location of teachers and their union representatives in a range of key decision-making bodies across the state sector has been crucial in limiting the impact of new managerialism at primary and second level.

## Higher education accommodating new managerialism

The situation in higher education, especially in the university sector, is quite different however. The government-initiated OECD review of higher education in Ireland in 2004 (OECD, 2004) was a watershed in Irish higher education. The report strongly critiqued the lack of investment in higher education research in the sciences and technological areas in particular and emphasized the role of higher education in developing a '*skilled work force for the economy*'. There is no reference in the body of the report to the role of the universities or higher education generally in developing the civil, political, social or cultural institutions of society, either locally or globally. While the government terms of reference for the OECD group did make reference to the importance of identifying strategies for developing skills and research needs 'for economic and social development', there is no reference to these social objectives in the published report.

The National Strategy for Higher Education (2011) known as The Hunt Report (from the name of its chairperson, a business man) is even more heavily laced with the new managerial language of efficiency, flexibility and accountability than the OECD Report of 2004. It has been adopted by the Higher Education Authority and will form the framework for the future development of higher education in Ireland. Although it recognizes that Irish higher education spending is highly efficient (as recognized by the ECOFIN study organized through the European Ministries of Finance; see St. Aubyn et al., 2009) and that 'Ireland was ranked highest of all countries in the international recruiter reviews of graduate employability and second highest of 28 countries in the international peer review of graduate quality', it goes on to argue that '[t]here is considerable potential for changing work practices to improve flexibility, efficiency and responsiveness to new needs' (Department of Education and Skills, 2011: 29). The focus of the report is on the role of higher education in rebuilding 'an innovative, knowledge-based economy', having graduates who will be 'the productive engine of a vibrant and prosperous economy' (ibid.: 1). Reviewing the work of academic staff 'continuously ... in all institutions as part of a robust performance management framework' is seen as central to the realization of the new goals (Department of Education and Skills, 2011:2). It proposes to curtail university autonomy by ensuring that 'Institutional strategies will be defined and aligned with national priorities' (Department of Education and Skills, 2011:4). There is a proposal to introduce 'up-front fees and income-contingent loan scheme' and to have greater '[c]onsolidation, economies of scale, greater productivity and commercial activity' (Department of Education and Skills, 2011:5) to help fund higher education in to the future.

While there has been resistance to the increased marketization of higher education from 2004 onwards, including strike action, the power of the unions in the higher education sectors, especially in the seven universities, is not comparable to that of their counterparts at primary and second level, not only because there is a range of unions representing different staff,[22] but also because union density among academics is not as high as that among teachers. In addition, many junior academics are on temporary and/or part-time contracts and are not unionized. As many general services have been outsourced over the past 20 years, this also reduces the scope and influence of unions at the higher education levels, especially in the universities.

What is notable about the changes in the past ten years is that higher education is being pressurized to change from being 'a centre of learning to being a business organisation with productivity targets ... to transfer its allegiance from the *academic* to the *operational*' (our italics) (Doring, 2002: 140 citing McNair, 1997). As the operational has encoded within itself many of the values of the commercial, adopting a purely 'operational focus', or treating change as a purely 'technical problem', means that the values of the commercial sector can be encoded in the heart of the higher education systems and processes almost without reflection (Lynch, 2006). The move from the academic to the operational is increasingly explicit in Ireland as is the development of joint ventures and conferences between business and the universities.[23] The Report of the Interdepartmental Committee on Science, Technology and Innovation (Forfas, 2004) on *Building Ireland's Knowledge Economy* exemplified such a trend. The Report was actively promoted by the Irish Universities Association (IUA) which represents the heads of the universities. In the section on 'Realising the Vision', the report outlines two of the main actions for the Public Research System (effectively the universities and other higher educational institutions) as being to '*Develop a national plan to increase the performance, productivity and efficiency in the higher education and public sectors*' and '*to sustain Ireland's commitment to building an international reputation for research excellence*'. Throughout the report the development of society is equated with economic development and the latter is focused primarily on science and technology. The Expert Group on Future Skills Needs (chaired by a person from a multinational company) also sets the agenda for higher education and constantly directs educators to service the market economy more effectively (EGFSN, 2011).

## Conclusion

Ireland has moved from being a state governed by theocratic principles to one governed by market principles. The progression to neo-liberalism has followed the international trend, emerging in the 1990s and consolidating in the first decade of the new millennium. While neoliberalism was initially sold as a simple modernization project, that changed over time. The focus on the human capital value of education persisted but it was married to a new education project focused on educating students for a market economy. The development of an entrepreneurial and actuarial self became the new mantra in an age of individualized modernity, not only globally (Peters, 2005) but also in

Ireland (Inglis, 2008). The move to the market has been accelerated in recent decades especially from 1997 to 2011 when Ireland was governed by a strong neo-liberal coalition government that systematically promoted marketization and privatization policies throughout the public sector. While neo-liberal policies have been systematically challenged in primary- and second-level education, due to the power of the teachers' unions in particular, there have been profound changes in educational management and organization nonetheless. As we will show in subsequent chapters, the management responsibilities of school principals have been redefined at primary and second level. There is pressure not only to produce academic results but also to profile the school in 'the market'. The task is not just to do the job well but to show that one is doing it well, to 'sell' the school or college in the local and, in the case of higher education, the global market. While there is resistance to marketization at trade union levels, especially at primary and second level, new managerial reforms inevitably get under your skin; there is no way of escaping, even for those who are not committed to the new managerial project. The call to be market-led rather than education-led has profound implications not only for the definition of what it is to be an educational leader or manager, but for principals and senior managers' personal lives. Managers are increasingly required to work in a way that is not bound by time or other commitments. The focus is the product not the person, both in terms of what is attained and what is counted and countable. A culture of carelessness is created, one that is already visible in higher education (Lynch, 2010). This has implications for recruitment as well as retention in senior management positions especially in terms of gender.

# 2
# The Culture of Governance in Irish Education

As new managerialism was instituted globally from the 1990s onwards, it was introduced into national educational systems that had histories, philosophies and modes of governance that were culturally specific. This chapter examines the governance structures of Irish education and how these mediated new managerialism. It focuses in particular on the key role played by the Catholic Church prior to and during the managerial era, especially in the primary- and second-level sectors of education where it was and is the single largest provider of education. In mapping the specificity of new managerialism in Ireland, we argue that specific postcolonial and cultural contexts generated different local logics of control across educational settings that framed the Irish experience of new managerialism. New managerial modes of governance were not adopted without dissent and mediation, a dissent and mediation that is ongoing (see Chapter 1). The implementation of new managerialism in Irish education presents an interesting case study, given Ireland's European status and its history of political and cultural colonization. The Catholic Church was and is a major cultural force in Irish life (Garvin, 2004; Inglis, 1987, 2008). It was a major player in how new managerialism was mediated and managed in Irish education, particularly at primary and secondary levels.

## The history of Irish education and the control of the churches

As noted in Chapter 1, Irish society failed to develop on many fronts after independence in the 1920s. Economic protectionism, allied with a deep-seated nationalism and the hegemonic control of education and cultural institutions by a conservative Catholic Church, resulted in a stagnant economy marked by massive emigration, religious and cultural conservatism and deep-seated anti-intellectualism in the socio-political sphere (Chubb, 1982; Inglis, 1987; Garvin, 2004). After independence, ownership and control of education, health and welfare services remained in private hands, mostly those of the Catholic Church and a small number of other churches and voluntary bodies. While there have been significant shifts in the ownership and control of schools over the past 30 years, especially with the decline of religious personnel, the Irish State does not own most schools either at primary or at second level.

The control exercised by the Catholic Church over Irish education has operated not only through its ownership and control over schools (Akenson, 1975; Hyland and Milne, 1992), but also through the wider moral monopoly it has exercised over cultural, social and political life (Inglis, 1987). The Church's organizational network, combined with extensive control of social and economic resources, enabled it to exercise a 'virtual monopoly of Irish morality [...] second only to that of the State' for most of the twentieth century (Inglis, 1987: 61). The ownership and control of schools was key to this wider cultural and moral monopoly:

> Control of the education system has been fundamental to the Catholic Church maintaining an adherence to its rules and regulations. It is within the schools that young Irish children have been slowly and consistently instructed in and also imbued with the Church's teachings.
>
> (Inglis, 1987: 53)

Although the power and influence of the Catholic Church has waned in the early 2000s, particularly following the highlighting of sexual abuses perpetrated by priests, the 'Church's right to dictate policy in a broad range of social, cultural, intellectual and marital areas was maintained and successfully enforced amongst Irish Catholics until well into the late twentieth century' (Garvin, 2004: 129). Moreover, the protection given to religion (Article 44) and the rights of parents over education (Article 42) in the Irish Constitution has ensured that Catholic control and influence continues, albeit in new forms.

Under Article 42 of the Irish Constitution, the family is defined as the 'primary and natural educator of the child'. As most parents (over several generations) have themselves been educated in Catholic schools and cared for through a variety of health and welfare services that are Catholic in ethos, it is not surprising that most (87%) profess to be

Catholic (Central Statistics Office (CSO), 2006). Whether the process whereby people have been educated to believe Catholic teaching is indoctrination or not (as Clarke (1984) claims), the fact remains that Irish people identify as Catholic, albeit in slowly declining numbers (CSO, 2006). This cultural identification with Catholicism grants the Church considerable power over education given the provisions of the Irish Constitution on parental rights in education.

Article 44 of the Constitution enhances denominationalism in Ireland as it guarantees the rights of all denominations to run schools and organizations according to their beliefs and values. Because well over 90 per cent of primary schools are denominational, people of no faith or minority religious belief, who cannot access a school of their faith/belief, are forced by lack of choice to send their children to a denominational school. This leads inevitably to problems of exclusion for minority group children especially in the context of an integrated curriculum structure in Irish primary schools (Devine, 2011; Mawhinney, 2007).[1] Although Article 44 does protect the rights of children, and they are exempted from attending instruction in a religion outside their own beliefs, this is very difficult to achieve when a denominational ethos pervades the school day, and prayers and other religious events are integrated into the mainstream activities of the school. The fact that Catholic primary schools prepare children during the school day for the religious sacraments of Communion and Confirmation is especially problematic as it leads to feelings of exclusion among children who are not sharing in these celebrations (Mawhinney, 2009).

The protections granted to denominational education also impact on teacher training, staff appointments and student enrolment. While teacher education is secular for second-level teachers, primary teacher education was entirely denominational up to the early 2000s when an online (for-profit) teacher education college (Hibernia) was established. Given the history of primary teacher education, the great majority of teachers currently employed in Irish primary schools have been educated in one of the two major Catholic-run teacher education colleges or in the small Church of Ireland (Anglican) College. Almost all of those who hold senior posts have similar backgrounds. Schools and colleges that are denominational in ethos (and over 90 per cent of primary-level and between 50 per cent and 60 per cent of second-level schools are) can and do reserve the right to appoint people who adhere to their values and beliefs. This right has been enshrined in law in Section 37 of the Employment Equality Act (1998).[2] Denominational schools are also entitled to give preference to children of their own faith. This has had serious consequences for racial and ethnic segregation with the rise of immigration in the early 2000s (Devine, 2011,[3] O'Gorman and Sugrue, 2007).

The control exercised by the Catholic Church on education is also evident from the gendering of Irish schooling. Most Catholic schools were planned in a gender-segregated way in large towns and cities (where schools were set up by religious orders or diocesan clergy), reflecting the Catholic belief in gender-segregated schooling.[4] While this practice changed over the past 30 years, due to amalgamations, declining intakes and policy shifts, Ireland still has a relatively large number of gender-segregated schools and classes: 26 per cent of primary school children and 38 per cent of second-level students were in segregated classes in 2003 (Department of Education, 2007: Tables 1.4 and 2.10).[5]

While the Department of Education and Science does exercise control over curricula, examinations and terms and conditions for teachers' appointments, it is not directly involved in appointing principals or teachers. The power to appoint has always been local in Ireland (Gleeson, 2010: 25), and this was institutionalized under the 1998 Education Act (1998) when responsibility for governance was formally devolved to Schools' Boards of Management.[6] However,

> [w]hile the board of management is charged with the direct governance of the school, every primary school is ultimately controlled by a patron. Typically, the Roman Catholic and Church of Ireland bishops are the patrons of the schools within their dioceses.[7]
>
> (Mawhinney, 2007: 386)

As the Catholic Church was not (and is not) a democracy, the norms that guided governance within it were deeply hierarchical. The hierarchical approach was also employed in governance of schools. Sean O'Connor, assistant secretary of the Department of Education and Science (1965–75) noted that the role of lay teachers in Church-owned schools was that of the 'hired man' [*sic*]. He called for a new system of governance where the religious would be in education as 'partners, not always as masters' (1968: 249). While new systems of lay, and more democratic, governance were instituted from the 1970s onwards, these were devised primarily due to the decline in the availability of religious personnel. The secularization of management in Church-run schools did not arise through any desire by the Churches (of all denominations) to divest themselves of control of schools. The Catholic Church has been successful in negotiating new zones of influence in newly established governance structures such as the community schools at second level, and more recently community national schools at primary level. Although there are very few religious heads of schools or colleges, religious influence is still exercised albeit 'mainly confined to trusteeship rather than school headship or teaching' (Gleeson, 2010: 28).

## A traditional and anti-intellectual society

However, it would be simplistic to claim that Catholicism could entirely explain the hierarchical conservatism in Irish education. Ireland was also a traditional rural society up to the 1970s when it became industrialized and urbanized. Securing the future of livelihoods in farming often meant promoting strict control on family members, not only in terms of work but also in terms of marriage and sexual behaviour (to avoid legal claims on the family farm). Conservative Catholicism found a welcome home in a conservative male-dominated rural society where land was the primary value and protecting the inheritance of land was the guiding principle of economic and social life (Whyte, 1984). Given that emigration bled the country of so many of its young people in the post-war years,[8] and those who were left behind were disproportionately older and very young, it was no surprise that conservatism went unchallenged. Moreover, intellectual life itself remained stagnant for many years up to the early 1960s:

> Few inquiries of any depth were made into social and economic problems, and even those were mostly of a pedestrian quality, or [...] by common consent were ignored. [...] Neither public servants (politician or professional) nor the universities provided new idea.
>
> (Chubb, quoted in Lee, 1989: 562)

The secular administrators of the Irish State were singularly hostile to ideas and concepts, no matter how verifiable the evidence supporting them (Lee, 1989: 562–80). Moreover, there was a very low tolerance of informed dissent even in areas of finance and public policy. There was a particular disdain for scientific evidence, not helped by the fact that 'between 1923 and 1968, only a quarter of all secretaries of government departments had university degrees' (Lee, 1989: 573).

Although the Catholic Church did control schools and exercised tight control on sexual morality in particular, their ability to influence policy outside of this sphere was not as great as is commonly assumed:

> Those responsible for the formulation of social policy had little contact with the supply of ideas in Ireland, much less with the wider

> world. Catholic thinking, or selected Catholic thinking, may have influenced some. However, what is striking about social policy in the first generation of independence is not the demand for Catholic principles among policy-makers, but the general indifference in policy formulation to any social thought, Catholic or otherwise.
>
> (Lee, 1989: 578)

The anti-intellectualism of Irish political culture was undoubtedly rooted in the type of education that operated in Ireland both intellectually and organizationally. At the academic level, school education did not encourage intellectual or political dissent: 'The Irish secondary school system in the early decades of independence inculcated many worthy qualities. Neither intellectual independence nor intellectual originality were normally among them' (Lee, 1989: 573). Many years later, the OECD (1991: 76) observed that the goals and values of Irish education have 'tended to be tacit than explicit' and that the 'critics of schooling appear to be in the minority' (OECD, 1991: 57). The demise of the Irish Association for Curriculum Development in the mid-1990s and the establishment of the National Council for Curriculum and Assessment (NCCA) as a statutory body in 1998 (it existed since 1987) further consolidated the consensualism around curricular issues within Irish education. The NCCA was a largely representative body of various interest groups in education, including the teacher unions and management bodies. It was operating within a 'partnership' structure where consensus politics were inevitable due to competing interests and compromises: it focused over time on syllabus development rather than substantive issues of educational reform (Gleeson, 2010: 135–6). Even when the NCCA did make innovative proposals, the implementation of these rested with other bodies connected to or within the Department of Education. Innovation could be and was stymied by fragmentation (Gleeson, 2010: 281–99).

At the organizational level, schools were characterized by a strong ethos of institutional control, involving respect for authority, the expertise of teachers and a largely unquestioning approach to religious beliefs and values. Irish students were trained to be intellectually acquiescent, especially in relation to social structures and institutions. But it would be questionable to attribute this deference to authority entirely to Catholic influence. While it is true that Catholic schools and colleges were especially strong in their hierarchical organization (Inglis, 1987), consensualism and lack of dissent was also a feature of academic life within the university sector well into the later part of the twentieth century (Lynch, 1987).

Moreover, a general culture of suspicion operated in relation to intellectual dissent, especially on social issues. This was true of all groups in Ireland for many decades, business people, farmers, organized labour and public servants (Lee, 1989: 577–79). This was aided by the fact that the 'left' in Ireland was not exactly a major progenitor of new ideas. The left, in-so-far as it was represented for many decades by the Labour Party had little interest in ideas, left or otherwise the 'poverty of its ideas' counting among its more conspicuous features (Lee, 1989: 578). Moreover, Ireland remained quite unique in Europe in not having any social science subjects (notably potentially critical subjects such as sociology, critical theory, media studies, women's studies, equality studies or philosophy) on the school syllabus, even as an option at leaving certificate level. The most prestigious national newspaper, and the only one to have a substantive weekly book review supplement, *The Irish Times*, rarely reviews social scientific books, including books on education. Most major social scientific works published by leading Irish scholars have never been reviewed in Irish newspapers.

The socio-cultural context within which change and 'modernisation' occurred in Irish culture was therefore quite specific. The deference to authority that was embedded in Ireland's rural traditions and its conservative Catholic education was mapped on to a culture of deep anti-intellectualism and consensualism. This, in turn, was allied to thinking framed through a prolonged political and cultural colonization where deference to authority (albeit an ambivalent deference) was embedded in the politics of survival (Kenny, 1985). While literary figures were indulged, and their eccentricities celebrated and even marketed internationally as an emblem of Irish 'genius', Ireland did not encourage or indulge those who dissented from the academic status quo. Even within the academy, dissent was policed and controlled (Lynch, 2006; Lynch, Crean and Moran, 2010).

## Times of change and the persistence of anti-intellectualism

It was only in the late twentieth and early twenty-first century that the dominance of the Catholic Church in Irish education began to wane. The forces of modernization and secularization, intersecting with declining numbers in religious orders, contributed to a decline in the Church's involvement in school management and teaching (Coolahan, 1981). The Education Act (1998) copper-fastened managerial changes by locating a variety of groups with statutory 'functions and responsibilities [...] in the schooling system' (DES, 2004: 24). The base of power in Irish education slowly shifted from the Catholic Church-State nexus to encompass teacher unions, national parent organizations and other managerial bodies, notably the Vocational Education Committees. The establishment of the *Forum on Patronage and Pluralism in the Primary Sector* in Spring of 2011 signified the most important move to an alternative model of management of governance for schools for many decades. Its express purpose is to make recommendations to the Minister for Education on future models for school governance.

The slow pattern of change in the education sphere has to be set within a wider context of more extensive social and cultural change. As Garvin recounts, 'it took the clerical scandals of the 1990s, a series of self-inflicted wounds on the Catholic Church, to wreak serious and probably irreversible damage to the Church's previously central position in Irish society and culture' (2004: 213). Educational institutions, the media and other cultural institutions were key players in this cultural shift, encouraging 'a greater psychic individualism and a decreased willingness to adhere to rules and moral standards set from above without some prior argument. Increased wealth or *embourgeoisement* led to increasing psychic independence and decreased ability by elites to control opinion or behavior' (ibid).

While Irish people's new-found psychic individualism may explain their critique of a declining and ageing hierarchy in the Catholic Church, it did not extend to effectively critiquing the new high priests of capitalism in Irish political and cultural life. The Celtic Tiger era saw new deities replace the old clerics: business leaders were praised for their political and economic acumen; builders, developers and bankers, and their service workers in the professions, became the new model citizens. Everyone was encouraged to be an 'entrepreneur'. Ireland began to gloat to itself and the world as to the merits of its economic (neo-liberal) miracle (McSharry and White, 2000). While there were dissenting voices in the academy (Allen, 2000, 2007; Kirby, Gibbons and Cronin, 2002; Coulter and Coleman, 2003), these were in the minority and many academics were far from critical of the Celtic Tiger, claiming it as the success story of a neo-corporatist strategy of governance (O'Riain and O'Connell, 2000). The hyping of the 'property boom' was exemplified in the lack of critical analysis of the housing market in the Irish media.[9] Advertising revenues soared from property promotions in the Celtic Tiger era with all the main daily newspapers having extensive 'Property Supplements'. There were few questions asked about the sources of funding or the long-term cost of the boom. Those who did critique the new elites and their powers were either ignored or subjected to derision.[10] Ireland's dubious financial capitalism was not subjected to systematic scrutiny until it was too late.

The lack of respect for dissent pervaded all areas of Irish public life, including public policymaking. Neo-liberalism with its new managerial codes of governance was able to seep in to Ireland without much resistance in the early 1990s. As noted in Chapter 1, in other countries, while politicians advanced neo-liberal reforms, often in the face of deep opposition from public servants, new managerial practices were welcomed in Ireland by senior civil servants (Gleeson and O'Donnabháin, 2009: 29). The Strategic Management Initiative (SMI), the government initiative that instituted the practice of new managerialism in the mid-1990s, was neither imposed nor forced on the Irish public service in its early years (Collins, 2007: 36–7). By the time it came to be resisted, by some of the teacher unions, it was well entrenched and institutionalized in law. The introduction of the Education Act (1998) was the most significant event in institutionalizing new managerial changes in Irish schools.

## Legislation, change and accountability

Up to 1998, the mixed ownership and control model that evolved in Irish education was allied with a lack of specific legislation governing the operation of schools. Regulations and circulars issued by the Department of Education were 'not under any statutory power but merely [operated] as administrative measures [...] they [had] no statutory force, and the sanction which ensure[d] compliance with them [was] not a legal one but the undeclared understanding that the Department [would] withhold financial assistance in the event of non-compliance' (Constitution Review Group, 1996: 339).

Legislation in the past two decades, particularly the Education Act 1998 and Education Welfare Act 2000, has radically altered this situation. The Education Act of 1998 governs 'primary, post-primary, adult and continuing education and vocational education and training'. It sets out the functions and responsibilities of all key partners in the schooling system and the terms and conditions of Boards of Management for all schools. It requires schools to engage in the preparation of school plans and to promote parent associations. Accountability procedures are laid down in law (DES, 2004: 24).

All educational institutions receiving public funding are subject to the control of the Department of Education and Skills (DES),[11] and the Minister of Education and Science is the government-elected state official responsible for Irish education. The DES is responsible for the administration of the publicly funded primary, post-primary and special education schools. The functions of the DES include policy formulation and review; resource allocation and monitoring of expenditure; evaluation of performance; quality assurance of the education service; performance of a range of executive and operational functions and advice and support to educational management and staff.

The growth of accountability and performance-led appraisal in Ireland became official when the role of the DES Inspectorate was established on a statutory basis in Section 13 of the 1998 Education Act. This clearly defines the functions and powers of the inspectorate in supporting and evaluating the quality and organization of education in schools and education centres. Performance appraisal has been introduced in the form of whole school evaluations that the inspectorate complete on individual schools.

While the changes that were introduced in primary- and second-level education were the result of protracted negotiations with many interest groups, over many years, changes in the higher education sector were more centrally controlled by government. The Higher Education Authority (HEA) was originally and continues to be the funding authority for the universities and a number of designated higher education institutions. In line with the recommendations of the OECD (2004) report on the future of higher education in Ireland, the role of the HEA was expanded to involve regulatory functions across all higher education sectors. The HEA has a range of functions[12] and is also given additional responsibilities under the Universities Act, 1997, to assist and monitor strategic development plans, quality assurance procedures and equal opportunity policies in Irish universities.[13] The implementation of OECD-initiated 'reforms' has resulted in dramatic changes in the governance, management and strategic planning of higher education institutions in recent years. The establishment of a Strategic Innovation Fund (SIF) that is awarded competitively is powerful mechanism for directing change. Individual institutions have to achieve internal reforms to gain funding from the SIF through the

> re-organisation of faculties and departments, the introduction of new internal management and resource allocation processes, the development of new management information systems and administrative streamlining.
>
> (Minister of Education and Science, 2005)[14]

The publication of the Hunt Report in 2011 heralded the further enhancement of 'reform' in line with a new managerial agenda. Higher education is expected to service the 'Smart Economy' and to 'strike a balance between the demands of the market and their academic mission' (DES, 2011: 92); higher education is to be more market-oriented in the future.

## The long legacy of hierarchical and male control

Irish education has not only been Catholic-controlled and anti-intellectual, it has also been generally male-led. Men have held and continue to hold a disproportionate number of senior posts across all sectors of education, especially in higher education although there has been a greater gender balance in senior appointments in the early 2000s. In 2010, 85 per cent of teachers at primary level were women but just 60 per cent of school principals were women (Table 2.1). This does represent a significant rise in the number of women principals from 1994 to 1995, however, when just 46 per cent of principals were women (INTO CEC Report, 2009/10). At second level, women comprise 60 per cent of teachers and 37 per cent of principals (Table 2.1).

While there is still gender disparity in senior appointments at second level, there has been a significant improvement since the early 2000s: women comprised less than a third of all principals in 2003–4. However, in second-level education, it is notable that women principals tend to be concentrated as heads in single sex girls' schools: only 20 per cent of principals in co-educational community and comprehensive schools are women (Department of Education, 2007). The gender disparity is similar in the vocational/community college sector to what it is in the community/comprehensive sector.

Higher education also remains a male-led domain. While 39 per cent of full-time academic staff in Irish universities were women in 2003–4,

*Table 2.1* The proportion of senior post holders in education who are women[15]

| | **Primary level** | **Second level** | **Higher education** |
|---|---|---|---|
| 1993–4 | 46.0% | 29.0% | 6.3% |
| 2002–4 | 50.0% | 32.2% | 10.0% |
| 2009–11 | 60.0% | 37.0% | n/a |

*Source*: Data for 1993–4 – figures for primary, second and higher education level from Lynch (1999: 149).
Data for 2003–4 – figures for primary-level principals from DES statistics. 2002–3 figures for second-level principals and higher education professors and associate professor positions in the university sector (from DES, 2007 *Sé Sí – Gender in Irish Education* report).
Data for 2010–11 – 2009/10 figures for primary level from INTO report for principal positions. Second-level data from DES. Higher education figures were not available.

only 7.5 per cent of full professors and 12.5 per cent of associate professors were women (Department of Education, 2007: 343). (Just 10 per cent of all professors were women (Table 2.1)). No data is available on the proportion of women who hold professorships in 2011. However, 80 per cent of the 78 top management posts that were occupied in the university sector in 2005–6 were held by men (Figure 2.1).

The pattern is similar across all sectors of higher education (universities, institutes of technology and colleges) where 78 per cent of the top 264 occupied posts were held by men in 2005–6 (Figure 2.2).

When mapping the emergence of managerial change in Irish education, therefore, it is evident that not only is Irish education strongly

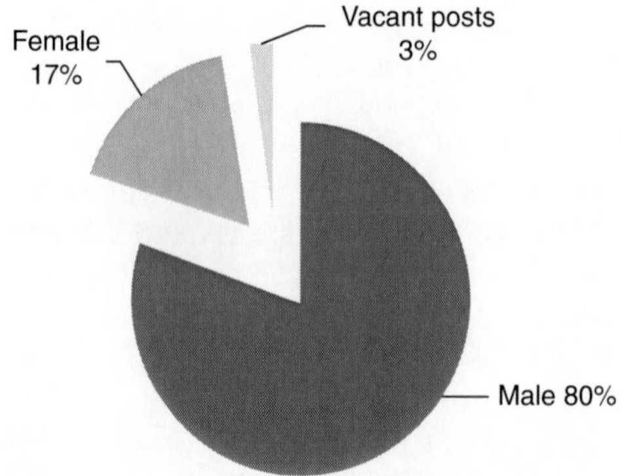


*Figure 2.1* Gender profile of senior posts in Irish Universities (2005–6)[16]

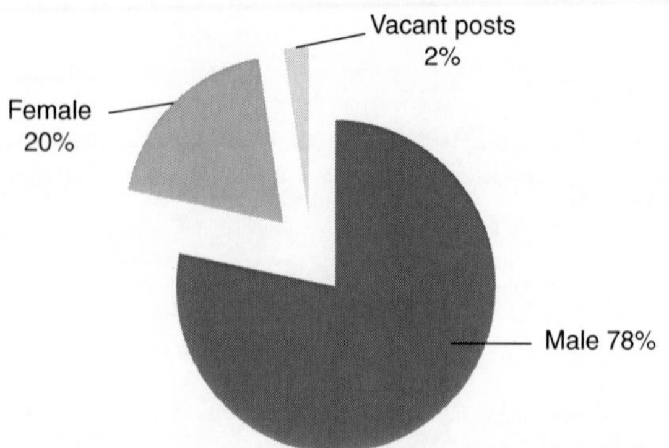


*Figure 2.2* Gender profile of senior posts across all sectors of higher education (2005–6)[17]

influenced by the Catholic Church in its management traditions and culture, it is also strongly influenced by men.

## Conclusion

While the neo-liberal government that controlled politics from late 1997 until 2011 planned and successfully implemented new managerial regimes in education, especially in higher education, the implementation was contested. As noted in Chapter 1, the first and most significant groups that contested the new managerial code were the teacher unions, especially the second-level unions. They succeeded in constraining the ability of the government to monitor teacher performance by negotiating a system of Whole School Evaluation (WSE) that left the performance of individual teachers outside the assessment system. They (and other management groups in education) also successfully negotiated the prohibition of State-directed league tables. While WSE was not welcomed by teachers, it was a very different and more benign system of performance measurement than that which operated in an individualized system.

Given the fact that the Catholic Church owned and controlled the great majority of primary schools and a majority (albeit lesser) of second-level schools, it too was a major player in framing the response to new managerialism. The Catholic Church did not oppose new managerialism in an overt manner however. It merely continued to proclaim its message as to what Catholic education involved, noting its rootedness in the teachings of Jesus Christ and its concern for people as spiritual beings:

> What distinguishes the Catholic school is that its concept of the human person is rooted in the teaching of Jesus Christ as embodied in the Catholic faith community. Each person is a spiritual being who comes from God and whose destiny is to be with God when this life is over. The ideal of the Catholic school proposed here is one whose ethos or characteristic spirit is rooted in its 'Christian concept of life centred on Jesus Christ'.
>
> (Irish Bishops Conference, 2007: 4)

The bishops also noted their concern for 'those suffering any kind of disadvantage', emphasizing the values of community, justice, respect and forgiveness (ibid).

> In the work of education Catholic schools provide an important service to society. They cater for the educational needs of children but

> they have a particular concern for those suffering any kind of disadvantage. In promoting a sense of responsibility and the right use of freedom they help to form students as good citizens. In emphasising the values of community, justice, respect and forgiveness they help students to grow in maturity and to take their place as responsible members of society (DCE, 1). Catholic education, then, has a dual purpose: its service in the mission of the Church and its service to society.
>
> (Irish Bishops Conference, 2007: 4)

What the Church did not do, however, is to state how it would consistently implement many of its values across its schools. Despite its concern for disadvantaged people, for example, the Catholic Church continued to uphold the elite and socially selective schools that they operate in the second-level sector (as do the Protestant Churches). The churches adapted to new managerialism rather than challenged it. Where the religious were no longer available to run schools, they placed them under Trusts that were religious-controlled. At primary level, the Conference of Religious of Ireland (CORI) outlined their support for Church involvement in primary education while acknowledging the need for diverse provision.

> CORI supports the Catholic Church's commitment to continuing its involvement in primary education in accordance with the wishes of Catholic parents. It is acknowledged that there is also a need for other forms of patronage in a diverse society.
>
> (Conference of Religious of Ireland, 2009)

The Churches' concerns have been with retaining their schools rather than challenging new managerialism. The impact of religious control over schools is not simply organizational however. Even schools which were not Catholic or Protestant, namely, Vocational Schools and Community Colleges, were not necessarily non-denominational.[18]

What was significant about Catholic control and influence in particular was the culture of management that it bequeathed to education. It promoted a hierarchical and patriarchal system of centralized governance. Many schools, especially at second level, that were run by religious had a very weak middle management system as the principal (if religious) ran the school with the assistance of her or his religious community, not all of whom were necessarily teachers in the school. Power was centralized and was not negotiable. In the case of primary schools the parish priest (or rector in the case of Protestant schools), in consultation with the local bishop, made key decisions (Inglis, 1987). The religious order or body made key decisions in religious-run secondary schools. While the Education Act of 1998 limited the power of all the Churches and institutionalized democratic forms of governance that had been evolving slowly since the 1970s – due to the decline in direct religious governance and the demand by parents and teachers for more control – nevertheless, the management culture that pervaded education was one that was Catholic in tradition.

One of the positive features of the Catholic tradition was its strong emphasis on the pastoral care of the children, especially in girls' schools (Lynch, 1989). Schools were expected to and did care for children in a variety of ways that were not required or paid for by the State. This was a feature of Catholic education in other countries and not just in Ireland (Grace, 2002). However, the problem that school management faced when the religious were no longer available to offer a range of school services, effectively as a gift to the State, was that there was no structure of management *in situ* to replace them. While posts of responsibility were created over time (A posts and B posts) to fill the middle management void, these were clearly defined and limited to particular tasks that were negotiated between unions and management. Moreover, as these promotional posts were given to staff on the basis of seniority rather than performance in both national schools (where the INTO negotiated the conditions) and in secondary schools (where the ASTI was the main union), they were seen as rewards for long service by many of the occupants. Although this practice has changed (and it did not operate in VEC-run schools), it nonetheless created a culture of promotion without engagement for teachers.

In effect, Ireland created a culture of management where the school principal had duties in local communities, especially in rural communities and small towns and villages, which were unwritten (helping run the local football club, the choir, the drama group, organizing charitable events, fund-raising etc.). These were not part of the principal's paid duties but they were part of an unwritten contract of total and often voluntary engagement with the local community. Principals were also expected to provide care and support services in schools for which they were not paid. There were not and still are not any social workers or counselors in Irish schools even if they are needed. Getting the state to pay for a school secretary to assist in administrative work has been a major task for school boards over the past 20 years.

As lay principals took over schools, they were increasingly required to take on all the duties of management and unwritten local duties with few supplementary supports. Unlike the religious of the past however, lay school principals did not have a supporting religious community. And, as we show in later chapters, if they were women, they were already morally impelled to be the primary carers of their own children, or parents or siblings who had care needs. With new managerialism new demands were mapped on to the already heavily loaded management role. The image of the all-available religious head was married to the 24/7 manager.

# Part II
# Appointing Senior Managers

# 3
# The Case Studies of Senior Appointments

## Background, objectives and rationale to the study

Education is an increasingly feminized profession, yet research indicates that senior appointments continue to be disproportionately male (Coleman, 2003; Thomson, 2009).While research has been conducted in Ireland on the reasons women do not apply for senior posts in schools in particular (Gleeson, 1992; Kellaghan and Fontes, 1985; Warren, 1997), we know little about the culture of senior appointments and the institutional framework within which appointments are made.

This is the first major study to examine cultural codes enshrined in senior appointments at all three educational levels in Ireland, focusing particularly on gender. It investigates the values encoded in the processes and procedures for recruiting senior post holders, and the values directing the work of management at primary, second-level and higher education. It also explores the views of those who served on the boards of assessors for senior appointments in all three education sectors, as to the challenges facing educational leaders in the contemporary era. The study set out to establish whether a culture of new managerialism (a culture that valorizes long work hours, strong competitiveness, intense organizational dedication, while assuming a lack of ongoing care commitments) was prevalent in Irish education, and if it were, how it impacted on the work of senior managers in education particularly women and men with primary care responsibilities. The policy goal of the research was to review existing procedures with a view to making them more genuinely inclusive of women and men working within different family, care and professional contexts.

Using a case-study approach, the objectives of the study were

- to examine empirically the definitions, terms and conditions, processes and procedures governing senior appointments in Irish primary, second level and higher education sectors;
- to identify the ways in which definitions, terms and conditions, processes and procedures are gendered, as well as how this gendering of appointments impacts on women and men;
- to examine the extent to which a culture of performativity and new managerialism has taken hold in schools and higher education institutions, and to examine the implications of this culture, where and if it exists, for gender equality;
- to develop recommendations for a paradigm of educational leadership and management that is both women- and care-friendly;
- to enable leadership and managerial authorities involved in the case-study schools and higher education institutions to learn from the research and to gain ownership of it in the process.

The *New Managerialism in Education (originally known as the Senior Appointments in Education* project) was conducted by a research team in the Equality Studies Centre in University College Dublin (UCD) School of Social Justice. It was funded by the *Gender Equality Unit* in the Department of Education and Science.

A qualitative methodology, comprising a series of strategically determined, intensive case studies of the senior appointment process across different educational sectors, was adopted; the selection of the case study school and higher level institutions is described below. A later and complementary stage of the research was completed in 2007, focusing on an analysis of media coverage and news-making of the major themes emerging from this initial study.

## Selection of the case studies

The research was focused on analysing the culture and values informing senior appointments in the Irish education sector in recent years. Appointments that had been made in the four years prior to the commencement of the study were sampled for inclusion in the study, notably those between 2001 and 2005. The planning of the study involved extensive dialogues with a wide range of stake holders in Irish education, including the Department of Education and Science, management bodies at various levels of education, parent representatives, teacher unions and representatives of various professional bodies representing school principals. The study was guided by an advisory committee comprising of representatives from a range of educational bodies with a management remit including the Irish Primary Principals' Network (IPPN), the Diocesan bodies for Catholic Schools, the Joint Managerial Body (JMB) for Secondary Schools, the Irish Vocational Education Association (IVEA), the teacher unions for primary and second-level schools and a number of other educational associations and interest groups. The committee met at the early stage of the study to approve the plan and design and after the data was analysed, to respond to the draft findings.

Twenty three cases of senior appointments were selected for the study. The cases represented appointments in primary, second-level and higher education. Prior to the selection of the case study schools and higher education institutions, initial meetings were held with teacher unions, representatives of management bodies and experienced principals and assessors. Senior managers who had been appointed within the previous four years were selected from national data on senior appointments provided by the Department of Education and Science and other educational agencies. A strategic sample was taken from the national data to ensure representation from different types of educational institutions across the country. An equal gender balance of recent appointees was selected for interview from primary, second-level and higher education institutions. The boards of management and trustees of each institution were then contacted, requesting an interview with an assessor from the interview board of the recently appointed senior post holder. Assessors were chosen for interview on the basis of their experience on interview boards for senior posts, bearing in mind the importance of gender balance. In many cases, the chair or another senior member of the interview board was interviewed. Representatives from the board of trustees or relevant education office were also interviewed in some cases, given the power and influence they exercised in framing the terms of senior appointments in particular school sectors.

Sixteen schools and seven higher level institutions[1] were selected for the main case studies, a profile of which is presented below at the end of this section (see Table 3.3 Profile of primary, second-level and higher education case studies). The study involved a total of 52 in-depth interviews across the 23 case studies as follows:

- Eight case studies were undertaken of principal appointments at primary level involving six coeducational schools, one all-boys' school and one all-girls' school in a variety of rural and urban communities. An equal number of women and men were interviewed among the eight principals and eight assessors. Four additional interviews were undertaken with education officers in the primary sector due to their strategic position in defining the terms and conditions for senior appointments in a range of primary schools in different regions. Twenty interviews were undertaken in total in the primary sector.

- Eight case studies were undertaken of principal appointments at second-level including four all-boys' and three co-educational schools and one all-girls' school in a variety of rural and urban communities. An equal gender balance of senior managers was also achieved in terms of the 16 second-level principalships. Three education officers were also interviewed; 19 interviews were undertaken in total in the second-level sector.
- Seven case studies of higher education appointments were undertaken including universities, institutes of technology, further education colleges and statutory education agencies. Three senior male and four senior female senior post holders were interviewed as well as four males and two female assessors from the selection boards. There were 13 interviews in all in the higher education sector.

A qualitative research methodology was chosen for this project as it is 'grounded in a philosophical position [...] that it is concerned with how the social world is interpreted, understood, experienced or produced' (Mason, 1996: 4). This interpretive approach is ideally suited to exploratory research where little is known about a topic. It allows for an empirical inquiry that investigates a contemporary phenomenon within its real-life context, using multiple sources of evidence (Yin, 1984: 23).

Each case study involved an in-depth qualitative interview with the recent appointee, an interview with one or more assessors from their interview board and the collection of relevant supporting documentation (advertisements for the post, application forms and other relevant information). Two distinct interview schedules were designed for senior appointees and assessors, with adaptations for the relevant education sector (primary, second-level and higher education). These interview schedules comprised open-ended questions, designed to explore interviewees' experiences of the interview process and educational leadership in a style that 'probes beneath the surface, soliciting details and providing a holistic understanding of the interviewee's point of view' (Quinn-Patton, 1987: 108). Interviews lasted between one and two hours in length, were digitally recorded and later transcribed in full for analysis purposes.

We also undertook an analysis of the background to the appointments by examining the advertisements, information given to candidates, the procedures followed for the appointments, the profile of the selection panels and all other related documentation. This work took place at the same time that we were conducting the interviews. As Ezzy (2002: 61) points out, 'simultaneous data collection and data analysis builds on the strengths of qualitative methods as an inductive method for building theory and interpretations from the perspective of the people being studied'. A system of open coding was used to identify the initial findings emerging from the data, before categorizing this material into different research themes (Maykut and Morehouse, 1994). A qualitative computer software package, MAXqda, was used to organize and code the interview data and case study documentation (Corbin, 2007). This analysis identified the main themes of the research, including different management and leadership characteristics sought after in potential appointees (such as efficiency, past performance in management roles, accountability and interpersonal relations and communications skills), perceptions about the impact of gender and care on appointments and senior management work, and the socio-cultural norms of educational leadership and management. A second stage of analysis followed, using theoretical reflection and literature to further refine the analysis of these findings. The main themes were organized under the headings of the application and selection process, experiences of educational leadership and management, implications for identity and the self, and gender and care. Simultaneously, a detailed literature review was completed to review contemporary theories, national and international research on educational leadership and management.

This research project followed ethical principles of autonomy, informed consent, confidentiality and sensitivity. All stages of this research were completed overtly, gaining the full permission of all respondents. The confidentiality of participants was maintained, with all material resulting from the research deleting any personal or identifiable references. At times, this meant excluding or generalizing information from the interviews that would have compromised this anonymity (i.e., names, places, organizations and so forth). We were also mindful of the need for sensitivity to the local issues among the education community in Ireland (it is a small country and many people in senior posts in education know one another), and the power dynamics involved in conducting research with individuals appointed to leadership positions and with those involved in their appointment. Given the small size of the senior management community in higher education, particular care was taken to anonymize the identities of those interviewed.

## Profile of senior managers, assessors and educational institutions

### Primary-level case studies

The eight primary principals (four women and four men) were based in six co-educational schools, one all-boys' and one all-girls' school. These schools were located in a variety of rural and urban communities across Ireland (see Table 3.1); they had been appointed within two to four years of the research interviews. The schools ranged in size from 45 to 454 students, with four schools having fewer than 100 students, two schools between 100 and 200 students and two schools over 400 students. As a consequence, the larger schools had 'walking' or administrative principals and the six schools with 200 pupils or less had teaching principals.[2] The strong religious background of Irish primary school management was evident in the fact that five of these schools had a Roman Catholic background, one was Church of Ireland and the other was multi-denominational.

The boards of management of these schools were all voluntary, and members varied in their knowledge and experience in education. Some members were highly experienced in education and management issues, while others were new to the post and relatively inexperienced. The socio-economic background of students varied, with four schools serving students from a mixed socio-economic background, two served students from disadvantaged backgrounds and two catered for students

*Table 3.1* Primary-level case studies

| School name | School type | School size | Religious status | Socio-economic status | Location |
|---|---|---|---|---|---|
| Scoil Allen | Girls | 45 | Catholic | Middle | Urban |
| Scoil Corrib | Co-ed | 413 | Catholic | Disadvantaged | Urban |
| Scoil Derg | Co-ed | 454 | Catholic | Middle | Urban |
| Scoil Derravaragh | Co-ed | 94 | Catholic | Mixed | Rural |
| Scoil Erne | Boys | 145 | Catholic | Disadvantaged | Urban |
| Scoil Foyle | Co-ed | 58 | Multi-denominational | Mixed | Rural |
| Scoil Neagh | Co-ed | 50 | Multi-denominational | Mixed | Rural |
| Scoil Sheelin | Co-ed | 116 | Church of Ireland | Mixed | Rural |

from middle class backgrounds. Two schools (one in a rural area and the other with disadvantaged status) described their student enrolments as declining. Three schools were maintaining a steady number of enrolments and three had expanding student numbers (as a consequence of their location in areas with a rapidly increasingly population).

The eight principals who participated in these case studies ranged in age from 37 to 49 years. While five of the eight principals had children (one principal had one child and the remaining four had two or more children), a sizeable minority (three principals) had no children. Of those with children, three principals had young children (12 years of age or under) and two had older children (teenage or adults). Most had spent several years teaching before applying for the principalship. Three principals had between 18 and 27 years of teaching experience, three had between seven and ten years while the remaining two principals had one year and four years respectively. In those cases where principals were appointed as principals with very few years of classroom experience, they had gained knowledge and skills in other areas of education. For example, the principal with four years of teaching experience had been seconded to the Department of Education and Science for seven years. The principal with only one year of teaching experience had been working in a special education unit for several years before becoming principal in another school for two years prior to the current position. He was one of only two people in the primary school case studies who had previous experience as a principal; the other had acted as principal prior to being appointed on a permanent basis. For the remaining six principals, that was their first position as principal and most had been successful on that initial application. Only two people had submitted other applications for principalship.

All but one of the principals had additional postgraduate qualifications beyond their initial degree in teacher education. Two had postgraduate diplomas and were currently enrolled for a master's degree, and five already had master's degrees. Their master's degrees were mainly in education, but with specialization in areas such as languages, information technology, arts, business and management. The person who did not have postgraduate education spoke about a desire to complete a master's degree at a later stage when her children were older.

Assessors were chosen on the basis of their experience and seniority in the interview process. Two assessors described themselves as 'relatively new' to the senior appointment assessment process, one as 'experienced', and four others as having 'several years of experience' of educational management and interviewing for schools. Three of the assessors we interviewed were former principals. Two additional interviews were conducted with representatives from the board of trustees of two schools (the interview panel of one school group and two education officers from another).

### Second-level case studies

Four of the eight principals interviewed at second level were female and four were male. Three were based in co-educational schools, four in all-boys' schools and one in an all-girls' school; all had been appointed within the previous three years. The eight schools were located in a variety of rural and urban communities across Ireland (see Table 3.2 below). The school size ranged from 542 to 221 students, with six schools having between 400 and 600 students, one having approximately 350 students and the remaining school with fewer than 250 students. The religious influence in Irish second-level schools was evident in the fact that five of the eight were secondary schools with a Roman Catholic background, with the remain classified as multi-denominational, two of which were VEC (Vocational Education Committee) schools and one a fee-paying school.

The boards of management of the second-level schools were all voluntary, with most schools describing their board of management as

*Table 3.2* Second-level case studies

| School name | School type | School type | School size | Religious status | Socio-economic status | Location |
|---|---|---|---|---|---|---|
| Scoil Blackstairs | Secondary free-scheme | Boys | 509 | Catholic | Middle | Rural |
| Scoil Comeragh | VEC | Co-ed | 446 | Multi-denominational | Disadv | Urban |
| Scoil Errigal | VEC | Co-ed | 356 | Multi-denominational | Mixed | Rural |
| Scoil Galtees | Secondary free-scheme | Boys | 542 | Catholic | Middle | Urban |
| Scoil Iveragh | Secondary fee-paying | Boys | 221 | Multi-denominational | Middle | Urban |
| Scoil Mourne | Secondary free-scheme | Co-ed | 412 | Catholic | Mixed | Urban |
| Scoil Nephin | Secondary free-scheme | Girls | 505 | Catholic | Mixed | Urban |
| Scoil Sperrin | Secondary free-scheme | Boys | 437 | Catholic | Mixed | Urban |

experienced and supportive. The VEC schools also described the wider support structures that they gained from the national VEC system. Most of the secondary schools were in a process of change as religious bodies amalgamated or restructured schools, managing them through the establishment of boards of trustees and regional education offices. The one fee-paying school in the second-level sector had a long-established private support system. The socio-economic background of students in these schools varied, with four schools educating students from a mixed socio-economic background, one educating high numbers of students from a lower socio-economic background and two schools serving a middle-class student body. Two school principals described their student enrolment as declining (one in a rural area, while the other was located in a wealthy urban area with an older and changing age profile). Four schools were maintaining a consistent or increasing number of enrolments, although they were in a competitive position vis-a-vis other local schools, while the remaining two schools had full student enrolments as a consequence of high status (one as a respected secondary school in a rural area and the other was a fee-paying[3] school in an urban area).

The principals ranged in age from 38 to 54 years. Six principals had children and two principals had no children (one was a member of a religious organization and was celibate). Only two principals had children under the age of four years (one male and one female). Most were extremely experienced teachers before applying for a principalship: three had experience of over two decades; three had between 10 and 20 years of teaching experience, while just a minority (two) had taught for a period of less than 10 years. These latter two principals had other educational management experiences; one was on secondment to a Department of Education programme and the other had formerly been a principal in another school. All had experience in posts of responsibilities or as assistant principals prior to taking up that position, aside from the member of a religious order. Two principals had previous experience as a principal in another school before being appointed to their current position. For the remaining six principals, that was their first position as principal. All but one of the principals had additional postgraduate qualifications beyond their initial teaching degree. This principal who was a member of a religious order had been appointed directly to the post by the bishop under Article 20 of the Articles of Management (DES Circular 04/98), which allows religious bodies to appoint a qualified member of the order to the principal position in defined circumstances. Two principals had postgraduate diplomas and six had master's degrees in education. At the time of the interview, only one of the principals had three years of experience in the post of principals, while the majority (seven) were either in the first or second year of their current position.

The eight assessors (two female and six male) and three education officers (all male) who participated in the second-level case studies were chosen on the basis of their experience and seniority in the interview process. All of the assessors had several years of experience of educational management. They also had considerable interviewing experience across several schools (including the three representatives from the board of trustees and education offices who were also interviewed). Eight of the assessors and education officers were former principals, while two of the remaining three assessors were retired professionals with extensive interview experience and the other was a retired teacher who had many years of experience in VEC management.

### Higher education case studies

Three male and four female senior managers in seven higher education institutions were interviewed. Most candidates had been appointed within two years of the research interview and one within four years of appointment. They worked in a variety of higher education institutions including further education colleges, institutes of technology, universities and statutory agencies and in a variety of locations across Ireland. All of the higher education institutions were well established, with steady student enrolments and expanding research activity. They were undergoing a process of change, as new strategic plans had been introduced, which emphasized the professional development of staff and the expansion of research activity. In many cases, the institutions had also reformed their senior management structures.

The participant post holders were at a senior management level, representing heads of faculties (or equivalent positions), vice-presidents and heads of institutions. They ranged in age from early forties to mid-fifties. Four senior post holders had between one and three children and three senior post holders did not have children. Aside from one male post holder who had a pre-school child, the remaining senior post holders had older children (in their late teens and twenties). Most had extensive experience in senior management posts before they applied for their current position, ranging from heads of faculties and departments to deputy head or head of an institution. All of the senior appointees in institutions of technology and universities had Ph.D. qualifications, with the other two post holders having master's degrees. All of the academic post holders were research active, and had extensive policy experience, advising different government departments and other bodies on strategies in their area of expertise. Three of the academic senior post holders had international experience in other educational institutions in Europe and the United States.

The six assessors who participated in the third-level case studies were chosen on the basis of their experience and seniority in terms of interviewing (one assessor was not able to complete an interview). All had several years of experience of educational management and interviewing. Four male and two female assessors from the interview boards were interviewed in total. The assessors of the institutes of technology and university appointments all had Ph.D. qualifications and were academics that had previously, or currently, held top-rank senior management posts. The other two assessors for the further education and statutory agency appointments had extensive senior management and interview board experience, as well as academic and equivalent qualifications in their field.

## Conclusion

This study was both intensive and extensive; it involved compiling data from all sectors of education about the principles governing senior appointments in Irish education. It explored the values and presumptions encoded in the way posts were defined, interpreted by assessors and then lived by appointees. The study took place at a time of great change in Ireland, a time when the move to new managerialist practices had become part of the official ideology of the Irish public service (Collins et al., 2007). It was the time of the so-called Celtic Tiger when the values of neo-liberalism were being actively promoted, but not always without resistance. The study tells the story of what was happening in educational management in Ireland in that period. It highlights the many challenges that new appointees had to face, not only with the rise of new managerial values, but with the decline of the very real influence of the Catholic Church in managing a large body of Irish primary and second-level schools.

New management systems were being instituted at primary, second level and in higher education but without much discussion as to what the impact of these changes might be. This study set out to examine the impact of new managerialism, especially its gender and care implications for contemporary leaders in Irish education.

*Table 3.3* Profile of primary, second-level and higher education case studies

| Primary schools | Description | Education leader | Gender of education leader | Assessor | Gender of assessor | Education officer | Gender of education officer |
|---|---|---|---|---|---|---|---|
| Scoil Corrib | Primary co-ed urban disadvantaged | Aindreas | Male | Cathal | Male | Ferdia<br>Etain<br>Cuan | Male<br>Female<br>Male |
| Scoil Erne | Primary boys urban disadvantaged | Muiris | Male | Ailbhe | Female | | |
| Scoil Sheelin | Primary co-ed rural mixed class | Aoife | Female | Colum | Male | | |
| Scoil Derg | Primary co-ed urban middle class | Aodhaigh | Male | Cian | Male | | |
| Scoil Allen | Primary girls urban middle class | Bridget | Female | Caitriona | Female | | |
| Scoil Foyle | Primary co-ed rural mixed class | Aisling | Female | Blathnaid | Female | Cillian<br>Ciara | Male<br>Female |
| Scoil Neagh | Primary co-ed rural mixed class | Caoimhe | Female | Macdara | Male | | |
| Scoil Derravaragh | Primary co-ed rural mixed class | Conor | Male | Donal | Male | | |
| **Second-Level Schools** | | | **N=8; 4M, 4F** | | **N=8; 5M, 3F** | | **N=5; 3M, 2F** |
| Scoil Comeragh | VEC co-ed urban disadvantaged | Niamh | Female | Barra | Male | | |
| Scoil Nephin | Secondary girls urban mixed class | Maeve | Female | Sheila | Female | | |
| Scoil Iveragh | Secondary boys urban middle class | Muireann | Female | Fionn | Male | | |

| | | | | | | | |
|---|---|---|---|---|---|---|---|
| Scoil Errigal | VEC co-ed rural mixed class | Brendan | Male | Eibhlin | Female | | |
| Scoil Galtees | Secondary boys urban middle class (fee paying) | Peadar | Male | Ronan | Male | Cormac | Male |
| Scoil Mourne | Secondary co-ed rural mixed class | Fionnuala | Female | Fiachra | Male | Fergal | Male |
| Scoil Sperrin | Secondary Boys Urban Mixed Class | Gearoid | Male | Lorcan | Male | Michael | Male |
| Scoil Blackstairs | Secondary Boys Rural Middle Class | Daithi | Male | Deasun | Male | | |
| **Higher Education** | | | **N=8; 4M, 4F** | | **N=8; 6M, 2F** | | **N=3; 3M** |
| Colaiste Achill | Higher education institution | Tadgh | Male | Conleth | Male | | |
| Colaiste Saltees | Higher education institution | Neasa | Female | Oscar | Male | | |
| Colaiste Inis Meain | Higher education institution | Andrew | Male | Siofra | Female | | |
| Colaiste Inisbofin | Higher education institution | Tiernan | Male | Iarlaith | Male | | |
| Colaiste Tory | Higher education institution | Sinead | Female | Ide | Female | | |
| Colaiste Rathlin | Higher education institution | Una | Female | Oisin | Male | | |
| Colaiste Valentia | Higher education institution | Sorcha | Female | Not applicable | Not applicable | | |
| | | | **N=7; 3M, 4F** | | **N=6; 4M; 2F** | | |

# 4
# The Selection and Appointment of Senior Managers in Education

## Introduction: Creating and normalizing educational leadership

While there is extensive research on educational leadership and management (Day et al., 2000; Gunter, 2001; Thrupp and Wilmott, 2003; Bush et al., 2010), the selection of educational leaders has received comparatively little attention. The most substantive body of research on leadership selection emerges from New Zealand and Australia in the wake of the reforms of equality legislation governing appointments (Gronn and Rawlings-Sanaei, 2003; Brooking et al., 2003; Barty et al., 2005; Blackmore et al., 2006; ACER, 2008). As this research indicates, the selection process is crucial as it is at this stage that the definition of a leader is constructed by selection boards and, in turn, interpreted and embodied by candidates as they present themselves as potential leaders. Such research also suggests that selection is a subjective process of decision-making that is strongly bound by the local context. While concerns have been expressed about the falling number of applications for leadership positions internationally (McGuinness, 2005; Gronn and Lucey, 2006; Earley et al., 2002; Blackmore et al., 2006; Fink and Brayman, 2006), the question of how the leadership role is itself constructed and how this is reflected in the processes of selection and appointment has rarely come under scrutiny.

This chapter explores how educational leadership is constructed through the selection process across primary, second level and higher education sectors of Irish education. In line with international experiences, Irish education is characterized by intensive change and new demands on leadership and management. While many of these changes mirror those taking place internationally, some are specific to the Irish context, such as the traditional dominance by Catholic ownership and management structure of Irish schools as explored in previous chapters. Neo-liberalism and an expanding knowledge society discourse has ensured increasing attention being paid to 'market' forces in terms of the quality of schooling, choice in education and the expansion of education (Coolahan, 1981; Lynch, 2006; Lynch and Moran, 2006). Focusing in this chapter on the views of assessors across 23 selection panels, we examine the interaction between formal policies regarding appointments and the informal practices of selection.

This analysis highlights the tensions that can exist for assessors – and senior managers – as they try to balance increasing performativity and new managerialist demands with the more traditional ethical and moral dimensions of leadership roles in education (Lynch et al., 2006; Blackmore et al., 2006). Key concepts of 'local logics' and 'homosociability' frame the analysis as it is shown how assessors often select 'safe' candidates according to known and familiar qualities, thereby normalizing particular leadership qualities (Brooking, 2003; Blackmore et al., 2006). 'Local logics' privilege particular understanding about the nature and values of the institution and community from which assessors implicitly draw in their selection of a leader who would be a 'comfortable fit' (Brooking, 2003: 4). Like homosociability (Kanter, 1977), this process ensures the reproduction of socially homogenous candidates. As Savage and Witz (1992: 16) contend, homosociability is often gendered as men (and other dominant groups) 'effectively "clone" themselves in their own image, guarding access to power and privilege to those who fit in, to those of their own kind'. This is allied with the careless culture of new managerialism that discourages those with care responsibilities to progress onto senior management roles.

## Qualitatively researching the senior management culture

The 23 case studies in this research consist of qualitative interviews with recently appointed educational leaders, an interview with one or more assessors from their selection board and analysis of supporting documentation (advertisements, application forms and other documentation). A strategic sample was taken from national data on educational appointments provided by the Department of Education and Science (DES) to ensure representation from different types of institutions. The three sectors of Irish education were represented, including (a) eight primary schools, (b) eight second level schools and (c) seven higher education institutions. The analysis of the selection process is based on the interviews with assessors. They were chosen on the basis of their experience and seniority in the interview process and included chairs of boards of management, representatives from board of trustees and former principals (or academics in the case of the higher education sector). Although assessors were chosen on the basis of experience, their gender profile reflected the general dominance of men in senior management with 21 males and 9 females interviewed.

## Governance and senior management appointments in Irish education

As the previous chapters explored, historical patterns of ownership and management have shaped a distinctive management culture in Irish educational institutions. The influence of Roman Catholic Church ownership of over 90 per cent of primary schools and 60 per cent of second level schools is significant, as is the declining number of religious personnel in school management and the consequent shift to trusteeships and amalgamated schools. These changes are countered by the state's increased role in education as reflected in the recent establishment of the *Forum on Patronage and Pluralism in the Primary Sector*. All levels of education have been marked by an increase in legislative and bureaucratic regulation in recent years (notably Universities Act 1997, the Education Act 1998, Employment Equality Act 1998, Equal Status Act 2000, Education Welfare Act 2000, Education for Persons with Special Educational Needs 2004 and the Institutes of Technology Act 2006). The new legislation has placed statutory responsibilities and devolved powers of governance onto educational institutions and boards of management.

This chapter examines how these changes have impacted on the policies and procedures governing the selection process for senior management posts in Irish education. It tracks the appointment process through the stages of establishing a selection board, examining the permeation of a voluntary ethos of public service in Irish education, and the intersection of homosociability and gender dynamics. We analyse how the criteria for selection of senior management are established and used in the appointment process (by translating criteria to the local logics of the institution, personal qualities of candidates and previous management experience). We examine how the selection process is socially constructed, with assessors making subjective decisions about authenticity of candidates' performances that have an important influence on the selection process and future educational leadership.

## Establishing the selection board: Voluntarism, homosociability and gender

The power to define and apply the criteria for appointment is very important as it enables assessors to construct and normalize their ideal qualities of leadership. The selection process for senior appointments in Irish education varies according to sectors, with the least formality evident at the primary and second level school sectors where state regulations list general selection guidelines such as professional qualifications, management experience and reference checks.[1] Departmental circulars are general in nature, listing guidelines for selection criteria, advertising, interviewing and records.[2] Vocational Education Committee (VEC) guidelines give more detailed guidelines for the selection board on developing job specifications, questions and criteria.[3] The higher education institutions demonstrate the greatest depth and formalization of application and interview process, with detailed guidelines listed about the job and person specifications, interview questions and selection criteria. As a consequence of the generality of the guidelines at school level, the chairperson of the board of management and former principals tend to be the most influential figures on selection boards due to their insider knowledge of the post and school. Hence the selection of assessors for the interview board is a primary mechanism of power, as

> the interview panel can be constructed by schools in such a way that the principal wants to steer the succession process, they can use influence so that people aren't even aware of [it] because they are not even tuned into it [...] it actually looks like a board decision but the principal has made it [...] When you dig and when you excavate a little bit, you discover that this has been set up for a particular purpose which is to anoint person A.
>
> (Fergal, male assessor, Scoil Mourne second level school)

While internal assessors were influential in the selection process due to their local knowledge of the institution, external members were viewed as more objective (relative to internal assessors) and brought a wider expertise of educational management to the selection process. They were selected from panels of educational experts (formed by diocesan and management associations) and many were former principals, chosen because they were 'associated with the school closely [...] I know the sort of person that would suit the school' (Sheila, female assessor, Scoil Nephin second level school). This closeness can be problematic as

Blackmore et al. (2006) point out, in terms of 'homosociability', as assessors select leaders with familiar qualities and characteristics to one's self. While this does maintain ontological security for assessors who can operate within a familiar context of taken-for-granted assumptions (Garfinkel, 1987; Goffman, 1961, 1971), it can also potentially act as a constraining and homogenizing force in the appointment of senior managers.

The dependence on known assessors was driven by the ethos of voluntarism that underpinned educational management in Ireland. Boards of management and selection boards of Irish schools were voluntary in nature, resulting in a high dependency on the goodwill and voluntary efforts of a limited number of people. Over half of the assessors involved in this study were former educational leaders (school principals and academics), motivated by their commitment to education to serve voluntarily. This resulted in assessors being drawn from a relatively small pool of highly involved 'insiders'. While this gave them important local knowledge of the education system, problems can arise when selection 'boards have been interviewing for so many years they [...] have gotten into a nice little rut' (Ciara, female education officer, Scoil Foyle primary-level school). While their wealth of experience and knowledge of the educational system is invaluable (especially in a voluntary selection process), it can create and reproduce the focus on homosociability and predictability – qualities that may not be suited to leading education in a time of rapid change (Sugrue and Furlong, 2002).

This 'vocational ethics of service' (Gronn and Rawlings-Sanaei, 2003: 172) has become normalized within the wider context of religious control of Irish school management. However, the decline of the religious congregations has made this voluntary system increasingly difficult to maintain and dependent on a very small number of highly motivated volunteers. Tensions were evident between voluntarism and the increased formalization required by legislation and state policy. As a consequence of the growing formalization, educational ownership were becoming involved in the selection process in an advisory capacity, offering guidance and training for school staff and selection boards. These management bodies consisted of boards of trustees and associations such as the Irish Primary Principals Network, Joint Managerial Body, National Association of Principals and Deputy Principals, Irish Vocational Education Association and local VECs.

A gradual shift towards more formalized structures was evident in the rise of a standardized online application process and application forms.[4] The beginning of this shift was evident in this research in VEC second level schools and higher education institutions which were developing more formalized procedures, albeit still advisory in nature. This formalization of the selection process gave greater control to external groups, as evidenced by the human resource consultancies who organized the selection process in two higher education institutions in this research. The selection board for higher education appointments was usually larger than the three-to-five person board in the school sector and included the director or president of the institution. Assessors were usually academics with senior management experience and viewed their assessor role as part of their general work responsibilities rather than as a voluntary act.

For many assessors interviewed for this research, it was still a transition period for educational management in Ireland. Consequently, they drew on their own experiences and expertise of educational leadership to guide their work rather than any formal structures or training. Training was usually one-day courses focusing on equality and employment legislation – what one assessor described as having 'more to do with covering your tail than anything else' (Colum, male assessor, Sheelin primary-level school). Increasingly, new members of an interview board received guidelines and training from their education office or other umbrella organizations like Catholic Primary School Management Association (CPSMA), Joint Managerial Body (JMB) and Irish Vocational Education Association (IVEA). All these groups provided short training courses on interview techniques and legislative requirements. Assessors described how this training was becoming increasingly important due to the employment and equality legislation governing the appointment process and the corresponding fear of litigation. Assessors had to ensure that they shortlisted and selected candidates according to the advertised job criteria and legislation.

The requirement for gender representation on selection boards was viewed as problematic, although it was a legal requirement. The general lack of female participation at senior management level internationally (Deem and Ozga, 2000; Lafferty and Fleming, 2000; Knights and Richards, 2003; ACER, 2008; Tihveräinen, 2009) is reflected in Irish higher education in particular (O'Connor, 2007a, 2007b; Lynch et al., 2006; Grummell et al., 2009a) and resulted in a very small pool of potential female assessors. As a consequence, many female assessors at higher education described the large number of interview panels on which they participated and the resultant lack of time for other activities.

> The biggest issue is that there are still so few women at a senior level that proportionately too much of our time is being taken on

> interview boards; it is actually quite a serious problem [...] this small number of women who are very good researchers are now finding their time available for research is being eroded by going onto interview boards, selection boards, committees of all kinds when trying to get gender representation.
>
> (Siofra, female assessor, Inis Meáin higher education institution)

Ironically the equality legislation intended to protect and promote women's participation in senior management has had many contradictory effects, putting immense strains on the current female senior managers and causing 'gender inflections [to go] underground' (Brooking et al., 2003: 152). The criteria that assessors established for senior management posts provide key insights into the culture of senior management in Irish education. These criteria can be organized into three issues relating to the local logics of the institution, personal qualities of candidates and management experience. What was significant was the clarity with which assessors spoke about these criteria, indicative of their influential role in the selection process. These criteria formed the basis of the interview questions and the marking scheme for selection, but revealed the cultural and attitudinal values of senior management. Also notable was the focus on translating these criteria to the tangible reality of the principals' work, both in terms of relating criteria to candidates' previous work experiences and to what Brooking (2003: 4) described as the 'local logics' of the school community.

## Translating criteria to the local logics of the institution

The process of selecting an educational leader was mediated by a range of factors, including the expectations, values and experiences of educational leaders and assessors, state regulations and the nature of the local community in which the educational institution was situated (Webb, 2005: 72). The 'local logics' of the post and institution was recognized as a significant factor in the selection process internationally (Brooking, 2003; Tihveräinen, 2009) and it was contextualized in the Irish case in terms of the rapid social and economic change facing the country. The traditional care and development logic of education had to be translated to the requirements of contemporary Ireland with its emphasis on a knowledge economy, performativity and educational capital as the subsequent chapters recount. The care and development logic retained an emphasis on values such as ethos, disadvantage and community. The ethos of the school was a vital component of Irish education, particularly in terms of the dominance of religious orders in primary and second level schools (Drudy and Lynch, 1993). Applicants were expected to demonstrate and embody the ethos or characteristic spirit of the school, but identifying these qualities in the selection process can be quite elusive.

> we would be confident that [ethos] is something very valuable that we want to preserve and we are looking to see, can the person [...] get at the heart of the ethos? Now there is a whole lack of confidence around this area because [assessors] have been uneducated [...] my generation wouldn't have been well educated around ethos, it would have been a very conformist faith [...]. The big issue for us would be around having the confidence to proclaim this [school] as being Christian [...] without getting too evangelical about it. That's obviously a huge concern.
>
> (Michael, male assessor, Scoil Speerin second level school)

The ethos of Catholicism acted as a shorthand code for pastoral values of care and Christianity that were valued within Irish education. Gendered consequences were evident in the prevalence of single sex schools in the Catholic system (Lynch et al., n.d.[5]). Although assessors accepted that gender should not be a factor in the appointment process (as Irish legislation states), norms and expectations around gender roles in the segregated tradition of Irish schooling still existed. Assessors commented on the feminization of the teaching profession, with contradictory implications being expressed (Drudy, 2008). Some assessors were concerned about the negative implications in terms of lack of male role models in schools as a consequence of the feminization of the teaching profession. In other cases, the desire for positive female role models was emphasised.

> [I]f you send your daughter to an all girls school, I would expect there would be a woman principal and I did that with my own daughter and the reason is there are so few role models for women [...]. I imagine if it was an all boys school that some people might be inclined to say 'sport' and things like that [...] and some people might be caring of the woman candidate and say 'well it might be too much and it might be charitable not to put her in charge of those very unruly boys' you know, it might be [...] seen as a tough job.
>
> (Ailbhe, female assessor, Scoil Erne primary-level school)

Assessors translated the job criteria and qualities to other 'local logics', including designated disadvantaged status. Irish state discourses have tried to deal with the persistence of disadvantage in particular communities through a targeted policy of supporting designated disadvantaged schools (Educational Disadvantage Committee, 2005). The chair of a board of management for one designated disadvantaged school revealed how selection criteria for these schools were bound up with an implicit sense of care and empathy that the principal had to create.

> I was at pains, I think, in my initial meeting with the [other] assessors to try and explain that to them, that we weren't looking for a general run of the mill principal, that being a disadvantaged area [...] the whole social make up of the families, family life and everything that's here, just demands as such a kind of a level of understanding and empathy that is much greater than would be necessary elsewhere [...] I do think that they are very particular values [...] the way the whole staff care for the children and the sense of trying to help the families in so far as they can.
>
> (Cathal, male assessor, Scoil Corrib primary-level school)

Similarly, assessors at other designated disadvantaged schools described how they gave weighting in the marking scheme for candidates' understanding of the local logics of disadvantaged schools. This was contextualized in candidates' empathy with students, their parents and the local community. This had to be combined with management and administrative criteria as these schools had an extensive administrative workload associated with the funding requirements for disadvantaged and special needs initiatives. This holds potential conflict as Webb (2005: 78) described in the UK context where the moral leadership role (of family and community care) promoted by inclusion policies simultaneously comes into conflict with standards agenda (performativity and accountability demands of the state). These dual tensions made leadership positions in designated disadvantaged schools a very demanding role.

Other schools were entering a process of change that was specific to the Irish setting as they moved from religious to lay leadership. Due to the declining involvement of religious orders in Irish school management, many Catholic-owned schools were appointing their first lay principals and were losing the support structure that the religious orders had offered. This meant that the new principal had to develop alternative structures of middle management from within the existing teaching staff. Assessors were keen to ensure that future principals would lead these changes with sensitivity for staff and the religious ethos of the school.

For other schools, the rural culture of its location was important. As the local school was at the heart of the community, the ideal principal was expected to be a school and community leader.

> Even though a community minded principal would always be a desirable asset to any school or any area but probably more so in a rural area. However that can be enacted [in] many different ways [...] within the school context by keeping the community in mind and the community traditions in mind, whether it is sporting, musical or athletic.
>
> (Donal, male assessor, Scoil Derravaragh primary-level school)

As Tihveräinen (2009: 70) noted, 'most selections are context-specific and emphasize suitability to the particular school'. Community-based activities were important 'local logics' in a rural context, where promoting and co-ordinating community-based activities like sports and music became important criteria for leadership. The importance of the principal as a community leader in rural areas was rooted in the high status traditionally given to teachers in rural Irish communities. This stood in contrast to urban-based schools where increasing administrative demands lead to general management and leadership skills being emphasised. Likewise, the assessors in the (urban-based) higher education sector highlighted other professional criteria, including curriculum development, teaching and learning effectiveness, and strategic planning. Assessors at two fee-paying second level schools and higher education institutions reflected the increased marketization context in their emphasis on 'skill and experience in financial management [...] managing the interface between finance and the service provided' (Cormac, male education officer, Galtees second level school). This highlighted the variation across sectors, as the location, management and social class background of the institution resulted in different aspects of management being emphasised.

## Embodying educational leadership through personal qualities of candidates

Assessors outlined a range of personal criteria that they associated with leadership positions. Candidates were expected to embody these qualities or 'manage their insides' as they internalise these qualities into their identities and presentation of self (Alvesson and Willmott, 2002; Tihveräinen, 2009). Many of these characteristics were framed within a discourse of career dedication (qualities such as ambition, drive, commitment and energy that were viewed as essential for the intensity of the leadership role). Assessors wanted someone who was

> strong, self confident and [with high] self esteem, the ability to keep putting one foot in front of the other. One of my hobbies is sailing, people who can sail into a headwind for 24 hours at a time and have that stamina and doggedness to stay with it [...] the absence of that in sufficient measure to my mind is one of the reasons why some people go under, not being able to see that they can come out the other end of it.
>
> (Ronan, male assessor, Scoil Galtees second level school)

These qualities evoke the concept of hegemonic masculinity (Connell, 1995), which is encoded in the new managerialist discourse of single-minded dedication to the job. This role, by virtue of its demanding nature, excluded many people (especially women and others with care responsibilities). Leadership is a form of 'greedy work' (Gronn, 2003) 'occupying an ever-expanding space and requiring intensified and sustained 24/7 performativity-driven levels of individual engagement' (Gronn and Lucey, 2006: 406). It is mobilized through organizational culture and language, which adopts the rhetoric of the battlefield or sports ground and reproduces stereotypical gender roles (Halford and Leonard, 2001: 54). When this discourse of individual dedication and strength was combined with the hierarchical position of the leader as ultimately responsible for all aspects of the organization, it created a very tough and demanding role. As a consequence, assessors sought evidence of the candidate's dedication and strength to perform these tasks; '[the principal] has to give over and above but unless they have it in themselves to give that, the whole thing will grind to a halt. So we have to ensure that those personal qualities are there first' (Lorcan, male assessor, Scoil Speerin second level school). Female assessors and senior managers spoke of gender implications of this all-encompassing leadership role when it has to be combined with care responsibilities.

> [Y]ou do work phenomenal hours and you are probably hearing this as well from school principals. That is another issue for women who still have caring responsibilities. I mean I don't, my children are grown up [...] most of us I'd say at the level I am at, it is just work, there is nothing else in our lives. That is an awful thing to say but there really is very little else if you want to really keep everything

going. That is a big question for the university sector and the education sector generally.

(Siofra, female assessor, Inis Meáin higher education institution)

The sense of living in a risk society (Beck, 1999), especially in the context of a rapidly changing Ireland, also intersected with this new managerial discourse. Assessors specified how they wanted committed and ambitious leaders who could modernise and develop their school, especially where the institution was expanding or amalgamating. These personal qualities of dedication, strength and modernization still had to be combined with the traditional caring ethos of education. This was particularly important at school level where assessors highlighted interpersonal qualities of care, sensitivity, communication and teamwork with staff and students.

The belief that these personal qualities should be embodied in candidates' personality and value system was also evident in research with Finnish assessors (Tihveräinen, 2009). Goffman's work (1961, 1971) on the presentation of self suggests a strong inclination on the part of the individual to present a competent 'self'. As assessors highlighted, the truth/authenticity of this performance or presentation of self can be difficult to ascertain through the interview process and was described in impressionist terms; 'when you interview somebody, there's an overall sense that you get [...] there's an impression that you get when you're interviewing, I'm not sure that I can put it into words better than that' (Cathal, male assessor, Scoil Corrib primary-level school). The selection process was a social performance, where candidates attempted to 'offer a plausible performance, one that leads those to whom their actions and gestures are directed to accept their motives and explanations as a reasonable account [...] a true [performance]' (Alexander et al., 2006: 32).

Assessors judged the authenticity of personal qualities through the body language and attitude that candidates expressed throughout the interview; 'sincerity is very important, you have to judge that and that can be difficult [...] you have to notice everything, little half smile can mean so much' (Donal, male assessor, Scoil Derravaragh primary-level school). They focused on personal qualities and described how they were trying to match a candidate's temperament with the school ethos and value system. Some differences were evident across sectors, as personal qualities became less important for senior management posts at higher education where assessors emphasized strategic vision, status and management skills instead. However, personal qualities still remained important as background evidence for qualitative judgments of candidates made during their interviews and from informal tours of the institution beforehand.

> [The candidates] were all offered the opportunity to visit [the institution] [...] and his [the guide's] opinion would have been fed back to the interview board [...] the type of things that they were looking at and type of personality that they had, their general knowledge and their interest, all of that type of stuff.
>
> (Ide, female assessor, Tory higher education institution)

Similarly, the use of reference checks was a qualitative judgment, with assessors acknowledging that

> there are other cases where you would read between the lines where a Principal might say 'if there is any further information please don't hesitate to contact me' or something like that, you would feel that there is something there that the Principal wanted to say but didn't want to put it in writing.
>
> (Deasun, male assessor, Scoil Blackstairs second level school)

## Embodying leadership through previous management experience

Assessors also judged candidates' suitability to the post in terms of their previous experience of management and leadership (including professional training and qualifications). Gaining management experience was only one element; as the ability to reflect upon one's past experiences in written and verbal interview formats was also considered essential. The capacity for reflectivity was taken as an indicator of how a candidate would perform in a leadership role; 'you have to look at the job and then you have to look at the experience of the person [...] because a basic predictor of how you're going to be is what [...] you have done in the past [...]. It's the ability to reflect on experience and learn from it' (Ferdia, male education officer, Scoil Corrib primary-level school). Candidates' ability to reflect upon their experiences gave practical illustrations of their management and leadership capacity and reduced the 'burden of risk' inherent in the selection process (Gronn and Lucey, 2006: 117).

Assessors spoke about the increased importance of management and administrative aspects of the leadership role, especially as a result of the growing performativity and bureaucratic demands of recent years.

They placed a particular emphasis on interpersonal and communicative management skills as a core part of being a senior manager. As noted previously, interpersonal criteria were often related by assessors to the local logic of the institution and they examined how candidates embodied these criteria. For example, a preference for a young and dynamic principal as a counter-balance to the older age profile of staff, gender sensitivity in a single-sex school, good interpersonal skills to deal with a history of difficult staff relations or changing management structures.

> The particular school [...] was going from being a [religious] Brother principal to a lay person and that always involves a huge deal of change because the Brother would have done an awful lot for the school, the lay person would have to develop middle management structures so that would be something that would have to go down on the criteria in such a school because you can't expect a lay person to operate the same way. So working with the staff, the staff wanted somebody who was very practical and down to earth who had experience in classroom teaching [...]. But they were also kind of sad that the previous principal was leaving [...] they had a great deal of affection so you had to be very sensitive to that.
>
> (Ailbhe, female assessor, Scoil Erne primary-level school)

Assessors at second level also specified leadership in relation to curriculum development, team building and staff development. Reflective of the growth of new managerialism in education, administrative management skills were emphasized across all sectors.

> I think the most important change from 50 years ago when I went on the board [of management] is that it has become a tremendously administrative job dictated by the Department of Education [...] that was one of the major things we were looking for because if you can't administer it you will be absolutely bogged down. You won't be able to run the school in any way if you can't do the administrative part.
>
> (Fionn, male assessor, Scoil Iveragh second level school)

This concern that leaders would become 'bogged down' or overwhelmed by the changing demands of the role was also expressed by other assessors who spoke of leaders 'go[ing] under' or 'sink[ing]' in Simkins' (2005: 14) terminology. The reiteration of these concerns highlighted the fears for educational leaders as their administrative and managerial role expanded. Assessors were keen to ensure that the candidates possessed the skills necessary to run the organization. They judged this through evidence of previous management experience (posts of responsibility and middle management) and how it was embodied through the personal qualities of the candidates (assessed through interview, especially suppositional questions about 'how would you deal with *X* situation', 'describe a past experience where you had to manage *Y* type of situation').

Higher education assessors were also conscious of the importance of management skills, particularly administrative and financial management ability. As senior management in higher education came from academic backgrounds, evidence of management skills was not a pre-given and candidates had to demonstrate their management capacity through their application and interview. Unlike the personalized and localized focus of the principalship interviews at primary and second level, the management skills that higher education assessors emphasized were framed within a discourse of strategic vision, negotiation and competitive context of higher education.

> I think strategic vision is very important in terms of; you are in quite a competitive arena [...] you would be looking as well for the other management skills in terms of [...] somebody who understands finances and who [...] can distribute budgets, manage budgets. You are looking for somebody who is a negotiator because they have a lot of negotiating to do both internally and externally in terms of funding and the likes. You certainly are looking for somebody if you can who has some knowledge, now that doesn't have to be personal knowledge, but who has gone to the bother of getting knowledge of what third level education is about, what the sector is about, where the sector fits in Ireland.
>
> (Ide, female assessor, Tory higher education institution)

Assessors for higher education institutions also spoke about the importance of senior managers having a professional track record of academic achievement in their own field to gain the respect of their colleagues. Having high academic status as well as experience was vital to command the respect that would enable them to lead.

> We would also expect them, and that would be specific to each faculty, to have some track record and the capacity to gain respect in the academic areas over which they would preside [...] we were

> looking for a capacity to provide managerial leadership in their area but also to have a personal track record that would command respect amongst those they would lead.
>
> (Oisin, male assessor, Rathlin higher education institution)

This was a point that was not mentioned by primary or second level assessors who did not problematise the link between experience and respect; if school principals had gained experience and could reflect upon it, respect seemed inevitable. A combination of academic respect and experience was considered essential for senior appointments at higher education.

Gender was a significant underlying factor here as women – and other carers – often lacked the same level of management experience as male candidates (Davies-Netzley, 1998; Brooking et al., 2003; ACER, 2008). There is a gendered division of labour where the teaching profession is considered feminised, but this does not translate into representation at higher management levels (Gronn and Rawlings-Sanaei, 2003; Drudy, 2008). While there are multiple factors impinging on this process which the previous chapter explored, the competitive nature of the current promotion process at higher education leaves women, especially those with children, at a disadvantage as they will have taken maternity leave and career breaks disrupting their career progression and senior management experience.

> [W]e're back to a situation with women and childcare [...] at the most likely time in your career where you are going to get this management experience, many women have taken time out to rear kids.
>
> (Ide, female assessor, Tory higher education institution)

## Judging the performative nature of senior management interviewees?

For school appointments, candidates were shortlisted on the basis of a short written application, before presenting themselves as potential leaders in interviews over a one- or two-day period of interviewing.[6] The interviews at primary and second level explored candidates' suitability as leaders of the specific school. Interviews at higher education level consisted of a presentation on strategic vision by the applicant, followed by an interview with the selection board. The establishment of marking and scoring schemes for shortlisting and interviews was more developed at the VEC and higher education sector, although the education offices of second level school were beginning to formalise this process. The marking scheme was most developed at higher level appointments where the marks were reviewed at the end of the interview process to select all appointable candidates. Members of the selection board then ranked these candidates and negotiated their relative strengths and weaknesses – in relation to the job criteria – before making a final recommendation to the personnel or human resources office. This process was not as clearly defined at primary and second level, where the interview board were required to keep records of their criteria and decision-making process, before giving a recommendation to the board of management, pending the completion of reference checks.

While there are wider questions about the suitability of standardized applications and interview as a selection tool (Blackmore et al., 2006), this process was accepted by most of the participants in this research as appropriate (although it must be noted that we only interviewed assessors and successful candidates). There was evidence of a cultural shift from informal to more formal practices as the use of interview preparation among the candidates illustrated, dovetailing with findings internationally (Caldwell et al., 2003; Gronn and Lucey, 2006; ACER, 2008). Formal preparation for application and interview was most evident in the higher education sector, while the informal and fresh approach that was favoured at primary level militated against such preparation.

The informal culture surrounding the appointment process caused some confusion among assessors and candidates about the level of preparation and contact prior to interview. Assessors spoke of the expectation that candidates would research the school and the post. This did cause some confusion for candidates who were not sure if it was appropriate to contact the school before the interview to find out information. Instead, most primary and post-primary candidates did their own informal research through their own network of colleagues. They also spoke of the 'coded messages' that could be read from advertisements. This was particularly important when the closing date for application was extended or the post was re-advertised. This was read as a coded message that 'the quality and number of applications did not satisfy the Selection Committee that there was a worthwhile competition taking place' (Ronan, male assessor, Scoil Galtees second level school). Applicants at higher education were given a contact person for enquires and informal discussion about the post, and assessors spoke of their expectation that candidates would research and contact the institutions to discuss the post before the interview.

Assessors felt that training was becoming increasingly important as the appointment process was formalized (especially at higher education level) and candidates were strategizing their career plans. Applicants described a range of preparation, including CV preparation, mock interviews, postgraduate study on leadership and management, analysing strategic plans and talking to former leaders and staff. The detailed application process for higher education posts encouraged candidates to develop and present a strategic vision for the institution. This presentation served several purposes as the assessor for a higher education institution explained:

> The presentation was something on strategic management [...] for the institution as it went into the future [...] it would have played an important role from a number of points of view. One from the point of view that you need a communicator [...]. It is also important to have some type of strategic vision and leadership skills that someone would demonstrate through both their thinking behind their presentation and their delivery of that presentation.
>
> (Ide, female assessor, Tony higher education institution)

Many assessors were sceptical about interview coaching and research; feeling that this 'grooming' would diminish freshness and sincerity evident during the interview. This relates to the wider question of the suitability of interviewing as a selection tool, as it involves a performance that may or may not be authentic. Alexander et al. (2006: 55) described an authentic performance as one where the person 'seems to act without artifice, without self-consciousness, without reference to some laboriously thought-out plan'. This concern with authenticity was most evident among primary-level assessors.

> I wouldn't be dazzled by people who are coached at interview, there are other ways of finding out. It is nice to be coached, to be confident but it doesn't give you a true picture and I prefer to see the true picture. Then you have to do other things like checking references and asking key questions and using common sense.
>
> (Ailbhe, female assessor, Scoil Erne primary-level school)

The formalization of the interview process and consequent demand for greater preparation was double-edged. As the earlier comments indicated, many assessors found it difficult to decipher rehearsed from sincere performances. This raises the problematic issue of performance and authenticity – is a performance less authentic and sincere because it is rehearsed? For some assessors, the increased formality of interview questioning made it difficult to probe rehearsed answers, while others acknowledged the value of interview preparation.

> There is a value in training in the sense that it can help you make use of an interview time, you can get better at getting to the point, you can get better at focusing on the answer [...]. But generally I think all the training in the world won't substitute for *capacity*, but for the person who has the capacity the training will get them that extra edge. I suppose what I am saying is [that] people who are reasonably experienced interviewers will reasonably rapidly distinguish between the person who is just a good interview performer rather than a *substantive* performer.
>
> (Oscar, male assessor, Saltees higher education institution; added italics)

The task of assessors involved the capacity to judge the 'substance' of the performance, to look behind the front stage performance of the interview to seek actual 'capacity' (Goffman, 1971). Assessors described how they used different types of questions to encourage candidates to demonstrate their suitability for the position. These included reflective questions on ethos, teaching experience, management capacity, and previous experience. Selection boards also positioned these questions in terms of the local logics of the institution, for example, interpersonal and conflict management skills in schools with a history of difficult staff relations or leading a school in a disadvantaged area. Candidates were asked to reflect upon past experiences and give concrete examples as a means of illustrating their senior management and leadership capacity; what one candidate described as 'probing questions, looking for your own attitudes, your own experience and how you would handle things in your way [...] how would I handle stress and things like that' (Aodhaigh, male principal, Scoil Derg primary-level school).

Reference checks from former employers also played an important affirmation role in the selection process. Assessors at primary and second level schools described the reference checks as a means of confirming that a suitable candidate was selected for the post. They were a form of reassurance for the decisions made during the selection and interview process. As mentioned earlier, verbal reference checks were particularly important and trusted, as many 'people are so wary of putting anything in writing, and the other side of it, people will give glowing references to get rid of teachers that they are not fond of' (Cillian, male education officer, Scoil Foyle primary-level school).

## Selecting the candidate: the impact of homosociability and authenticity

The selection of successful candidates was a qualitative judgement of capacity and authenticity, as assessors tried to match the qualities and experiences of candidates with the requirements of the individual institution. Assessors described how increased regulation and employment legislation governed their work. They used formal marking systems to rank each candidate's performance in terms of the listed criteria (judged from their curriculum vitae, references, interview and/or presentation). Freedom of information legislation[7] meant that any written comments by assessors as a collective body were available to candidates. This had made the selection process more transparent and quantifiable, but also held potential difficulties in terms of how interview records were maintained and how assessors subjectively interpreted criteria assessed the authenticity of candidates' performance.

Assessors tried to maintain ontological security by reducing risk and maintaining consensual selection processes as they stayed within the parameters of a familiar and accepted order (Blackmore et al., 2006). Assessors described a norm of homosociability and consensual decision-making because 'people have a familiarity with the kind of [educational] landscape and have a reasonable familiarity with interviewing [so] that a consensus is extraordinarily common' (Oscar, male assessor, Saltees higher education institution). The similar backgrounds and educational experiences of assessors promoted familiarity and consensus. On a positive front, this has protected the traditional care and development logic of education from the performativity demands of new managerialism, but it also potentially resists change and promotes conservatism (Sugrue and Furlong, 2002). Gronn and Lucey (2006: 119) describe a similar process of 'cloning' in the Australian selection process, where assessors look for qualities of 'loyalty, predictability and avoidance of risk'. In many cases, homosociability was the central mechanism in the assessment of candidates' suitability (Blackmore et al., 2006).

> They [other assessors] were able to say that 'she came from a very good family', you know [...] this was something that gave these people a bit of comfort then because they could situate them within a context and they could begin to visualise them, even though they

> didn't know them [...] they knew their family and that gave them the level of comfort they needed.
>
> (Fergal, male education officer, Scoil Mourne second level school)

Although this assessment by family background contravenes equality legislation,[8] it gives a clear insight into the operation of homosociability as assessors sought the comfort and reassurance of locating candidates in a known context – in this case family background. While the influence of homosociability and ontological security on subjective processes like selection boards is unavoidable, there is a danger that 'unfamiliar' or non-traditional candidates may not be appointed (including women, minority groups, disabled people etc).

The selection process is inherently performative and subjective, as assessors negotiate the relative strengths and weaknesses of each candidate and qualitatively assess their suitability to the position.

> It is more a knack than a science isn't it? [...] you can get two quite strong candidates for a job [...]. So what you have to then do as honestly and honourably as you can go back to their interview and discuss the respective strengths of them against the marking scheme almost [...]. It is a finely balanced judgement at the end of the day. But it would be quite unusual for it not to be a consensual judgement. You spend time at it to be quite truthful, you'd spend whatever time it took to do justice to people.
>
> (Oscar, male assessor, Saltees higher education institution)

Once again we returned to the issue of confidence and authenticity, in this case the truthfulness of the finely balanced subjective judgement that assessors had to make. What was evident from this research was the performative nature of the selection process both in terms of the candidates' presentation of self – as a suitable educational leader – and in terms of the assessors' judgement of this performance. It was part of the 'discretionary powers' that was central to professions (Frowe, 2005), as assessors – in this case – draw upon their past experiences and reflective capacity to judge the authenticity of the performance and the suitability of candidates to the post.

## Conclusion: Performing and judging the selection process

This chapter argues that the selection process for appointing senior managers in education is a socially constructed process where particular qualities of leadership are normalised. It is a relatively unproblematized stage of educational leadership which needs analytical attention to understand how educational leadership is subjectively constructed and judged by the selection board assessors and, in turn, embodied and performed by potential candidates. As Blackmore et al. (2006) contend the apparent clarity of merit selection in the selection process disguises its socially constructed nature and the tendency to reproduce familiar qualities and experiences. This selection process has to be contextualized within the wider political, economic and socio-cultural background of the education system. With respect to the Irish education system, this includes the intensive and rapid societal change that has resulted in growing demands on educational management, tensions between the traditional care ethos of education and new managerial demands, the role of voluntarism in educational management coupled with new governance structures (arising from the decline of religious congregations' involvement in the school sector, and the restructuring of higher education). These developments are framed by the growth of neoliberalism and other socio-cultural changes in Irish society in recent decades.

This research illustrates the complex interaction between formal procedures of appointment and the practices of selection; it identifies a range of professional and personal criteria that are used to identify and select candidates for senior management posts in education. The formation of the selection board is vital as homosociability plays a key role in the selection process; where assessors come from a similar background, they tend to construct criteria of educational leadership in line with familiar qualities and characteristics. The power to select and interpret criteria is central as it enables assessors to create and implement their visions of educational leadership that are 'safe' and predictable. While this does maintain ontological security for assessors and candidates who can operate within a familiar context of taken-for-granted assumptions, it can also act as a restraining and conservative force against change. This is particularly problematic when educational leadership is faced with intense organizational and socio-cultural change. This is also problematic in gender terms, especially in higher education, where the prevailing leadership model is a masculine one. It means that women and other minority groups are excluded and marginalized as consequent chapters explore.

Differences between education sectors are evident, with the primary and second level sectors translating criteria to the local logics of the institution and emphasizing the personal qualities of candidates. The higher education sectors were more formalized in their application process, highlighting their own 'local logics' of strategic and professional management criteria. While assessors looked for evidence of management capacity, the higher education discourse was marked by a concern that leaders would become overwhelmed, especially due to the expansion of management and administrative tasks. Female assessors and senior managers were acutely aware of the gendered division of labour and spoke about the pressures of balancing the competing demands of leadership and care work. The male assessors were less conscious of these pressures, with only a minority of male interviewees talking about care-related issues (see Part III). While an intensification of the management role was evident across all sectors, it was particularly acute in the higher education sector whereas the shorter hours of the school sectors were perceived as facilitating care and leadership work.

The protection offered by equality legislation and the feminization of the teaching profession have had contradictory gender implications. Brooking's research in New Zealand concluded that 'restructuring [of equality legislation] has not opened up new leadership opportunities for women in primary schools in the way one might have expected [...]. It has created opportunistic gaps for women to fill when either the market or male credibility has failed, but even then there has not been a significant shift considering the high proportion of women in the workforce, compared to men [...] the autonomy, power and "local logics" employed by boards, is effectively gate keeping the masculinised culture in place' (2003: 11). This conclusion is equally applicable to the Irish context as this research demonstrates.

The construction of senior management criteria was also influenced by the specific context and requirements – the 'local logics' – of the institutions that were matched to the personal qualities of candidates, senior management skills and previous experience. As the qualities of educational leadership can remain quite elusive and difficult to judge, assessors tended to translate criteria to the local logics of the educational community, primarily aspects of the school such as ethos, designated disadvantaged status, gender profile of the school, changing management structures from religious to lay management, socio-economic background and the differing needs of rural and urban-based communities. Assessors outlined a range of personal criteria that they expect candidates to embody in their identity and presentation of self. Qualities of dedication and strength intersect with the new managerial culture of strategic reform, performativity and change. There was a continuum of performativity with a high emphasis on it in higher education and a much lower emphasis in primary education. Interpersonal qualities of care, communication and sensitivity appear especially important in the school sector where the traditional care ethos of education continues to predominate as explored in later chapters.

The ability to reflect upon previous experiences is relatively unproblematized in the primary and second level sectors where management experience is presumed to bring respect. The lack of management experience among the academic applicants at higher education results in assessors focusing on candidates' professional track record and academic standing as a marker of capacity. The framing of these leadership criteria varied; with the primary and second level assessors evaluating how candidates embodied these qualities in their past experiences and personal qualities, while higher education assessors placed leadership within a wider sense of strategic vision about education. The focus was frequently on getting leaders who could achieve or maintain competitive advantage for a given university or college. This latter frame fits into the neo-liberal discourses on higher education more neatly while the former expressed a stronger focus on the local circumstances of the individual school.

The interpretation of selection criteria by assessors and applicants highlights the socially constructed and situationally specific nature of the appointment process. Assessors spoke of the difficulties of judging these performances, especially the authenticity of the performance, qualitatively interpreting the body language and substance of the performance to identify suitable leaders for the institution. The findings show that homosociability, local logics and authenticity are key values in leadership selection despite the increased formality and regulation of educational appointments. It indicates that the selection process must be considered by policymakers, training agencies and educationalists in developing a more proactive and inclusive approach to educational leadership.

# 5

# Assessing Applicants: The Care Rules

## Introduction

The relative absence of women from senior management posts is attributable to a host of complex processes, including the way power circuits operate in organizations and are masculinized in their deployment (Clegg, 1990; Halford and Leonard, 2001). It also arises from gender-based discriminations, both direct and indirect (Knights and Richards, 2003), and from the way in which inequality regimes are institutionalized and legitimated in particular educational contexts (Acker, 2000). The introduction of new public service management has played a significant role in reproducing the gendered order of control within education in the twenty-first century (Acker, 1990, 2000; Bailyn, 2003; Blackmore and Sachs; 2007, Deem, 2002; Drudy, 2005; O'Connor, 2010b; Morley, 2005) despite the fact that it may also open up opportunities for some women for promotion (Newman, 1995; Deem, 2003).

Gender inequalities at managerial levels are not simply a function of organizational dynamics, however important these may be. They are also influenced by more subtle and less visible social processes, including the way public citizenship itself is constructed, and how such conceptualizations frame the concept of leadership and management.

The concept of citizenship is formally defined as gender-neutral. When people think of citizenship they do not think of it as a gendered concept, as denoting a particular gender or sexuality. Yet, feminist scholars have demonstrated that the concept of citizenship is deeply gendered: the theoretical 'universal' citizen is in reality a male (heterosexual) citizen (Hobson, 2000; Jónasdóttir, 1994; Lister, 1997; Sevenhuijsen, 1998; Yuval-Davis, 1997). What is especially salient about the male-defined concept of citizenship is that it is care-neutral. The citizen is defined through political, economic and cultural actions not through care actions. The good citizen is assumed to be economically active, a producing citizen and 'a job seeker'.[1] A Rational Economic Actor (REA) model of citizenship is assumed both inside and outside education (Lynch, 2007; Lynch et al., 2007). Within the neo-liberal model, even those who are tied to caring, and without care supports, are under pressure to be economically active (Dodson, 2007). Those who are disabled are also commanded to be productive citizens, even though the evidence is far from compelling that when this policy is enacted that it is successful either in employment (Clayton et al., 2011) or education (Goodley, 2011). While neo-liberalism has played a key role in reconstructing citizenship in line with entrepreneurialism and embedding this increasingly in education (Apple, 2004; Peters, 2005), the equation of citizenship with rationality and autonomy, and the eschewing of any concept of dependency and interdependency from citizenship, has a longer history that impacts on how care work is perceived both outside and inside education.

## The care context

From the time of Hobbes and Locke, to that of Rousseau and Kant, up to and including Rawls, Western political theorists have glorified the autonomous concept of the citizen. They have upheld a separatist view of the person, ignoring the reality of human dependency and interdependency across the life course (Benhabib, 1992; Kittay, 1999). Political theorists have defined the emotional and rational life of individuals as opposites, the former being equated with femininity and a narrow self-focused privatized moral and political thinking. There is a belief that:

> emotions seem to bind the moral imagination to items that lie close to the self and stand in a relationship to the self. They do not look at human worth or even human suffering in an even-handed way. They do not get worked up about distant lives, unseen differings. This, from the point of view of many moral theories – including utilitanarianism, Kantianism, and their relatives in non-Western traditions – would be a good reason to reject them from a public norm of rationality, even though they might still have some value in the home. I believe that this objection [...] underlies quite a few arguments that connect women's emotionality with restriction to a domestic role, suggesting that exactly the abilities that make them good in that role undermine their status as citizens.
>
> (Nussbaum, 1995: 368)

The denial of the importance of emotions has contributed to the denigration of the emotional work that women[2] do to maintain affective relations of love and care. Moreover, the belief that women are unable to exercise independent judgment due to their assumed 'emotionality', and are thereby unsuited to public office, and particularly to positions of responsibility, has a long history: it is found not only in Western but in Islamic, Chinese and Hindu traditions (Nussbaum, 1995: 364).

As denigrated emotional work has been corralled into the family sphere, and equated with femininity, there has been an inevitable equation of work and value with the public sphere. Rawls's *A Theory of Justice,* which has been the dominant work in Anglophone political theory since its publication in 1971, is a clear example of a text that gives primacy to the public sphere. Sociologists working on egalitarian issues have followed a similar course. Whether in Weberian (Tilly, 1998) or Marxist (Wright, 2010) traditions, they have relied on social class, status and power interests as the primary categories for investigating the generation of inequalities and exploitations. Indeed debates about equality in education have been overwhelmingly focused on the Marxist-Weberian trilogy of class, status and power (Lynch and Baker, 2005). Sociological studies of gender inequality in employment have also focused strongly on the public sphere, be it on the dynamics of power within organizations (Halford and Leonard, 2001), on how bureaucracies could be reconstituted to be more 'rational' and thereby gender inclusive (Kanter, 1977), or on how women's lack of promotion to senior posts is simply a matter of 'preference' and personal priority (Hakim, 2000). While early feminist scholarship challenged mainstream thinking as to why women were subordinated at work (Acker, 1990; Cockburn, 1991), their work was primarily focused on how the *public* bureaucracies of work are constructed as masculine in the first instance. While deconstructing liberal framing of the gender equality problem as one of 'making women behave like men', they remain focused on the public spheres as the primary site of injustice.

## The feminist contribution

The interface between care work and gender justice has received considerable attention from feminist economists and sociologists (Folbre, 1994, 2001, 2009; England, 1999, 2005; Himmelweit, 2002; Hochschild, 1989, 2001; Gornick and Meyers, 2003), and legal theorists (Fineman, 2004; Fineman and Dougherty, 2005). It is feminist-inspired work that has also played the key role in political theory in taking issues of care, love and solidarity out of the privatized world of the family to which they had been consigned by liberal and indeed most radical egalitarians (Benhabib, 1992; Gilligan, 1982, 1995; Held, 1995; Jónasdóttir, 1994; Kittay, 1999). It has also drawn attention to the salience of care and love as goods of public significance (Kittay, 1999) and highlighted the importance of caring as a human capability meeting a basic human need (Nussbaum, 1995, 2001).

Scholars in the feminist tradition have also exposed the limitations of conceptualizations of citizenship devoid of a concept of care and highlighted the importance of caring as work, work that needs to be rewarded and distributed equally between women and men in particular (Finch and Groves, 1983; Fraser and Gordon, 1997; Glucksmann, 1995; Hobson, 2000; Hochschild, 1989; Lynch, Baker and Lyons, 2009; O'Brien, 2005; Pettinger et al., 2006; Sevenhuijsen, 1998). They have demonstrated the limitations of the citizenship model that assumes the prototypical human being is a self-sufficient rational economic man (*sic*) by highlighting the reality of dependency, both in childhood and at times of illness and infirmity, and the way vulnerability and dependency operate across the life course (Badgett and Folbre, 1999; Fineman, 2008; Folbre, 1994; Folbre and Bittman, 2004). And they have shown that economic, political or cultural institutions cannot function without the care institutions of society (Fineman, 2004; Sevenhuijsen, 1998; Tronto, 1993).

Overall, what feminist scholars have helped to do is to enrich intellectual thought within the Weberian and Marxist traditions. While social class, status and power are primary categories for investigating the generation of inequalities and exploitations feminists have drawn attention to the way the care world and affective domains of life are also discrete spheres of social action, albeit deeply interwoven with the economic, political and cultural spheres.

## Care and education

An indifference to the affective domain and an allegiance to the education of the rational autonomous subject and public citizen are at the heart of Cartesian rationalism, encapsulated in the phrase 'Cogito ergo sum'.[3] The person to be 'educated' is defined as an autonomous and rational being, one who is prepared to achieve her or his potential in the public sphere of life, with little attention given to the relational caring self.[4] It is exemplified in Rousseau's *Émile* where it is assumed that Sophie does not need education for judgement comparable to that given to Emile as she is deemed unsuited, as a woman, for public positions of responsibility. It is part of the doxa of the education trade, an unspoken assumption that the person being educated is rational and autonomous. It is also assumed that teaching and schooling are a rational processes preparing citizens as public persons, largely ignoring the ways in which caring is both endemic to education and to human life itself (Noddings, 1984, 2003). The presumption that emotions, and the caring and other-centred thinking that stems from them, are not rational is also a deeply gendered assumption as it is women who are defined as emotional and therefore non-rational.

The citizen carer and the care recipient citizen (and most people are both one and the other simultaneously) are only recognized in the educational arena when professionals are being trained as social workers, nurses, doctors, teachers, psychologists, social care workers and/or counsellors/therapists. Education for caring and loving as mothers, brothers, partners, fathers, sisters, friends, neighbours or work colleagues, or how to create a solidarity-based world, is not generally part of the educational trajectory.[5] With some notable exceptions, there is little attention paid to the subject of caring *per se* as a goal of education (Lynch, Lyons and Cantillon, 2007). The problem is exacerbated by the fact that the scholarly understanding of work has been equated with economic self preservation and self actualization through interaction with nature (Gúrtler, 2005; Pettinger et al., 2005); within this frame, education is inevitably seen as preparation for public, economically validated work.

What is significant about the focus on the rational, public subject is that it is not a new phenomenon. The classical liberal view of higher education glorified the arts and humanities for the cultivation of the mind (Newman, 1875). And the development of logical mathematical intelligence and abstract reasoning has been the overriding preoccupation of formal education since its initiation (Gardner, 1983). Even the growing recognition of emotional and personal intelligence within developmental psychology (Gardner, 1983, 1993, 1999; Goleman, 1995, 1998; Sternberg, 1998, 2005) has not unsettled the focus of education on the development of the rational public actor. The research on emotional intelligence (EI) is largely indifferent to issues of gender, care and interdependency, and particularly to how EI operates in the informal care sphere. There is a strong focus on the relevance of EI for measurable achievement. With some exceptions (Cohen, 2006) emotional intelligence is generally defined as a capability that enhances and supplements other marketable capabilities including academic attainment (Cherniss et al., 2006; Grewal and Salovey, 2005; Goleman, 1995; Lopes et al., 2006; Vandervoort, 2006).

### Neo-liberalism, education and the Rational Economic Actor (REA) citizen

Although classical liberalism focused attention on educating the public citizen as an autonomous subject, within neo-liberalism the ideal type human being is increasingly defined as a self-sufficient, rational and competitive, economic *man*. At the individual level, education is defined in terms of personalized human capital acquisition, making oneself skilled for the economy 'the individual is expected to develop a productive and entrepreneurial relationship towards oneself' (Masschelein and Simons, 2002: 594). The focus of the EU Lisbon agreement on preparing citizens for the 'knowledge economy' exemplifies the prioritization of competitiveness as a key educational objective: knowledge is reduced to the status of an adjective in the service of the economy.[6]

The ideal type of neo-liberal citizen is the cosmopolitan worker built around a calculating, entrepreneurial, detached self. It is a worker who is unencumbered by care responsibilities and is free to play the capitalist games in a global context, be it as migrant labourer or market capitalist (Connell, 2002). Neo-liberalism has deepened the disrespect for the relationally engaged, caring citizen that it has inherited from classical liberalism by devaluing not only the emotional work that has to be done to care, but by validating consumption and possessive individualism as defining features of human identity. Competitive individualism is no longer seen as an amoral necessity but rather as a desirable and necessary attribute for a constantly reinventing entrepreneur (Apple, 2001; Ball, 2003a). Neo-liberal thinking in education has succeeded in doing what classical liberalism did not do; it subordinates and trivializes those aspects of education that have no (measurable) market value. Education within the humanities has already been subjected to this devaluation (Rutherford, 2005; Wang, 2005). As education about care and love work was not even on the educational table in the Cartesian tradition, it is even more easily trivialized in the neo-liberal era as it has no immediate commercial relevance in an age of marketization. Unlike the expunging of the humanities by deliberate downgrading, it is made irrelevant by omission.

The careless model of citizenship inscribed in neo-liberalism also offers a Hobbesian perspective on social and educational life, focusing on creating privatized citizens who are educated primarily for themselves (Giroux, 2002; Masschelein and Simons, 2002). Education is increasingly defined as just another service to be delivered on the market to those who can afford to buy it for their personal utility rather than a capacity-building public good that is a right of all of humanity. The vision that is presented is that of a privatised, consumer-led citizenry, fed on a culture of insecurity that induces anxiety, competition and indifference to who are vulnerable and who are seen to threaten that individual security. In this wider cultural context, being caring of others, and having education specific to that task is easily defined as redundant.

While classical liberalism saw intimate care work as a private matter, it did grant a place to basic public forms of care within the machinery of the welfare state. The attack on the welfare state, a hall mark of neo-liberal policies (Harvey, 2005), exemplifies the undermining of care and solidarity in the public sphere. Moreover, the care dimension of professional carers has been increasingly eroded with the rise of neo-liberalism. The focus of education for professionals with a strong care remit, including teachers and social workers, has become increasingly regulatory and controlling (Garrett, 2006; Mahony et al., 2002). The work of social carers is also subjected to detailed scrutiny and measurement in a manner that often undermines the relational and emotional dimensions of paid care work itself (Toynbee, 2007).[7]

While people who manage schools, or those who appoint them, may be removed from the world of hands-on caring, there is no person who, at some time, is not in need of care, and many people have care responsibilities. People are relational beings even if their job status or public standing gives them considerable autonomy. It is this relationality, particularly the relationality that involves primary care work, which we want to explore here in terms of how it frames senior appointments in education.

## Management, education and care work

Teaching is a caring profession and care work is endemic to education. Managing a school requires many skills, some of which are purely technical and apply in any organization (planning, budget and time management, personnel management, establishing systems of governance and regulation, etc.). Others are unique to education, including the developmental and nurturing skills required to enable young (and not so young) people to grow and develop, and to support teachers in this task. There is an emotional investment in people that is not required in many organizations as the 'product' is the development and care of others.

Because the principles of new managerialism are devised in a commercial context where the bottom line is business gain and profit, they manifest themselves in education through the promotion of forms of governance (measurement, surveillance, control and regulation) that are antithetical to caring in a number of ways, especially insofar as they focus on outputs and subordinate process. While caring has an outcome dimension, it is generally not measurable in a specifiable time frame. The gains and losses from having or not having care are only seen over time. And caring is not open to measurement in terms of quality, substance and form within a metric measurement system. Even if caring could be monitored and measured through matrices, the very doing of this would force people into the calculation of other-centredness that would undermine the very principle of relatedness and mutuality that is at the heart of caring.

In a new managerial framework, people are ultimately instruments in the achievement of an end. The goal is the achievement of a successful product; the care of those who produce the product is, inevitably, secondary, except and insofar as it impacts on productivity. What is at issue here is a conflict of discourses and practices regarding the governance and purposes of education, and the role of relational human beings within this process.[8]

## Gender, care and educational management

### The context of the study

This is the first major study in Ireland to examine the cultural codes enshrined in senior appointments at different levels of education focusing particularly on gender. It investigates the values encoded in the processes and procedures for recruiting school principals and senior post holders in further and higher education and in statutory education agencies. It also explores the experiences of the principals and senior post holders in living out those values, and the views of assessors for senior posts across the first-, second- and third-level sectors as to the challenges facing school leaders in the contemporary era. The principal aims of the study were: (a) to test the claim by many researchers that a culture of new managerialism (a culture that valorizes long work hours, strong competitiveness, intense organizational dedication, while assuming a lack of ongoing care commitments) governs the work of senior managers in Irish schools, further and higher education institutions, and statutory educational bodies, and (b) to establish if new managerial forms of management have gender implications when and if they are in operation.

What lies behind the study is a deep-rooted concern regarding the lack of gender balance in senior appointments across the education sector.[9] As of 2011, none of the heads of the seven Irish universities is a woman; only three of the fifteen institutes of technology have women presidents while just two of the five heads of the teacher education colleges are women see O'Connor (2010a). In the latter case, women lead very small colleges. While women comprise 85 per cent of primary teachers, only 60 per cent of heads are women; at second level, women comprise 60 per cent of teachers but 37 per cent of principals. Despite the lack of gender balance nationally, we decided to interview a relatively even number of women and men at senior level, to explore in some depth how those who were appointed perceived their roles and the factors that influenced them in applying for and taking up principalships. We wanted to see what factors enabled women to be principals as well as what operated as disincentives.

The study focused on new appointees in senior management posts in primary, second-level and tertiary education in Ireland. One senior post in the Department of Education and Skills (DES) was also examined as the DES played a key role nationally in framing public systems of management, including increasingly educational management. All of those interviewed had been appointed within the preceding four years as the aim was to examine how new posts were being defined in the wake of the strategic management initiative of the Irish government (see Chapter 1) and the related rise of new managerialism as a mode of governance in education internationally. To understand the values and assumptions informing senior managerial appointments, a key assessor (either a chairperson of the board or a board member who was nominated as an influential member of the board by the chair) was interviewed regarding the criteria for, and management of, each appointment. In a small number of cases, trustees from schools were interviewed as the chairperson believed they would best explain the values informing the appointments process. This only happened at primary and second level.[10]

## Focusing on the assessors

In this chapter, we focus especially on the assessment process, particularly on the views of 28 assessors for the 23 senior posts. Not only had the assessors played a key role in the appointments under review, they also played a powerful role in other appointments as most served on an ongoing basis on selection panels for senior posts in their particular field of education. We planned to interview the chairperson of the board in each case, and where this was not possible we sought a nominated senior board member.

We interviewed eight assessors (five male and three female) who were involved in appointing the eight primary school principals within the past four years. While three assessors described themselves as 'relatively new' to the selection process, the remainder had several years of experience of educational management and were interviewing for several schools. Two additional interviews were completed with representatives from the board of trustees of two schools. The two people involved also had extensive management experience, as well as playing a central role in defining the criteria for senior posts, and, at times, in selecting candidates for principalships.

We interviewed eight assessors (six male and two female) and three education officers (representing the school trustees) involved in selecting second-level principals. All of the assessors had several years of experience of educational management and were interviewing for several schools. Eight of the assessors and education officers were former principals, while two of the remaining three assessors were retired professionals with extensive interview experience; the remaining person was a retired teacher who had many years of experience in Vocational Education Committee (VEC) management.

The six assessors (four male and two female) who participated in the third-level case studies, and the person from the civil service who assessed for the Department of Education senior post, each had several years of experience of educational management and interviewing. They served on many appointment boards in their own fields.

The reason for focusing on how the assessors defined the values and qualities they sought for senior management positions was because the people involved exercised considerable influence in setting the terms of appointment, and in determining who was appointed to the posts we were researching. Moreover, they were also involved in selecting candidates for related senior posts in their own sectors of education. They played a significant role in framing the cultural landscape at senior management level across the various sectors of education.

## Assessors' views – gender and related issues

As noted in Chapter 4, the different sectors of education operated with slightly different local logics. As the logic of practice for senior appointments in primary and second-level education was quite different to that in higher education and the civil service (particularly due to the endorsement of new managerialism at a formal institutional level in both higher education and the DES), these sectors are discussed separately. While female and male assessors shared some assumptions in common about the gender issues impacting on appointments, they also differed. For that reason, we analyse both gender groups separately.

### Male assessors at primary and second level

Gender was not regarded as being relevant by any of the assessors when assessing candidates for interview. All of those interviewed, both women and men, were adamant about this. As Fergal, the education officer for the trustees at Scoil Mourne contended, 'you might have a teacher that is fully immersed in the life of the school, they might have a family or they might not, I mean none of this is really relevant actually'. The assessor for Scoil Derg, who had been a principal in two different schools, and also an experienced assessor, expressed a similar view:

> I think certainly in my own operation in interviewing and assessing I think I would be looking at the person and the qualities rather than if it is a man or a woman.
>
> (Cian, male assessor, Scoil Derg primary-level school)

However, he did not deny that gender influenced decisions in some instances:

> The classic one is to say, and I heard somebody passing this remark because the neighbouring school Principalship also came up: It's an all-boys' school, and somebody said I don't think they would be ready for a woman heading up an all-boys' school just yet . And I'm thinking that doesn't make sense.
>
> (Cian, male assessor, Scoil Derg primary-level school)

When assessing people for principalships, some assessors were vehement that neither pregnancy nor motherhood mattered. They held the a view that you had a system in place to replace people who went on leave, whether for career breaks or for maternity leave, so you just worked with that system. The chairperson of the board of management for Scoil Galtees, a boys' second-level school (who is a principal in another school himself) pointed out that people move in and out of jobs, including teaching posts regardless of gender; mobility of staff is part of what you have to deal with in management. When asked if the gender of the candidate for a principalship mattered, he said:

> Quite honestly no. The way I will answer that question as well is by saying, when I look at the teachers that I have appointed I never think 'well Mary will probably be out next year because she had a child 2 or 3 years ago and she said that she would like to have a second'. I mean, take it away from that aspect altogether, if Thomas were to come to me and say 'I am applying for a job as History teacher 50

> miles down the road' I'd say 'Good on you and good luck to you'. I might hate as hell losing him but everyone can be replaced. You have to assume that as a Principal that no matter who it is, whether it's maternity leave, whether it's any sort of illness, you have to find a replacement [...] I don't worry about that aspect, I honestly don't worry about that aspect at all.
>
> (Ronan, male assessor/chair of Board of Management (BOM), Scoil Galtees boys' second-level school)

Not all assessors were as unequivocal in their belief that gender did not matter when it came to making senior appointments, however. The assessor in Scoil Sperrin, a boys' second-level school in an urban area was a director of a company in the private sector. His view of women was that they were 'effective', although his language implied a certain ambivalence about their suitability as managers. While he admired their 'dedication', he was a little concerned about what he called 'women's extreme views':

> Certainly in my time involved with the parents council and with the various boards of management, I'd been most impressed by some of the ladies who were here. And I could see certainly say, you know, in business I mean as a manager and as a director, a lot of them, [...] very effective people working for me [...] were ladies [...] [They] were more effective than their counterparts, more dedicated I hate to say. Women at times [...] sometimes, take a more extreme view than men but I found in terms of dedication and [...], I see no reason why a lady couldn't be principal.
>
> (Lorcan, male assessor, Scoil Sperrin boys' second-level school)

### Accepting the gender division of care labour

Even if assessors believed that gender did not matter at the selection stage, they still believed that it impacted on women's choices and applications for senior posts. As Conleth, the assessor of Achill further education college, recounted:

> I know there are a few people who didn't apply for the job because they had young families, and I'm talking about women now, yes [...]. That does affect the applicants for the job.
>
> (Conleth, male assessor, Colaiste Achill higher education institution)

The assessor for the principal's post in Scoil Nephin, a girls' second-level school, made the same observation, noting how two 'beautiful' women did not apply for the principal's post in the school:

> There were people on the staff here that could have applied for Principal at that time, at least two fully qualified, beautiful [...] [women] but because they had small children they didn't go.
>
> (Sheila, female assessor, Scoil Nephin second-level school)

And so did the assessor in Scoil Derg:

> A lot of women don't apply because of family commitments, because of care issues, saying 'no I couldn't possibly do that not when my kids are young'.
>
> (Cian, male assessor, Scoil Derg primary-level school)

What is significant about these conversations is that the assessors did not problematise the gendered division of care labour that contributed so obviously to the fact that women were not applying for senior posts. It was noted as a fact, a social given, without comment or without being contested.

The chairperson of the board of management in Scoil Sperrin, a boys' second-level school in an urban area, also claimed that caring responsibilities impacted on people's application rates for senior posts. However, while he believed that society was changing, and saw 'no reason why a lady couldn't be principal', he still felt it was inevitable that 'the lady' would be the person to be the primary carer. It was something that women could manage with 'au pairs and stuff like that'.

> Unless the family patterns changes, it is going to fall to the lady to attend to that [child care]. A lot of women are taking a year out or doing job share for a while but they are coming back to the workforce [...] (like my own wife) [...] much sooner, they have au pairs and stuff like that.
>
> (Lorcan, male assessor, Scoil Sperrin boys' second-level school)

While this assessor regarded women as suitable to be secondary school principals (and the person appointed principal by the board he chaired was a woman, albeit a woman with no children), he did not think of men as having to take time out for caring; he believed that women were the primary carers of children.

### Believing Women's as carers: a prescribed 'choice'

The other narrative that male assessors deployed to explain women's lower application rate for senior posts was to individualise the decision as a private choice for women.

Ronan, the assessor for the Scoil Galtees post, believed that the reason women were not in senior posts was because of their personal choices: 'they are not applying for them'. He did not mention any connection between women's low application rate and their roles as primary carers or the lack of publicly available, reasonably priced child care supports. He spoke at some length, however, about how the decision about child care was made in his own family and this conversation illustrated his belief that a woman's decision not to seek promotion was a personal one. He claimed his wife 'chose' to take on the role of primary carer for their four children and that she only moved into a post of responsibility 'when she felt this was the right thing for her to do at that particular time'. He claimed she had never expressed 'an interest in moving up the promotional ladder'. Although he did not think that caring for children was the only reason women did not apply for post primary principalships he admitted, 'You could not discount it' (Ronan, male assessor/chair of BOM, Scoil Galtees boys' second-level school).

While male assessors did not generally display overtly discriminatory attitudes to women being principals, and some were vehement that it did not matter, there was a sense of resignation to the prevailing gender order in terms of caring. It was assumed that women 'chose' to take leave to be the primary carers, or waited until children were older to apply for senior posts. None of the assessors assumed that men or indeed themselves (most of whom were principals) would interrupt their career for caring. Child care was seen as a woman's job and if she wanted to be a principal as well, that was her individual 'choice'.

Promotion to senior posts for women was contingent. It was desirable if and when women were 'ready'. Readiness was dictated by their care identities and presumed responsibilities:

> Women are at a later stage in their careers, generally [when appointed], not all the time but generally they are and that is their decision and that probably makes sense to them and probably it is sensible'.
> (Donal, male assessor, Derravaragh primary-level co-ed. rural school)

Donal's view was typical of most male assessors at both primary and second level. It was assumed that 'there are issues there for women, or nurturing responsibilities and [...] some women manage better than others'. However it was assumed to be their personal and free because, as Barra claimed, women think 'I have little ones at home. I think I'm not ready for that big job' (Barra, male assessor, Comeragh VEC second-level school). This dilemma was not named for men as they were not asked to choose between care work and promotion.

### Pregnancy and principalship

Pregnancy was not cited as a barrier to women's promotion to a principalship by the male assessors. However, there was one male assessor who addressed this issue. He claimed that a woman appointed as principal in a school which he knew well had had two maternity leaves in her first few years as principal. He believed that this made managing the school very difficult for her:

> Because of her own personal situation she was two years behind and in that two years events had happened and incidents had occurred and she found it very difficult to assert herself in an area of responsibility.
> (Donal, male assessor, Derravaragh primary-level co-ed. rural school)

His view was that being pregnant and being a principal were not compatible. In the context of recounting a story about the woman who had two young children in the early stages of a principalship, he stated:

> [I]t is very important for Principal to apply and to accept the role of the school leader when they are ready for it in their own professional and personal lives. If they are not ready, they are not ready and just bide their time for some other situation.
> (Donal, male assessor, Derravaragh primary-level school)

Given the silence around pregnancy as a barrier to promotion, and the comments made by several assessors that women should apply when they are 'ready' for the job in relation to caring responsibilities, it is clear that there is an unwritten code that senior post holders should not have major care responsibilities and the people who are likely to have these are women.

## Women assessors at primary and second level

Like male assessors, the women who were assessors did not articulate gendered views about women's and men's suitability for senior posts. Ailbhe, the assessor for the principalship at Scoil Erne primary-level school (who was herself a principal with children), was of the opinion that a 'principalship is a job that married or single, with or without children, people can handle'. In her view, commuting long distances to work as a principal would be a much more serious constraint than the demands of child care 'but sometimes other things might be more important, like travel in Dublin. If somebody was living two hours away and applied [for a principalship] you would be curious as to why they were applying for a job in the capital [...] commuting is difficult' (Ailbhe, female assessor, Scoil Erne primary-level school).

### Women, juggling and managing

Caitriona, the assessor for Scoil Allen, where they had recently been an assessor for a post where a woman with younger children was appointed principal, felt that it was possible to manage care and be a primary principal. Although it was demanding, it was assumed women were good at coping:

> I'm not sure how someone like _____ [current principal's name] can [manage], with children [...] how she would manage. I'd have the confidence that she would handle it very well.
>
> (Caitriona, female assessor, Scoil Allen primary-level school)

This assessor believed that being a principal was something women could *juggle* with child care. Moreover, she expressed a widely held (gender essentialist) view that being a principal of a primary school was a good job for a woman with children as she could do child care and retain a relatively high status job as school principal.

> [Women] [...] can juggle the hours and the time that they are working, and it has always been seen as a good job for women to go into and I think it is.
>
> (Caitriona, female assessor, Scoil Allen primary-level school)

A very experienced assessor in the VEC system who had served on several appointment panels for second-level schools thought that being a parent, and especially a mother of children, was actually an advantage in being a teacher: 'That's not a poltically correct thing to say, because there are so many single people in the system, but it does make you a much better teacher, a much more tolerant person'. She went on to say that she believed women were really suited to being principals as they had practice of managing at home and being well organised.

> Again, this is going to be politically incorrect, but if a man gets up in the morning and his wife is there, well she'll have his clothes ready for him, his lunch maybe [...] whatever, and off he goes [...] and when he comes home in the evening generally he might do the garden, but he mightn't do anything [...] but a woman whether she likes it or not, takes responsibility to get the breakfast, get the dinner at night, [...] keep the house tidy, look after the children, all those other things, do the shopping. Now some men, some men are marvellous, and some men, you know, do all that as well but [...] this is still Ireland. So a woman in order to be a teacher at all, to be a worker at all, especially a married woman, has to be very, very well organised, and they tend to run their schools the same way.
>
> (Eibhlin, female chair of the board of assessors, Scoil Errigal second-level school)

**Ambivalence about women principals**

Other assessors were more ambivalent about mothers being able to combine child care and senior management responsibilities including the assessor for the principalship at Foyle primary school. The assumption here, as elsewhere, was that mothers rather than fathers were the primary carers:

> I suppose primary education you have the summers off, in theory, unless you are helping to build a school. It probably should be seen as less demanding [...] maybe than senior corporate management or something. But the family commitments definitely would be an issue. I mean if people have young families and that, I don't think they could do it. But then I suppose it depends how you view what your role is if you were a *mother* [our emphasis]. Maybe people are happy for childminding and initiatives like that to cover them.
>
> (Blathnaid, female assessor, Scoil Foyle primary-level school)

Interestingly, Aisling, the principal who was appointed to Scoil Foyle, was a woman who did not have children. She indicated at interview that she was available to work as many hours as were required to do the job 'so like if there are days when I need to keep going until 11pm that's fine' (Aisling, female principal, Scoil Foyle primary-level school).

There were no real differences between female and male assessors in their appraisal of the challenges involved in accommodating child care with being a principal, as it was assumed by both to be a women's responsibility. While some did not approve of this arrangement, including

Eibhlin, the chair of the board of assessors at Errigal, even she saw it as inevitable that care and domestic work would be assigned to women:

> You know you're very tied down as a principal, [...] the hours are much longer [than being a teacher], [...] that's why more women are not in managerial posts, young women in particular, because it is very hard to juggle small children [...] and the morning that you walk away at half eight or eight o'clock when you have a sick child is very difficult [...] but you can now [be a principal] especially if they've [your children] gone into post primary.
>
> (Eibhlin, female chair of the board of assessors, Scoil Errigal second-level school)

Primary principalships were seen by a number of assessors as ideal management posts for women given the feasibility of synchronising work hours with child care throughout most of your career. While secondary school principalships were regarded as more demanding, it was believed that child care problems would be resolved for women when their children entered the post-primary sector as they would have the same schedule. In both cases, women were regarded as the default carers in families and it was their private choice as to how they managed this. There was no discussion of the cultural imperatives that operate, requiring women to be the primary carers of children if they are to be defined as 'good mothers'. Nor of the fact that masculinity is defined as relatively care-free in Ireland (Hanlon and Lynch, 2011).

## Assessors in higher education

There was considerable unanimity among female and male assessors in higher education as to why such a small number of senior management posts were held by women. For this reason, we do not analyse male and female assessors separately the data does show however, that care, and especially child care and the gendered culture of senior management, formed a greater part of the women's narrative about management than men's.

### The role of interviews

When explaining women's poor representation in senior management in higher education, neither women nor men believed that the problem was at the interview stage. The only issue raised about interviews was that most selection boards for top-level posts, such as director or president, were chaired by a man, and that women were not evenly represented on boards of assessors. A number of assessors excused this on the ground that 'it was hard to find suitable women' to be on senior boards:

> The biggest difficulty [...] and we've always found it, and when I worked in – [name of place] [...] was getting a woman for the Interview Board. It was always very difficult to get a woman. We can get three men no problem but we always have a difficulty getting at least one woman.
>
> (Conleth, male assessor, Colaiste Achill higher education institution)

There was no mention however of the efforts that were or were not made to identify and recruit 'suitable women' outside their existing male-dominated networks. Interestingly, some believed that having gender balance merely required one to have one woman on the Board of Assessors. Even when the one woman was found for the board, she did not always exercise much influence especially if she was from human resources and did not hold a senior post herself:

> [We get] as it were a token woman, you know one out of five, maybe [...] if it was somebody from personnel she wouldn't have had great weight.
>
> (Iarlaith, male assessor, Inisbofin higher education institution)

While the assessor in Inisbofin did not think that the board composition was a major barrier to women applicants, he did feel that it was a notable feature of senior appointments' boards within his own experience.

Viewed from the perspective of women who were called on to serve on many boards, the problem was simply that there were not enough women promoted to senior level to service the boards. This resulted in an onerous work load falling to a small number of women especially in science:

> [A]t the moment in relation to women in science, the biggest issue is that there are still so few women at a senior level [...]. We are all very keen to make sure that women are represented on Interview Boards but the flip side of that for the very small number of us in senior position.
>
> (Siofra, female assessor, Inis Meain higher education institution)

**Lack of women applicants**

Both women and men who were assessors for senior management posts in higher education claimed that the main issue was that there were generally no women applicants for top-level management posts in the university system.

> Certainly on most of the Boards I have been involved in for senior University positions there simply have been no female applicants.
> (Siofra, female assessor, Inis Meain higher education institution)

There was a sense that the posts were male-defined and male-owned before they were advertised. This gendered pre-population of positions was exacerbated by the fact that women were getting too little administrative experience at a relevant time in their career. The head of Tory held that, the criteria were written in such a way that it assumed one had particular types and length of experience at management level. This meant that women simply could not consider applying:

> [B]y the mere fact that you are looking for management experience in terms of criteria [...] you may in itself be limiting your field, if you want to put it that way [...] because not that many women have come. They are coming now slowly through the system. There are less women with that experience so you are by definition excluding them.
> (Ide, female assessor, Tory higher education institution)

The assessor for Rathlin held similar views about the lack of women applying, and attributed this to the fact that women had not reached the professorial ranks from which senior managers tended to be recruited:

> [Y]ou do have a much smaller number of female applicants and there is no point in denying that. And that is partly because, although the system is improving, the number of women in senior academic posts, and I don't mean University leadership posts but just Professors, is still much less than what it should be. And they tend to be a significant part of the pool you draw from for whatever other senior officer appointments you make.
> (Oisin, male assessor, Rathlin higher education institution)

A related problem identified was that women were not even competing for professorships in the university. While professorships are not senior management posts *per se*, they are the type of senior academic posts that would prepare one for senior management at VP or presidential level. The assessor at Inis Meain had served on a board for a Humanities professorship a few years previously; while there were 45 applicants for the post, only two were women. This was despite the fact that there are a large number of women in the discipline.

The net effect of women not moving up the promotional ladder at an earlier age like men was that there were too few women with sufficient administrative and, in particular cases, research experience to apply for really senior posts in higher education. The assessor in Inis Meain pointed out that she had been on the interview board for the post of president at another university and only one woman applied; this woman was short-listed as the selection committee was concerned about lack of gender balance in the final selection. The assessor claimed she was not really qualified for the post and she believed it was a mistake to interview her.

> I don't think somebody should be interviewed because they are a woman either, I think they should match the requirements of the post before they are interviewed.
>
> (Siofra, female assessor, Inis Meain higher education institution)

**The care track**

The complex ways in which child care tracked women into streams of work (the mommy track) that did not qualify them for senior posts was also noted by women who were assessors but not by men. However, while senior women managers commented on the problem, they did not question the gender division of care labour in any depth, although some were aware of it:

> I think it is the criteria [for senior management appointments] are excluding the women in many incidents. Why don't they have them in management? I think women are better at balancing their lifestyles than men in a lot of situations and we're going back to, [...] a situation with women and childcare and you are looking at all those issues where at the most likely time in your career where you are going to get this management experience, many women have taken time out to rear kids, or maybe are rearing kids and are working, and if they are, well then they are in all probability not going to put themselves forward to take on extra loads, particular extra loads that are going to cause as I say an absolute work/life imbalance.
>
> (Ide, female assessor, Tory higher education institution)

**The 24/7 culture**

It was not simply the technical criteria that led to women not applying (or succeeding if they did apply); there were also social criteria that women were less likely to meet, although these were not always explicit. Assessors in higher education and the senior civil servant assessors claimed that the criteria for top-level posts excluded those who could not work outside of the scheduled hours of work. The working day did not have time boundaries:

> As in I suppose, it's stating the obvious, the gender of applicants simply doesn't register on anyone's radar anymore or now, [...] I would feel it that it is more likely to be a feature in terms of the decisions to go for the jobs. It doesn't feature at all in the selection process. But I would think the element of the cultural that might discourage participation would tend to be that you get long hours cultures in organisations and we would be an offender there.
>
> (Oscar, male assessor, Saltees higher education institution)

The long-hours culture of senior management posts in universities was deemed to be a major disincentive for women who had dependents; it was assumed they would be the primary carers.

> I mean since I came into the post I'd say, on average I work an 85 hour week, between 75 and 85 hours a week [...] That is another issue for women who still have caring responsibilities. I mean I don't, my children are grown up, my [immediate family] aren't even in _______ [name of city].
>
> (Siofra, female assessor, Inis Meain higher education institution)

None of the assessors said that they felt the long-hours culture was a barrier for men.

The prioritization of paid work and meeting the demands of the 'long-hours culture' were not only essential when appointed to senior-level posts, they also applied much earlier in careers if women or men wanted to build a management and research profile that would make them eligible for senior posts in the first instance. As noted by the assessor at Tory above, child care dictated the patterns of women's careers. There were too many 'extra loads' for women to take on if they did management work on top of research, teaching and child care. And she was not optimistic about any change:

> In my optimistic days I think it is changing slightly, not hugely. I think it is still very much a male-dominated society and our perceptions and expectations around the whole childcare issues would still be very much middle ages [...] (laughs).
>
> (Ide, female assessor, Tory higher education institution)

### Senior management as conflict-led

The fact that senior posts in higher education were perceived as conflict-laden was also a disincentive to women according to some assessors. They believed that women had a different and more negotiated approach to managing power relations but would get drawn in to the adversarial approach if in senior management.

> I think the issues are such that I cannot see any immediate change in the balance between males and females in senior positions in education generally because women I think are more inclined (by and large, it is a generalisation) to look at the overall life situation [...]. Men enjoy power, men enjoy cruelty really, [...] I would have many, many experiences of that, men taking on each other and it being a fight to the end just like primitive people five million years ago when males were emerging and they were fighting to maintain their corner.
>
> (Siofra, female assessor, Inis Meain higher education institution)

The female assessor at Tory had a similar view. Management at senior level was seen as conflict-laden and male-defined:

> A senior manager needs to be absolutely able to fight their corner, has to win every conflict, has no fear of conflict, maybe welcomes it. Whereas a lot of women wouldn't, a lot of women would go a different way about it.
>
> (Ide, female assessor, Tory higher education institution)

There was a belief among some of the women assessors in higher education (who were all senior managers themselves), that the caring approaches to people that women would often espouse were not valued in senior management. This was another reason women did not apply:

> I think women aren't going into management because their natural instinct to be caring has now been totally blocked by the risks that you take by showing that kind of thing.
>
> (Siofra, female assessor, Inis Meain higher education institution)

In spite of the overall sense of fatalism that women assessors had about change, there was also a view that if targets were set and institutions set out to create a gender balance, this could be achieved. One university, Rathlin, which had made progress in appointing women at senior level stressed this strongly.

> [W]e are still not where we should be but we are much, much better and there are now significant numbers of women in senior positions. Not by any means yet at [the] level or [even a] proportion of the level, except for the senior management level. And I have been keen on that because it [...] set a tone for the rest of the system. So [...] my view is that the senior management team should be gender balanced in a visible way. [...] we have always pursued targets above what we were required to, for example the governing authority said it must be 50/50 and so we have pursued this very strongly.
>
> (Oisin, male assessor, Rathlin higher education institution)

Despite Oisin's claims however, even though Rathlin had improved the proportion of women in senior posts, there were still very few women at senior management level, especially at professorial level, at the time of the study. And this is the grade from which people are normally recruited to management positions.

## Conclusion: The long arm of history

To understand why so few women are appointed to senior managerial posts, it is important to examine the culture of organizations and the gendered regimes of injustice within them. However, it is also important to move beyond the issue of organizational culture, to examine how the relational lives of women and men differ, and how the care narrative, arising from these relational differences, operates to control and contain women's ambitions in a way that does not apply to men. The unequal division of care labour is profoundly important and it is deeply embedded in the way the public citizen-manager is defined.

Women are defined by their care roles and relationships in a profound manner that does not apply to men. Citizenship, full and respected 'universal' citizenship, that is, is equated with the economic, political and cultural sphere, not with the care sphere. Insofar as it defines care out of citizenship, the universal view of citizenship is male-defined and citizenship is gendered. The implications of this for women in senior posts may appear tenuous, but they is not. Because caring is treated as peripheral to public life (and to public status in particular), the work involved in caring is defined out of the management paths laid out for those who wish to become senior appointees. Most of the assessors interviewed, in this study, especially the male assessors in higher education, implicitly assumed that the citizen manager is a non-relational being in the sense of having a caring life outside of employment that needed time and attention: they treated their care world and that of others as a private matter. They did not talk about how care relations impacted on getting into senior posts, or even into middle management, unless asked specifically about it. When appraising the relative merits of candidates, the relational lives of potential appointees were invisible. Given that equality legislation[11] defines people's relational identities as private, for reasons of non-discrimination, this is understandable. However, the irony of this legal protection is that it has silenced the ways in which affective relations are deeply gendered and have profound implications for who is fully eligible to be a senior manager. Senior management posts, especially in higher education, but increasingly at primary and second level, are assumed to be care-free; those appointed are assumed to be available to participate in a 'long-hours' work environment that precludes having responsibility for primary care work. If those who apply for senior posts get in to those positions, it is presumed primary care will happen but it will be kept private and will not encroach on the world of senior management.

The silence that exists around caring was evident in the way male assessors within the higher education sector only attended to the subject of care in passing, if at all. It was not part of their mind map when outlining reasons why women were not in senior managerial roles. Women's narratives about care were somewhat different: they wanted to talk about care, they were familiar with the language of caring and got emotionally and personally engaged with the issue. However, the female assessors were quite fatalistic about the gendered order of caring. They generally expected women to manage it themselves, to 'juggle' things and to 'get through'. With a few exceptions, neither male nor female assessors critiqued the intensification of work at senior managerial levels within new managerialism; a deeply gender-biased mode of governance was in operation but was not known or named in gender terms.

# Part III
# Being a Senior Manager

# 6
# Leading Educators: The Emotional Work of Managing Identities

This chapter explores the experience of being a newly appointed senior manager. Central to the analysis is the construction of identity in the senior management role and how this may be shaped, constrained and facilitated through broader discourses related to new managerialism, market ideologies and the incorporation of an enterprise culture in education. Such discourses it is argued increasingly set the context within which senior appointees work, requiring them to modify and adapt their behaviour in line with performative neo-liberal ideals. The chapter draws on data predominantly from interviews with the newly appointed senior appointees, supplemented by data from interviews with assessors, where appropriate. The analysis presents a complex picture of the construction and formation of senior manager identity across education, as newly appointed principals/managers seek to survive and thrive in the educational organizations in which they are positioned as leaders. In this sense the chapter considers the ethical dimension to the everyday life of leaders in education and of how this is intertwined with the construction, performance and management of self and identity.

## Self and the construction of identities

The formation and construction of identity is a complex and often contradictory process, with recent analyses querying the concept of a 'unitary self' originally posited by Cooley (1902) and Mead (1934) in favour of accounts which stress the multiple and fragmented nature of self and identity that emerges in societies increasingly characterized by risk, flexibility and uncertainty (Beck, 2006, 2010; Baumann, 1991; Jenkins, 2004). In such contexts, the regulation and management of identity is a significant mechanism of control. As Jenkins (2004: 22) notes,

> Identities exist and are acquired, claimed and allocated within power relations. Identification is something over which struggles take place and with which stratagems are advanced – it is means and end in politics – and at stake is the classification of populations as well as classification of individuals.

Foucault's (1979, 1980) analysis draws attention to the microphysics of power as central to processes of identity formation and how identities are fashioned in line with 'regimes of truth' which signify, classify and govern. His focus on power as diffuse, embedded in the processes of identity formation through the dominance and evolution of particular discourses and norms, draws attention to the disciplinary technologies inherent in modern societies as individual behaviour is regulated and shaped through practices of subjectification. In this sense new managerialism exemplifies a regime of truth, 'bio-power' in action, increasing and promoting the body's utility, while at the same time rendering it dependent on external control and monitoring.

> This power over life evolved in two basic forms [...] the first to be formed centred on the body as a machine: it's disciplining, the optimisation of its capabilities, the extortion of its forces, the parallel increase of its usefulness and its docility, its integration into systems of efficient and economic controls, all this was ensured by the procedures of power that characterised the disciplines: an anatomo-politics of the human body.
>
> (Foucault, 1979: 139)

The discourse of new managerialism has given rise to a series of such disciplinary practices, providing a normativity and way of relating to the self. Rose (1996, 2001), for example, considers the emergence of 'psy' discourses in the context of new technologies of the self which emphasize individual responsibility and control and the pursuit of 'self' excellence and empowerment. These are – forms of governmentality which accord neatly with the goals of the enterprise culture typical of capitalist societies in the western world. Performance indicators, budgetary targets, strategic plans, 'democratic' accountability serve to create a technology of self that simultaneously positions the individual as autonomous but constrained. Issues of constraint and autonomy are not fully captured by Foucault, however, and require a more nuanced analysis of positioning and presentation in everyday life (Clegg 2006; McNay 1999). The formation, construction and performance of identity involves a dialectical interplay between structure and agency and are deeply embedded in the exercise of power and the classificatory tendencies of both discourses and practices in a range of institutions. Central, for example, to Goffman's (1971) earlier work in this area is the notion of performance and strategies of impression management as 'agents'/ 'actors' consciously pursue goals and interests. His work suggested a strong inclination on the part of individuals towards the presentation of 'self' as competent and of how this can vary depending on context and location. These latter cannot be divorced from the broader cultural and social context within which the individual is located – the performance of roles (mother, pupil, doctor, manager) and interests pursued is reflective of the norms, values and discourses prevalent in the wider sphere. Such 'competence' also reflects a drive towards maintaining ontological security, a sense of place in the world, creating feelings of uncertainty and confusion when interactions are not as they should be. Trust, belonging, connectedness and knowing the rules of engagement/ presentation are all part of the formation of social identities. Giddens, likewise, relates agent's positioning to role ascriptions which are drawn from broader structures, norms and values in the surrounding society:

> Social positions are constituted structurally as specific intersections of signification, domination and legitimation which relates to the typification of agents. A social position involves the specification of a definite identity within a network of social relations, that identity, however, being a category to which a particular range of normative sanctions is relevant.
>
> (Giddens, 1984: 83)

The idea that identity is socially constructed through the active and reflective engagement of the individual in a social context resonates with Bourdieu's (1977, 1990) concept of habitus and the improvization engaged in by actors across 'fields' of action. In societies characterized by new managerial/neo-liberal reform, the rules of engagement become increasingly shaped and defined in line with those of the market. Trust and confidence in who we are and how we should be are challenged by the range of scripts and 'choices' that are continuously made available.

However, underlying the work of identity – the 'doing' of self is an ethical dimension which provides part of the rationale for action and self presentation. Rose (1996) defines ethics as the means by which individuals come to construe and act upon themselves (ibid.: 153), while Sayer (2005) suggests that normative concerns related to care, well-being and quality of life are reflective of the moral dimension of actors' guiding principles which are implicated in their commitments, identities and ways of life (ibid.: 6).Both the construction and presentation of self then is a multi-layered phenomenon and over the course of interaction, and in the enactment of roles, different aspects of self may intersect in complex ways. Identities are something we do, not just something we are (West and Zimmerman, 1987); a form of situated social practice in which individuals perform roles that are relational and embedded in norms and expectations related to self and 'other' (Butler, 2004; McNay, 2007; Poggio, 2006; Pullen and Simpson, 2009; Ybema et al., 2009). Conflicts and contradictions abound, multiple identities merge and overlap giving rise to a crafted self (Kondo, 1990; Devine et al., 2011) that is at once fragile and versatile, depending on the context of interaction and the resources individuals bring to it (Bourdieu, 1990). The agency inherent in such positioning should not however, mask the ambiguity and messiness that characterizes much of our identity positioning (Martin, 2006; Pullen and Knights, 2007; Pullen and Simpson, 2009).

It is in this context that we can begin to consider the impact of changes in workplace organizations brought by new managerialism and neo-liberalism, especially as this relates to the performance and the construction of senior manager identities.

## Organizing identification self and identity in educational leaders

The evolution of new forms of management in the public service sector has been documented in Chapter 1 in terms of the move towards neo-liberalism and increasing marketization in many Western government policies (Clarke et al., 2000; Farrell and Morris, 2003; Davies et al., 2006).What has taken place is a sea-change in the discourses and practices governing the management of institutions that traditionally have held a public service remit. As we have seen, the language of the market has come to pervade the analyses and subsequent funding of the services provided in, for example, Health and Education, in terms of an emphasis on efficiency, accountability, competition, performativity and measurable outcomes that ultimately demonstrate value for money. As Chapters 1 and 2 have illustrated, the public sector in Ireland, including education, has not been immune to such change.

For our purposes in this chapter, key questions arise in relation to the management of manager identity as an aspect of this change. Alvesson and Willmott (2002), for example, assert the significance of the management of identity as a modality of control that includes 'managing the insides' (ibid.: 3) of workers, including managers, in terms of their hopes, fear and expectations of success and value in the organization in which they work. Flexibility, adaptability, self empowerment and self actualization are incorporated into the new worker identity as commitment to corporate goals for excellence and achievement is deemed to be a characteristic of the person (a matter of their character) rather than a requirement of the organization. In this sense, Rose (1996, 2001) speaks of the 'ethic of autonomous selfhood' that pervades the enterprise culture – a governing of the soul that reflects new technologies of the self and the intensification of liberal subjectivities (Rose, 2001; Davies, 2006). Work can provide a sense of meaning and identity but also insecurity and anxiety for self in a competitive environment that erodes trust relations. While this latter applies to workers at all levels, the experience of management can be a double-edged sword. On the one hand the seductive aspect of leadership and management as a site for identity investment has been noted (Sinclair, 2009; Whitehead, 2001) through the promise of power, status and purposeful action. On the other hand the insecurities that arise from increasing surveillance, performativity and accountability, coupled with the ambiguities of power relations, can lead to insecurities around identity work, and the impression management of managers (Alvesson and Willmott, 2002; Furtner et al., 2010; Lyon and Woodward, 2004).

## Managing identities in the education sector

Research in the education sector documents the challenges to identity inherent in the new managerial climate and its pervasiveness especially in Anglo Saxon societies such as the UK, Australia and New Zealand. Questions have been raised about the erosion of the professional identities of academics and teachers (Archer, 2008; Ball, 2007; Beck and Young, 2005; Fitzgerald and Gunter, 2006; Wong et al., 2008) as they strive to meet increasing demands for accountability and performance in their roles. Market-oriented forms of new managerialism pose specific challenges in the education (as well as the health) sector because care (as detailed in Chapters 5 and 8) itself is neither a quantifiable commodity nor an outcome that is open to strategic measurement. In an increasingly managerialist system, educationalists may struggle to retain a balance between their commitment to the broader goals of education (a *careful* education), with the more narrowly defined goals of performativity and competition (*care-less* in terms of a focus on narrowly defined outputs) in the education marketplace (Ball, 2007; Crow and Weindling, 2010; Day et al., 2006; Devine et al., 2011). Such processes of identification involve a complex interplay between often competing demands and values. Individuals struggle with identities in a new managerial context – seeking to retain personal meaning and connectedness in the face of colonization of the life-world (Habermas, 1987: 173), while simultaneously surviving in an increasingly competitive work environment.

For those who are appointed to senior management positions the pressures can be even more intense. The field of leadership theory and management has itself undergone significant change in response to the wider political and economic environment, the significance of leadership as mechanism for change in education evident in its prioritization by the OECD (2008). The development of the school effectiveness movement, with its emphasis on the difference schools can make to educational performance (Creemers and Kyriakides, 2010; Teddlie and Reynolds, 2001), has led to a series of debates and counter debates (Bush, 2009; Gunter and Fitzgerald, 2008; Gronn, 2003; Thrupp, 2005; Thrupp and Willmott, 2003) about the appropriate direction of both policy and practice in relation to education management and leadership in schools. While administration and management approaches predominated in the 1980s and 1990s, Bush (2009, 2010) argues that leadership theory is being increasingly placed at the centre of the field, rather than at the periphery as one of a number of traits that characterize effective school managers. This shift in emphasis is attributed as a reaction to the overly narrow and technical rational managerialist approach to education which, with its emphasis on performance and public accountability, can equate the work of school principals with routine tasks driven from the outside. Others argue however that the shift towards a focus on leadership in itself derives from the desire to radically alter school culture in line with the neo-corporate agenda (Ball, 2007) and the accompanying need to draw distinctions between the leadership 'elite' – those charged with promoting such change (through, for example, force of charisma and personality or indeed private sector experience) – and those concerned with the systematic maintenance of school routines (Gunter and Fitzgerald, 2008).

Leadership in this sense has become increasingly professionalized, with senior managers in education being required to cater to the needs of informed parents ('consumers'), positioning and promoting their schools as centres of excellence. This 'reculturing' (Hartley, 1999) of both the school and leadership space requires leaders to have the necessary emotional and organizational skills to drive their organizations towards success. In schools, headteachers are no longer defined as 'managers' but as 'transformational leaders', engaging in a form of 'super leadership' that realizes both the broader visionary elements of education, with the practical accountability demands for money well spent (Creemers and Kyriakides, 2010; Day, 2005; Townsend, 2011). Increasingly leadership is also defined as a distributed process, the effective principal one who can draw on school colleagues to support and initiate change through teaching leadership (Alexis and Gronn, 2009; Gunter and Fitzgerald, 2008; Moller, 2009; Spillane and Diamond, 2007). School leaders are urged to be productive in their roles (Lingard et al., 2003), working with the demands of increasing complexity and diversity in schools in an 'authentic' manner, encouraging new approaches to learning and building relationships, both inside and outside of the school (Walker and Shuangye, 2007: 186). This more critical and ethical 'turn' in leadership studies (Strain, 2009) is giving rise to a renewed focus on the moral dimension to leadership practices, and the accompanying need to separate leadership performance from a narrower view of performativity (Bush, 2010; Caldwell, 2008; Stefkovich and Begley, 2007). A renewed interest in social context in mediating both leadership practices and experiences is also increasingly coming to the fore (Dinham et al., 2011; Thrupp et al., 2006).

To assume a unilateral incorporation of new managerialist ideals into the identities of senior appointees undermines the complex process that is involved in 'doing' identity. As noted previously, this includes the resolution of ethical questions related to values and the quality sought in one's everyday life, and the extent to which these conflict or coincide with how one is required to present oneself in the management role. In this respect distinctions are drawn in the experiences of identity construction and management across different sectors of education (Archer, 2008; Crow and Weindling, 2010; Day et al., 2006; Hey and Bradford, 2004; Sinclair, 2009; Deem, 2004; White et al., 2011). In the school sector, principals have been found to negotiate their positioning to incorporate the competing demands of performativity with broader visions of education and learning that do not compromise their core values (Crow and Weindling, 2010; Day, 2005).

Research into the impact of reforms in the higher education sector shows a complex picture. The concept of 'manager academic' has now become increasingly accepted as the norm, as senior staff in universities restructure their identities in management terms (Gleeson and Knights,

2008; Fletcher et al., 2007). This poses substantial personal and professional challenges to academic middle managers who have spoken of the feeling of being squeezed between the demands of lecturers and senior university management (Gleeson and Knights, 2008; Weiner, 2008; Grummell et al., 2009b). Deem (2004) identified ambiguous views among manager academics who were inclined towards subtle rather than crude mechanisms in encouraging academic staff to perform. High levels of stress have also been reported, with excessively long work hours. In spite of this, many identified themselves as change agents and were positive about bringing a more strategic vision to their organizations.

The debate over the most appropriate models of leadership and management in education highlights the tensions that derive from marrying economically driven policies with broader educational goals. If the general thrust of management policies is geared towards greater instrumentality, competition and productivity, how do leaders on the ground position themselves with respect to this change? What are the implications for those who are newly appointed in their roles across the education sector? The remainder of this chapter will examine some of these issues with respect to the experiences of recently appointed senior managers in Irish education.It does so with respect to three core themes:

1. Deciding to become a leader – envisioning the 'competent' self;
2. 'Doing' management and the ethics of management practice;
3. Managing the emotional self.

## Deciding to become a leader: Envisioning the 'competent' self

A consistent feature of the narratives to all of the appointees was their desire for challenge and extending themselves in their career roles. This was their primary motivation in putting themselves forward for senior management positions:

> I'm quite a motivated person and I will take the opportunities that are there and I will try and work to the best of my ability, I like my work, I like to enjoy my work.
>
> (Neasa, female senior post holder, Saltees higher education institution)

> I began to look around and say 'yea, it would be great to get involved in a more interactive way as a manager or as a Principal, other than just being a teacher with an Assistant Principal's Post'.
>
> (Peadar, male principal, Scoil Galtees second-level school)

In this sense it was clear that work was an important source of meaning to the interviewees in the construction of their identities. However the decision to move into senior management also reflected a perceived competence regarding their management capabilities, expressed primarily in the capacity to effect change through vision and leadership:

> There was the chance to do something that we had been talking about doing in the country for 5 years and now was the chance to be in control to do it.
>
> (Andrew, male senior post holder, Coláiste Inis Meain higher education institution)

For some primary school principals, this sense of competence derived from a network of family/friendship support with a tradition in education and senior management – teaching and management in education was part of their 'habitus'. For others, socialization into a management 'psyche' derived from the pursuit of postgraduate studies in education or management, and/or the management experience they experienced in their schools. This latter was especially notable among second level principals who had worked as teachers in the VEC (vocational education) sector:

> Now I was lucky enough I think that I worked in the comprehensive sector in two different schools over the first fifteen years of my career, which allowed me get the managerial experience, prior to becoming Principal, and giving me a taste for leadership.
>
> (Peadar, male principal, Scoil Galtees second-level school)

> I had a huge insight into the day to day nature of a principal's job because my husband had been a principal for about 15 years at that stage.
>
> (Bridget, female principal, Scoil Allen primary-level school)

Concepts of competence and how this manifests itself in the construction of senior management identity are also reflected in the discourses surrounding 'the ideal' type manager/principal. Such discourses are useful in conveying the constructs of management which permeate educational institutions and the extent to which they correspond to notions of 'super leadership' mentioned previously. In this respect, interview data from both the senior appointees themselves and their assessors consistently emphasized competencies around leadership/vision, people skills, coping abilities, financial management, energy/dynamism and the pursuit of excellence. In their own narratives about their roles, senior appointees used a discourse of strategic vision and direction to describe their leadership competence. They felt that their new role placed them in a position of power where they could have 'a voice in directing what's going on' (Aisling, female principal, Scoil Foyle primary-level school).This conception of vision as enabling power and influence was linked to their strategic and ambitious career strategy. Their desire for influence and control allowed educational leaders to enact change and gave voice to their sense of strategic vision. Muireann, the principal of Scoil Iveragh, described her strategic vision as having an interest 'in the big picture, and the philosophy behind education and how you would develop that within a school and the leadership dimension of it'.These leaders had a keen understanding of educational policy, outlining how their institution can strategically and efficiently develop within the wider educational field. As Oisin, the assessor at Colaiste Rathlin, described,

> My view has been that senior appointments need to be seen as ones that add value to the strategic priorities of the institution so they need to reflect the desire of the institution to be efficient in what it does and also to have leadership that is able to deal with strategic vision.
>
> (Oisin, male assessor, Colaiste Rathlin higher education institution)

A core part of strategic management was knowing how to motivate and manage people; to be able to lead and influence colleagues in a direction which will develop the strategic vision that one is putting forward. An ability to identify and implement strategic needs in line with educational legislation was vital. Assessors and senior appointees both acknowledged that teaching and curriculum demands have brought enormous changes to the role of educational leaders. These requirements were enshrined in educational legislation and directed by the Department of Education and Skills. Educational leaders increasingly needed to have a strategic sense of where their institution was located in the education field and to have a sense of strategic vision for the teaching needs and curriculum delivery of the school. This appeared especially important at second and third level education where the educational leader was expected to have a wide knowledge of curriculum and pedagogical methods that they could strategically develop within their institution. Tiernan, a college head at Colaiste Inisbofin, espoused this approach in his description of introducing 'modularisation of programmes, for credit accumulation models, for interactive models of teaching and learning, for the elimination of didactic approaches to learning, for more project based and group based and team based learning approaches'. Assessors looked for qualities of decisiveness and energy in the personality and style of senior appointees, as Fergal the education officer at Scoil Mourne outlined.

> I like somebody who has energy, that matters a lot to me, good organisational type of ability and skills, time management and bit of it.But I also like somebody with an eye to quality of the outcomes of the school, the quality of the teaching and learning that's what I look for is somebody who will bring those, and a sense of humour.
>
> (Fergal, male education officer, Scoil Mourne second-level school)

The presentation of self as competent in a range of tasks, straddling inter-personal, administrative and creative/visionary domains suggests that only those who have a solid and unique combination of competencies are positioned and position themselves as suitable for senior management positions in education. People who have this sense of self belief are those who will apply for senior management positions (this clearly has a gendered dimension, which will be dealt with in Chapter 7), but the capacities that they are required to bring, related to the increasing challenges in the role, seem to set them apart from others:

> I think they are unique and special and they are enthusiastic, they are doers, they are people who have vision.
>
> (Calum, male assessor, Scoil Sheelin primary-level school)

Acquiring these competencies through a range of experiences, and incorporating this into one's presentation of self is the first step towards becoming a senior manager. But to what extent is this 'self' enacted in the actual experience of senior management in practice? What is involved in 'doing' management in the education sector?

## 'Doing' management and the ethics of management practice

It was clear that 'doing' management was an all-encompassing task that positioned these senior appointees at the forefront of change implementation in their schools and organizations. However this was experienced differently across the education sectors. It appeared to be linked not only to the modalities of power and control which permeated the different sectors, but also the social context of schools and colleges and the constructions of management the interviewees had incorporated into their own sense of identity. This latter gave rise to ethical tensions, noted by Rose (2001) and Sayer (2005) and the desire to be 'authentic' (Strain, 2009) to their own vision for what leadership meant to them. An over-riding sense to emerge from all interviews was the growing emphasis on control and regulation, arising from demands for financial accountability and the fulfilment of legislative requirements set by government agencies. Activities in the Third level sector were now governed by the Universities Act (1997) and the Institutes of Technology Act (2006), while a range of legislation in education (Education Act 1998; Welfare Act 2000; Education for persons with Special Needs Act 2004) was altering the landscape of accountability and management practices at the school level:

> The Education Act has really defined our areas of responsibility and we all know them and we'll say the big area of responsibility over the last six years is the Special Education area. That is taking up a huge amount of time for contacting the powers that be and all the paperwork that is involved in it.
>
> (Conor, male principal, Scoil Derraghvaragh primary-level school)

> There's the Welfare Act, the Education Act itself, Special Needs now is the other big one that people are talking about, [...] the pile of stuff has gone bigger, that's the Special Needs folder there.
>
> (Maeve, female principal Scoil Nephin second-level school)

> The new requirements under the 1997 Act which delineate a form of management that is alien if you like to the traditional notion of a University [...] it is, a national requirement and statutory requirement, it is actually written into the Universities Act, we have no choice about that. 30 or 40 years ago it was a completely difference scene and the type of person, the University President would have been simply regarded as sort of a vague scholar. You wouldn't survive in that today.
>
> (Siofra, female assessor, Coláiste Inis Mhean higher education institution)

Increasing accountability through the role of the media, detailed in Chapter 10, was also noted as a contributory factor by this female senior post holder in Saltees institution:

> I think the senior jobs, the top jobs in public service are getting more difficult not less difficult, I would be pretty sure of that. And if you look at what it is that make it more difficult, and a lot of it rightly so, the accountability levels are obviously much more significant than they ever would have been. The media is a very strong driver as well. The cultural blame and so on and getting things wrong.
>
> (Neasa, female senior post holder, Saltees higher education institution)

An added and related dimension to the accountability/regulatory mechanisms in senior appointees' role was the increasing emphasis on profiling the institution in the public sphere, often in an environment of volatile student enrolments. This emphasis on competitive survival was evident across all sectors but differed by degree within sectors – for example, at third level it appeared to be most pronounced in the further education sector, while in the school sector it was most evident among principals working in disadvantaged communities:

> The demographics would be changing outside but we get only about 43% of the children baptised in this parish come to this school. Reasons for that, we are seen as a heavily disadvantaged school, local people who have social aspirations go to schools further down the hill.
>
> (Andreas, male principal, Scoil Corrib primary-level school)

The broader context of a shift towards greater accountability and demands for transparency had a profound influence on the interviewees' positioning as managers and of how they reacted to this change. Key sectoral differences were identified, with some experiencing the changed context as a source of ethical conflict, others as a source of empowerment for strategic change.

*Conflicted versus empowered self*

While all senior appointees spoke of the increasing grind of bureaucratic administration there were differences noted between the responses of those in the school sectors and those working in third level/statutory sectors. Most notable in the comments of those involved in primary and second-level education were criticisms about the amount of time taken up in satisfying accounting and regulatory demands. This revolved especially around the funding and management of initiatives related to educational disadvantage and special needs:

> I think there is too much bureaucracy, I think it is ridiculous, I think they don't focus enough, I think they move away from the child in the classroom and their reams of documents and the nonsense, I think it is just nonsense.
>
> (Conor, male principal, Scoil Derraghvaragh primary-level school)

> I do believe that the introduction of the legislation which is excellent and praiseworthy and wonderful, but […] they […] threw the people who were running the schools literally to the wolves of the Law Courts and I think that it is almost a backhanded way of running the schools.
>
> (Ronan, male assessor, Scoil Galtees second-level school)

While the benefits of inclusive legislation were identified as praiseworthy, there was also an experience of disempowerment and loss of control as school management was increasingly subjected to regulation imposed from the 'outside', with one assessor in Scoil Galtees defining principals as 'managers' rather than leaders. Increasing surveillance and control of principals' activities also emerged in the narratives of some primary principals, with reference to an assertive parent body, as well as traditional expectations, in rural areas especially, regarding the role of the principal in the community.

> There are expectations that you are at the Masses, at the funerals. They are not explicitly made but you feel the pressure at the same time. Definitely the matches, the Masses.
>
> (Conor, male principal, Scoil Derravaragh primary-level school)

> While the parents are great, there are a couple who have phoned the Department and would go and check, nearly negating my professionalism, do you know. And that doesn't do anything for your morale or your self esteem, and they wouldn't come and complain to me, they go right to the top.
>
> (Aoife, female principal, Scoil Sheelin primary-level school)

For most principals, the time devoted to managerial work cut across the time they wished to devote to the broader more visionary aspects of their role, reiterating findings identified elsewhere (Crow and Weindling, 2010; Day et al., 2006; Townsend, 2011). In this sense these principals experienced a tension between the practical fulfilment of managerial responsibilities, primarily dictated from outside, and their ideal construction of themselves as leaders, with the responsibility to initiate change that had a visible impact on the quality of teaching and learning in their schools:

> The Department are really so over burdening the Principal with reports, with compliance, with the necessity for policy devising and plans etc. that the Principal doesn't get a chance to really stand back and think, to have time just to nurture their own sense of what the school should be about.
>
> (Lorcan, male assessor, Scoil Sperrin second-level school)

Not all reactions to the managerial aspects of the principal's role were negative. In spite of his earlier criticisms of the amount of bureaucracy encroaching on his time, the principal of Scoil Derravaragh (whose initial graduate training was in the field of business) spoke of aspects of his role that clearly dovetailed with managerial approaches:

> The main rule of business is that you keep your customers happy [...] I would never classify children as business or as commodities but you have to build in efficiencies, you have to build in your management structures, you have to arrive at decisions, you have to implement decisions and you have to evaluate.
>
> (Conor, male principal, Scoil Derravaragh primary-level school)

Overall there appeared to be a lack of clarity over what 'doing' management entailed in this more regulatory driven environment and how principals should construct and position themselves among the alternate and multiple discourses which pervade management/leadership in education. This experience of a 'conflicted self' was mediated however by the social context of the school, with those working in schools with a high proportion of educationally disadvantaged and special needs children most prone to feeling swamped by administrative and fundraising demands. Leadership practices and positioning were clearly influenced by social context (Crow et al., 2010; Dinham et al., 2011; Thrupp et al., 2006/2011). Where there was a clearer management structure in schools – as in for example the VEC sector (although the VEC was interpreted also as a further administrative/regulatory layer), or in the more advantaged fee-paying second-level schools, the administrative support necessary to fulfil managerial functions appeared to be more readily available:

> In a smaller school, a voluntary secondary school, you're very much doing the chief bottle-washer, lots of the kind of low level tasks, involved in schools [...] whereas here (VEC school) you have the managerial support, the admin support, and a good strategic plan going forward.
>
> (Peadar, male principal, Scoil Galtees second-level school)

Recently appointed senior appointees in the third level/statutory sector appeared much clearer about their roles. In most cases their decision to apply for these senior management positions reflected an internalization of managerialism into their constructs of manager identity (Beck and Young, 2005; Grummell et al., 2009a; White et al., 2011). The discourse of new managerialism was present to a much greater degree in their interviews than in those of their counterparts in the school sectors. For them, managerialism was phrased in more positive terms, as facilitating the development of strategic thinking and essential to the modernization and survival of the institution. Importantly these senior appointees did not feel dis-empowered by the greater context of accountability, but seemed to view it as a challenge, embracing the benefits of a more 'business oriented' approach to facilitate broader educational goals. Significantly they also seemed to be provided with the administrative support that was required to allow them become more strategic and visionary:

> You end up in the position where you have proper administrative support and people who are dedicated to doing that rather than you doing the administration yourself.
>
> (Una, female senior post holder, Coláiste Rathlin higher education institution)

For the senior post holder of Coláiste InisMheain, providing an efficient and tightly regulated service was identified as empowering academic staff who could 'choose' to avail of the support services that were now provided by the university to further research productivity:

> The role of the office is to help you, not to drive some agenda or to beat you with a stick or something [...]. We have our research

> information system [...] so suddenly it is the people who are obviously deserving who are the ones who are being recognised. And for the others there is a clear route to recognition. So the rules are being made open and transparent.
>
> (Una, female senior post holder, Coláiste Rathlin higher education institution)

An alternate view however was espoused by this senior manager in Coláiste Inis Bofin who advocated a 'softer' approach to managerialism while still incorporating the value of accountability:

> I am very struck at the moment actually on the debate in Higher Education with regard to alternative styles of management, [...] [the] very corporate driven management approach as opposed to one which is predicated on academic departments having the highest levels of autonomy and self directedness that is consistent with being accountable. I would be very clear in my preference to the second approaches of those to academic management and to management generally and would have outlined that very clearly I think at that interview.
>
> (Tiernan, male senior post holder, Coláiste Inis Bofin higher education institution)

What is evident then is a contrast in the experience of managerialism among interviewees. While a discourse of new managerialism was more pronounced in the narratives of senior appointees in the third level sectors, interviewees across all sectors were clear in their assertion of core values that should underpin practice in institutions with an educational remit. Such values were grounded in an 'ethics' of self (Sayer, 2005; Strain, 2009) that all those interviewed sought to incorporate into their management selves.

### *The ethical self and manager identity*

Traditionally, school principals and academic leaders have had a high status in Ireland and play a central role in school and community life, displaying what Sugrue (2005) terms a 'passionate principalship'. This sense of vocation and commitment was evident among our interviewees as they spoke at length about the importance of vision, ethos and pastoral care[1] of their students, staff, parents and the wider community. For many, this was why they had become involved in educational leadership and they were keen to emphasize this sense of vocation or personal commitment to their role.Three interrelated areas emerged as underpinning their 'ethics of practice': the quality of student experience; fostering positive collegial relations and the aspiration towards excellence in their own practice. Each is dealt with separately although clearly there are links between all three.

*An emphasis on the quality of student experience* An ethic of care was at the heart of their leadership as most senior appointees strove to keep students at the centre of their work; they wanted to be a 'children's principal' that Caoimhe, the principal at Scoil Neagh described. Likewise, assessors described how qualities of care and compassion were vital as the educational leaders created a sense of pastoral care and student-centredness in their schools. Such views were also reflected in the comments of those in the higher education sector:

> It is important to me that people get into education, that people go through College, that they have a good experience while they are there, that they get to realise their potential. And unless those things are actually given quite active attention they don't happen. They will not happen just by me publishing five more articles [in an academic journal] or something like that.
>
> (Una, female senior post holder, Coláiste Rathlin higher education institution)

Creating an ethos of care was a vital issue for schools in disadvantaged areas as the educational leader and teachers had to provide a sense of care, belonging and empowerment that may be missing from children's daily lives. Niamh, the principal at Scoil Comeragh highlighted her role in driving a sense of school pride and mission to encourage students' sense of 'self esteem, raise their sense of value and being a member of the school community'. As Andreas, the principal at Scoil Corrib outlined, care and connectedness were:

> [s]till very much part of my philosophy, so the very troubled children, I would still try and spend time with them[...] I believe it's the one area where I do think I'm making a difference, in individual children's lives in that respect, does that make sense.
>
> (Andreas, male principal, Scoil Corrib primary-level school)

This commitment to care and to education, was the reason why many had become teachers and later educational leaders. They had applied for and gained positions as educational leaders to achieve a position of influence where they could develop this sense of pastoral care and vision within their institutions. A second component to this pastoral care dimension – an 'ethics' of practice concerned the management of staff relations.

*Fostering collegial relations* An ethics of care was evident in the participatory forms of leadership that some of the senior appointees had explicitly adopted. For example, Tiernan, a senior post holder in Coláiste Inis Bofin described how he had attempted to develop a more participatory form of management that gave staff a sense of professional autonomy and collegiality within the institution. This leadership style permeated all aspects of his work, even the building work on campus as he:

> [w]orked on the assumption that if you cannot provide people with a beautiful environment on which to operate, especially in the world of education, then somehow you are sending out an entirely negative message to them in terms of their own worth and their own value. I think this sector has generally been sent negative signals in terms of its worth and values for many years.
>
> (Tiernan, male senior post holder, Coláiste Inis Bofin higher education institution)

One of the greatest challenges facing senior appointees, and identified across all of the interviews, was that of managing staff relations effectively. The manner in which this was done not only reflected the ethical 'core' to their senior manager identity but also how they constructed and wished to present themselves as 'managers'. This appeared to be influenced by sectoral level, with a greater hierarchical 'split' evident between teaching staff and management as one moved towards higher education levels. At primary level a greater number of interviewees prioritized their 'teacher' over 'manager' identity and preferred to present themselves as colleagues with teaching staff rather than as belonging to a hierarchical layer of management:

> I would prefer to be a colleague rather than Principal and that would be my ethos and my philosophy and I would prefer to look at myself as [...] the term Principal doesn't sit comfortably with me but I would seek to empower people and set a good example and so on.
>
> (Conor, male principal, Scoil Derravaragh primary-level school)

At second level, the historical separation of the religious as management and lay staff as teachers ensured that a more distinctive 'manager' identity was part of the construction of self by interviewees in these schools. The well established system of devolved management structures in the VEC and further education sectors reaffirmed this tendency in the second level interviewees:

> And there would be very much an 'us and them' feeling in the school and it would be us […] So it would be the principal and then everybody else. And there was no sense, well very little sense […] there would have been very little sense of kind of teamwork and working together, it would be teachers doing their job, going into the class […]
>
> (Niamh, female principal, Scoil Comeragh second-level school speaking of her prior experience working in a secondary school)

In the university sector, given the relative 'newness' of some of the senior management posts, the interviewees had to position and present themselves in a distinct managerial role, while at the same time seeking to incorporate what was previously a more autonomous academic staff in the process:

> Not everybody liked me but I wasn't hated so much that I caused a lot of trouble and in academia everybody has a say, you know what I mean […] so it is important that you get on with people quite a bit.
>
> (Una, female senior post holder, Coláiste Rathlin higher education institution)

Across all sectors, interviewees spoke of the challenges of managing 'difficult' staff relations. What was required in these instances was a combination of sensitivity, patience and perseverance as the senior appointees sought to realize their core vision, often feeling constrained in doing so by staff that they felt were having an adverse impact on practice in the educational institution. This was one area where a number of interviewees favoured a more businesslike approach to education – through the initiation of performance indicators/benchmarks that were linked to promotional opportunity as well as retention within the profession:

> And I'm not saying necessarily that we would be a whole lot better off if there was wholesale firing going on […] but there is a total lack of any notion of performance.
>
> (Fergal, male education officer, Scoil Mourne second-level school)

Handling hostility from staff was also a source of challenge for the interviewees in their management roles and seemed to centre on the implementation of change and taking decisions that staff did not always agree with:

> Staff expectations can be quite unreal and their interpretation of procedures or innovations can be quite at variance with what was agreed and I find that very frustrating.
>
> (Gearóid, male principal, Scoil Speerin second-level school)

> I think that a lot of academics are really surprised when they come into these roles and then people hate them [...] at times I might be extremely offended when people blame me for things over which I have no control or tell me that I am not fighting hard enough for something for them when I have really fought hard and still not got it, that they don't give me the benefit of the doubt.
>
> (Una, female senior post holder, Coláiste Rathlin higher education institution)

Difficulties which arose in relation to working with colleagues, frustrations over the implementation of change challenged senior appointees' emphasis on excellence in their own practice.

*Aspirations towards excellence* The sense of vocation which underpinned much of senior appointees talk around leadership indicated their strong commitment to education and the passion they held for teaching, irrespective of which sector of education they worked in. Excellence was related ultimately to student experience and the creation of an educational organization that was known for its reputation:

> The importance of punctuality, delivery of an excellent curriculum; you become associated with [...] a centre of excellence as I have spoken about as in the IT is very strong at the school, sport is very strong at the school, music is very strong at the school and when we got those three things going on top of people going into their classes on time doing the business, a bit of team teaching and swapping and so on, when we got those things going the reputation improved.
>
> (Conor, male principal, Scoil Derravaragh primary-level school)

> The opportunity to, to manage, to develop and to lead, to have this college as a beacon school of excellence [...] particularly in the area of teaching.
>
> (Tadgh, male senior post holder, Colaiste Achill higher education institution)

The analysis overall highlights the extent to which the Senior appointees had to be both strategic and political in their positioning as senior appointees, finding a balance between pursuing what they felt was important (ethical self) while trying to retain staff on board. Dealing with the tensions between aspiration and practice gives rise to a range of emotions that in themselves indicate not only the level of personal investment that goes into any senior management role but also the dramaturgical aspect (Berger and Luckman, 1970; Goffman, 1971) to one's positioning as senior manager. It is reflected in the capacity to present oneself as capable and in control in spite of the range of emotions 'bubbling' underneath.

### Managing the 'emotional' self in the senior management role

Literature in relation to leadership and management increasingly emphasizes not only the emotional dimension to the senior manager's role (Furtner et al., 2010; Crawford, 2007; Zorn et al., 2007; Lyon and Woodward, 2004; Collinson, 2003), but also the extent to which the management of emotions is a key component in the realization of broader institutional goals especially in the caring professions (Bolton, 2001, Sachs and Blackmore, 1998) and especially for women (ibid). At issue in the analysis presented here is not only the actual emotion experienced by interviewees in their everyday lives as senior appointees, but also what this tells us about the culture of the organizations in which they work and how they are required to 'do' management in line with broader institutional goals. Emotions are embedded in ethics – especially if we define ethics in Rose's (2001) terms as 'acting' upon oneself. The feelings we derive from our interactions with others are underpinned by a range of normative dispositions that relate not only to our valuations/typifications of ourselves but also our expectation around how others should behave towards us. Role ascription is key here, especially if we consider the extent to which roles carry with them a range of normative obligations with which we, in taking up that role, identify. The question that is raised then is the extent to which interviewees experience a conflict between their emotions, their ethical selves, and the role they are expected to carry out as senior appointees on a daily basis. It also raises questions about how this becomes an attractor to or detractor from the role itself, an important aspect of gendered patterns in senior management appointments which has been dealt with in Chapter 5 and is also addressed in Chapter 8.

Putting oneself forward for a promotional position is always a 'risky' business, extending and challenging one's self into new responsibilities and experiences. Presenting oneself for interview, moving into a new school/institution has the potential to challenge any inner sense of security (ontological security) as one is put to the 'test' in a range of situations:

> It is indeed, no doubt it is, they are putting themselves and bearing their souls and it is a stressful experience.
>
> (Donal, male assessor, Scoil Derravaragh primary-level school)

> I mean obviously for the first few months, you know, there were people either being very quiet or testing situations to see reactions, and how you would move on things.
>
> (Muireann, female principal, Scoil Iveraghsecond-level school)

Other emotions that were consistently mentioned in the interviews, but predominantly in the school sectors (both primary and second level) related to feeling emotionally drained by the multiple demands in the role, as well as an accompanying sense of guilt at not being able to do all that was required:

> The guilt I had as a teaching principal was huge because I never taught as well as I'd like to because you were always being distracted, at least that guilt is gone. The guilt now is that I'm not doing my job well enough as a principal.
>
> (Andreas, male principal, Scoil Corrib primary-level school)

Part of the presentation of self in the management role is the need to appear 'in control' of all situations – all interviewees implicitly accepted that in their position they carried the final responsibility for all decisions taken. In many ways this need to appear 'in control' reflected for some a dehumanizing aspect in the management role – that to be a manager was to assume to be totally available for others, without having a reciprocal need for oneself, dovetailing with the requirements of 'super leadership' noted elsewhere (Caldwell, 2008; Crawford, 2007):

> People just come and they off load and they dehumanise you at times, they don't acknowledge that you actually have feelings as well

> and that happens [...] I read a good book recently where the principal of a school spoke about the permanent ache on their face from the smile and I think that is important, I do want to project a good humoured, efficient persona in this school.
>
> (Andreas, male principal, Scoil Corrib primary-level school)

> It is tiring and it is wearing and there are days that you'd love to say 'I wish you knew what I was going through too' but you just can't and you get on with it.
>
> (Fionnuala, female principal, Scoil Mourne second-level school)

In the third-level sector, interviewee narratives reflected a greater acceptance that the continual extension and investment of self was part of the role. It was also acknowledged that this may be a deterrent to others considering going forward for promotion:

> But I would think the element of the cultural that might discourage participation would tend to be that you get long hours cultures in organisations [...] The higher you go the reality is that the options are much starker [...] you are actually taking on a whole range of responsibilities and commitments rather than a schedule of time. And that is what they pay you for.
>
> (Neasa, female senior post holder, Saltees higher education institution)

> I'd say at the level I am at, it is just work, there is nothing else in our lives. That is an awful thing to say but there really is very little else if you want to really keep everything going [...] all my colleagues are saying 'why would I go there, why would I apply for that kind of a job?'
>
> (Siofra, female assessor, Coláiste Inis Mheain higher education institution)

The importance of the support of others emerged in discussions around being overwhelmed by the role – such support coming mainly through professional networks and family members. In this respect support through a clear and devolved system of middle management is also crucial (identified as often lacking in secondary schools), as is the support in primary schools of an effective board of management. This latter can be especially problematic however in light of the voluntary nature of board of management activity and the lack of educational expertise of many board members:

> My board is wonderful, it's made up of lovely, lovely people, but as a board, they leave me adrift and I think that that is proving hugely stressful for principals as well.
>
> (Blathnaid, female assessor, Scoil Foyle primary-level school)

> But I think one of the crucial issues in relation to the secondary school level principals job is that it is ludicrous what they are expected to undertake without appropriate support, the admin support is absolutely ridiculous and the support from posts of responsibility holders is way too weakly defined [...] it is ludicrous, it is outrageous.
>
> (Sorcha, female senior post holder, Coláiste Valentia higher education institution)

In spite of these challenges it was also clear that many of those in senior management enjoyed and got an emotional 'buzz' from their role, as noted by Aisling, the primary principal in Scoil Foyle when she said:' I love it [...] I know what's going on and that I have a voice in directing what's going on' and also by Neasa, senior post holder in Saltees:

> It's very hard, it's very complex and it is very demanding and you would want to be enjoying it. If you are not enjoying it and you are not getting the buzz about the craziness I would say you would burn up like that.
>
> (Neasa, female senior post holder, Saltees higher education Institution)

This is the seductive aspect of the role (Sinclair, 2009), in that the people who apply for them are those who enjoy placing themselves in situations where they were not necessarily comfortable, where they had to take risks and where they could ultimately exercise leadership. In this sense senior management positions are a seductive site for the investment of self (Alvesson and Willmott, 2002) providing a context within which action is purposeful and goal oriented. What is evident across all sectors is that their management responsibilities required them to stretch themselves significantly. The extent to which the work of senior managers required them to fabricate an 'inauthentic' self, as originally noted by Ball (2001) is however open to some questioning.

What emerged clearly in interviewee narratives was a commitment to improvement in their respective institutions, coupled with frustrations and tensions that arose from the interpersonal and administrative aspects of their roles. Their capacities to cope with the conflicting emotions and challenges in their roles is suggestive of an elastic (rather than necessarily 'plastic') self, that is continually stretched with the increasing demands of the role (Devine et al., 2011). For some there was awareness that this 'stretching' could become intolerable, necessitating eventual departure from the role – a problem that created its own difficulties in terms of alternate sources of employment/deployment:

> And I have seen personal friends of my own age who have given Principalship 5 or 6 years and run out of it at the first opportunity, and that is I suppose prevalent is too strong a word but it is common place.
>
> (Ronan, male assessor, Scoil Galtees second-level school)

## Concluding discussion

This chapter has considered issues to do with the presentation of self and identity in the senior management role and how this varies across the education sectors. A key focus has been the extent to which changes in culture, brought about by broader shifts towards new managerial practices of efficiency and accountability, have given rise to changes in the construction of the senior management position. New managerialism has profound implications for the construction and experience of management in education organizations. Underpinned by the neoliberal logic of the rational and voluntary choosing subject, senior managers are stretched personally and professionally, super-leaders maximizing the investment of their selves in their working lives. Three key themes emerged in the discussion; these related to perceptions of capacity and competence to engage in senior management, the tension between personal ethics and values in relation to education, and the management of emotions in the senior management role.

The analysis points to the significance of management as a site for identity investment – senior management positions provided interviewees with the capacity to engage in purposeful, directed activity that enhanced their own sense of self worth and drew on the considerable stores of energies they brought to their role. While they experienced a range of emotions in the ongoing challenges of their working lives, it was clear that among the greatest challenges facing them were demands for accountability and transparency in an era of increasing litigation, competition and demands for productivity in the educational world. New managerialism in this sense was experienced as a form of governance – shaping practice and identities that reflects disciplinary and bio-power (Foucault, 1979). However differences were identified that related to structural differences across the education sectors, but also individual actor's interpretation of their roles, hence role management. Significant differences were evident across the sectors in how this shift was being experienced. In the school sectors an ever-increasing administrative workload arising from legislative change, especially in the areas of student welfare and special needs, created real time bind difficulties for these principals. This was felt to cut across principals' desire to engage in broader visionary change, as well as interpersonal interaction with students in their schools. The construction of the principal role as a 'catch all' position, without due regard for the diverse nature of the role and hence the need for sufficient administrative back up, was identified as especially frustrating. This was experienced differently in the school sector itself; it was most trying at primary level for 'teaching principals' and those in disadvantaged schools. In such instances voluntarism, in terms of the willingness to work outside of school hours, as well as dependence on the voluntary activity of voluntary boards of management, ensured an ad-hoc almost idiosyncratic approach to aspects of management at primary level. In the second-level sector principals in secondary schools lacked a fully developed tradition of middle management to guide them in the allocation of administrative tasks. This was compounded by historical dichotomies between the management and teaching staff in religious-run schools. Within the vocational education sector, the experience of management appeared to be more streamlined, with a history of delegated posts and management structures. These served as important apprenticeships for entry into senior management positions across the second-level sector.

In the third-level sector, the lack of administrative support was never mentioned as an issue. This suggests that management roles were clearly defined and adequately supported in terms of administrative back up. Most notable in the narratives of these interviewees was their concern with strategic innovation and change, with an increasing eye to the public profile and competitive ranking of their institutions. However attitudes towards the acceptance of new mangerialist practices in the third-level sector were mixed, some viewed the changes favourably – as facilitating the implementation of radical change, while others were more circumspect in keen to retain an emphasis on core values of student support and care. For those in the school sector, the increasing culture of performativity was experienced indirectly through increasing media attention on school rankings and the need to market to maintain enrolments (again most notable among disadvantaged schools). It was also experienced more directly in the bureaucratic demands for efficiency, planning and accountability from the Department of Education and Skills.

The significance of these changes for the management of identity was considered and again differences were noted across the education sectors. While senior appointees across all sectors were required to 'perform', in the school sector especially the desire to retain an authenticity in the role, via an ethic of care and continual interaction with staff and students, was at times difficult to sustain. What was required was an 'elastic' self that was identified as a constraining factor in all sectors but as we will see in Chapters 8 and 9 there was a clear gendered dimension to how this elasticity was experienced, especially in terms of balancing care work in both personal and professional lives. Prevalent in the narratives of both assessors and principals were core concerns around the quality of interpersonal relations in their schools and the need to embrace a holistic approach to education that combined effective management practice with broader visionary goals. Emotions of guilt and depression, feeling overburdened and swamped sat alongside the energy and buzz senior appointees experienced in their roles – as they 'managed their insides' (Alvesson and Willmot, 2002), seeking to exercise a form of 'super leadership' (Caldwell, 2008) in the satisfaction the diverse demands upon them. Significantly however the threat of 'burn out' through the continual extension of self that was required emerged, with a number of principals reluctant to view themselves in these management positions for the long term. The incorporation of performativity was more pronounced in the identities of senior appointees and assessors at Third level. The experience of being stretched in this role derived from the focus on strategic planning and change, rather than being overwrought with diffuse demands and issues. In this sense their identities revolved around being targeted and driven – the greatest challenges being the encouragement and facilitation of others to embrace broader corporate/organizational goals.

A key question arises as to what extent the experience of 'self' in senior management is gendered and whether this 'stretching' is experienced differently, both in terms of gender and in terms of the sectors in which senior managers work. The chapter that follows considers the extent to which the experience in management posts is mediated by gender, in terms of organizational culture, and how this dovetailed with or contradicted senior managers' own constructions of themselves in gendered terms. It explores how senior appointees were required to 'do' gender within the organizations they were managing.

# 7
# Crafting the Elastic Self: Gendered Experiences of Senior Management

Senior management was defined as an all-consuming activity across all sectors of education. It was framed within an individualistic discourse that placed the burden of impact and change on the shoulders of each of the senior managers. In spite of the differences across the sectors in how new managerialism was being implemented, however, the intensity of reforms required a project of self-realization in which commitment to the organization – be it a school or higher education institution – was paramount. Given that there are gender differences in patterns of recruitment and retention in senior management across the education sectors, in this chapter we consider how the experience of elasticity in management is gendered by the need to 'do' and 'undo' gender identities in line with organizational cultures.

## Gender, organizational culture and management

While significant advances have been made at the level of legislation in the promotion of gender equality across the Western world and women's participation in the labour force has radically altered in the past 30 years, significant gender inequalities continue to persist in terms of pay, occupation and seniority across a host of private and public sector organizations (Halford and Leonard, 2001; Hey and Bradford, 2004; Ross-Smith and Huppatz, 2010). Hojgaard (2002) points out that at the current rate of progress, it would take another four hundred years to realize true gender equality in the labour market. Discourses of power and gender intertwine in organizational culture giving rise to gendered representations and subjectivities that derive from a complex interplay of history, tradition, economy and social context (Ball and Wicks, 2002). Organizational culture appears to be a key factor in determining both the production and reproduction of gender inequalities in the workplace.

In the management literature generally, organizational culture is viewed as pivotal to performance and productivity and is considered primarily as something the organization 'has' that is malleable and open to change in line with management goals and interests (Pemberton, 1995; Peters and Waterman, 1982; Smircich, 1983). Management goals however cannot be realized simply through top-down directives but must be internalized by employees as the 'common-sense' approach to behaving in the organization. In this sense organizational culture, as noted in Chapter 6, is deeply implicated in the construction of personal and social identities, a process that is also strongly gendered (Alvett and Willmott, 2002; Ball and Wick, 2002; Hatcher, 2003; Kerfoot and Knights, 2004; Probert, 2005). In their analysis, Halford and Leonard (2001) outline the extent to which organizations, both in their structures and cultures, are underpinned by a masculinist hegemony, which equates management with particular forms of dominance-led masculinity (Connell, 1995, 2000). To be a man in this hegemonic tradition means jettisoning the feminine from the 'self' and defining it as 'other'. It also means rejecting and subordinating other masculinities, notably gay masculinity, and working class and black masculinity. Hegemonic masculinity is framed by race, class, sexuality as well as gender.

Rejecting Kanter's (1977) liberal analysis that organizations are essentially neutral and non-discriminatory, Halford and Leonard argue that a particular type of male power is embedded in organizational structures through the methods of recruitment and selection, through the processes of job grading and career progression and through the organization of hours of work (Halford and Leonard, 2001: 54). In each of these areas, deeply gendered processes are at work, enacted through informal networks and sponsorship and informed by the construct of an 'ideal' type of manager who accords with a 'hyper' masculine norm – as one who is competitive, tough, individualistic and wedded to the organization. It is a care-free masculinity, one that is not bound to primary care responsibilities as these are assumed to be outside of men's responsibilities (Hanlon and Lynch, 2011). Care-free power is mobilized through the culture of the organization itself, through mission statements that are often defined in the anti-care rhetoric of the battlefield or sports ground. It also operates through patterns of communication and language usage, through imagery that presents stereotypical gender roles and through the separation of public and private life. Leonard (2002) notes that women in promoted positions often feel like strangers in a foreign land. They struggle personally, socially and politically to fit in to this corporate world. Men seem to have the symbolic capital to ensure they are recognized in the dominant form of organizational cultures (Everett, 2002). However, while men appear to integrate more easily into this culture (Corsun and Costen, 2001; MacKenzie Davey, 2008), and benefit substantially from its effects, this is not to suggest that all men are positioned as dominant within organizations or conversely that women are always subordinate (Billing, 2011; Martin, 2006). Not all men are welcome at the top.

While organizational culture is never gender-neutral, it is dynamic, fluid and changing and men and women are both positioned and position themselves differently depending on the traditions and context of the organization itself. Such analyses draw attention to the socially constructed nature of gendered identities, noted in Chapter 6. Gender cannot be simply reduced to traditional binaries of masculinity and femininity, but is performed (Butler, 1990), 'done' and 'undone' (West and Zimmerman, 1987; Butler, 2004; Deutsch, 2007) as part of a series of negotiated practices between self and other in contrasting social and organizational contexts (Flemming, 2007; Knights and Kerfoot, 2004; Martin, 2006; Poggio, 2006; Pullen and Knights, 2007). This is not always a conscious and deliberate process, and understanding the 'unreflexive' practising of gender, often routinely by people in powerful positions (Martin, 2006; Pullen and Simpson, 2009) is an important aspect of revealing stereotypes that apply to both men and women.

We have seen the impact of new managerial reform on organizational cultures through the shaping and practising of leadership identities in line with new managerial norms. While such reform has taken a number of hybridized forms depending on the sector in which it is being implemented, common to its successful implementation is the shift in organizational culture to one which is firmly embedded in principles of market dynamics, accountability and enhanced productivity. When considered in terms of gender dynamics, it is clear that new managerialism presents both challenges and opportunities for men and women to (re)negotiate their positions in a highly competitive and market-oriented culture. With the breakdown of traditional patriarchal power the emphasis is on what you can do rather than necessarily who you are; in theory women have the same chance of being promoted as their male counterparts (Fine et al., 2009). The delayering of management structures often typical of new managerial change can thus undermine traditional patterns of male dominance (Billing, 2011; Collinson and Hearn, 2003; Deem, 2007; Eagly and Carli, 2007; Fletcher, 2004).

In this changing environment, research suggests that women, especially those who are younger and highly educated are competing with their male counterparts. They are adopting a host of strategies, challenging gendered stereotypes, rendering themselves more visible in the organizational structure and establishing their own support networks (Airini, 2010; Billing, 2011; Coates, 1995; Huppatz, 2009; MacKensie Davey, 2008; McDowell, 1997; Ross-Smith and Huppatz, 2010).

However, Halford and Leonard (2001) argue that under new managerialism what is required is a form of superwoman who is as willing, as her male counterparts may be, to sacrifice all to the realization of company goals. In a performance culture, where career advancement is based on the achievement of pre-set targets, women are encouraged to compete equally to men. Changing views on effective management strategies, including the importance of emotional intelligence, copper fasten the view that the presence of a more 'feminine' orientation is a strength to any organization. Literature in this area speaks of the 'female' advantage (Cliffe, 2011; Hatcher, 2003; Huppatz, 2009; Metcalfe and Linstead, 2003; Sloan, 2010; Swan, 2008). While the move to more collaborative and 'democratic' practices may be of benefit, research cautions that this new 'emancipatory' framework, while valorizing qualities that may have traditionally been marginalised, does little to challenge any underlying masculinist model of management (Hatcher, 2003; Huppatz, 2009). New seemingly democratic forms of consultation often merely harnesses the feminine in the pursuit of performativity (Knight and Kerfoot, 2004; Walkerdine, 2004), doing little to challenge the hyper-masculinist model of management that can prevail (Hatcher, 2003; Ross-Smith and Huppatz, 2010; Wilson et al., 2010). As Walkerdine notes (2004: 2), it is easier to be 'one of the girls' than 'one of the boys', and women who enter management often have to practice gender in a managed way to retain their status as women and as managers (Martin, 2006; McTavish and Miller, 2009; Ross-Smith and Huppatz, 2010). An additional stretching is also required of women who enter managerial positions in organizations where men traditionally manage. They are the organizational 'other' and must manage their otherness or not succeed (Blackmore and Sachs, 2007; Halford and Leonard, 2001; Probert, 2005). They may have to minimize their gender difference in order to be treated equally to men, while retaining a distinct feminine identity to avoid being ridiculed for appearing overly masculine (Bailyn, 2003; Halford and Leonard, 2001). Managing a more feminine identity can thus be a double edged sword, a 'tactical resource' (Skeggs, 1997: 10) that can have strategic but limited value in management fields that are predominantly masculine in orientation (Ross-Smith and Huppatz, 2010).

Similarly Halford and Leonard (2001) argue that gender (and racial) blindness still persists in organizations that may have moved to more consensual and delayered models of management, ignoring the differing social and domestic realities of men and women. The relentless extension of self that is required in greedy organizations characterized by new managerial reform (Currie et al., 2000) creates severe challenges for those who have primary care responsibilities outside work (Coronel et al., 2010; Probert, 2005; Russell et al., 2009). Given the predominance of women in caring (Pettinger et al., 2006) and the moral imperative on women to do care work (O'Brien, 2007), it would appear that women face unique challenges combining their paid work and personal lives (Devine et al., 2011; Guillaume and Pochic, 2009; Lynch et al., 2009). While men must also manage their identities in new managerial regimes (Knights and Kerfoot, 2004; Linstead and Thomas, 2002) and the management of masculine identities incorporates resistance as well as accommodation to dominant masculinist norms (Pullen and Simpson, 2009), elasticity is not quite the same for men as it is for women. For women in highly performative work environments, being elastic not only involves meeting the requirements of organizational productivity (and as with men), the fashioning of self as the 24/7 worker, it also extends to doing caring work both within and without the organization in feminine-defined ways. This latter issue will be further developed in Chapter 8.

## Gender and management across the educational sector

While education has, since the turn of the twentieth century, been an increasingly feminized profession, differences in gender representation at the level of teaching and management are apparent across the various educational sectors. With respect to teaching in schools, for example, national and international patterns confirm the greater representation of women as teachers in primary and secondary schools (Coleman, 2001; Skelton, 2009; Tett and Riddell, 2009). The over-representation of women in the teaching profession, especially at the primary and pre-primary levels, dovetails with the classification of teaching as a 'caring' profession and of essentialist constructs of gender which define women as natural carers, instinctively suitable to the nurturing of young children (Acker, 1995; Shakeshaft, 2006). While women may pre dominate in the teaching profession (Drudy et al., 2005; Wilson et al., 2011; Skelton, 2009), their relative under-representation in management and leadership positions in education has been widely noted (Blackmore et al., 2006; Moorosi, 2010;

Shapira et al., 2011; Smith, 2011). This under-representation becomes more marked as one moves to higher-level (and more prestigious and generally better paid) sectors of education (Coleman, 2007; Lafferty and Fleming, 2000; Moreau et al., 2007; Neale and Ozlem, 2010; Shakeshaft, 2006; Thomson, 2007; McTavish and Miller, 2009).

Perceptions of sexism, coupled with the changing climate of management in schools and universities, can detract from women themselves seeking to move into senior management positions. Research has documented a greater reluctance on the part of many teachers in schools, for example, to put themselves forward for promotion due to the increasing demands of the role (Brooking, 2003; Fletcher and Campbell, 2003; Moreau et al., 2007; Thornton, 2002; Thrupp and Willmott, 2003; McLay, 2008). While this research was not explicitly focused on how the rate of applications may be gendered, given the well documented struggles of women to juggle both their professional and family lives, coupled with their career paths as typically being more fragmented than that of their male colleagues (Coronel et al., 2010; Wilson et al., 2010), there are many reasons why women would be less likely to offer themselves for promotion in the new managerial environment.

A review of literature in the area, however, paints a contradictory picture. On the one hand new managerialism, as a radical force for change in the structuring of organizations, is put forward as creating new organizational spaces for women where they can position themselves positively within the changed managerial order. Deem (2003, 2007) speaking of the university sector indicates that for women who see themselves on a distinct management career track, new managerialism provides increased opportunities for promotion through the range of managerial posts that become available to them. Furthermore, the emphasis on visibility of performance through the 'audit' culture provides an opportunity for women to have their work in the area of research, teaching and learning valorized and rendered more visible than heretofore (Harley, 2003; Thompson, 2007). This facilitates their potential entry to management positions. Research also suggests that women negotiate and resist their construction as 'other' forging networks, using their female capital (Huppatz, 2009) to gain promotion. Such capital, while limited in overall symbolic value, included using their 'femaleness' to their advantage by managing their appearance and social skills (Ross-Smith and Huppatz, 2010).

Conversely, however, the predominance of women at the lower ranks ensures that they are not as well positioned as men to put themselves forward for promotion (Lafferty and Fleming, 2000; Tomas et al., 2010).

The impact of hegemonic masculinity across the university sector, but most especially in the older and more traditional universities, can make it difficult for women to break into senior management. Those who do and those who do are typically childless and take longer than their male counterparts to achieve promotion (Bagihole, 2002; Deem, 2007). Male hegemony is reflected not only in the great number of men at management level, but also in the mode of operation of committees and conferences, where self-promotion through combative and competitive displays of skill and reason are prized (Airini et al., 2011; Blackmore, 2004; Thomas, 2004; McTavish and Miller, 2009; Tomas et al., 2010). In her research Deem (2007) noted that gender was perceived by respondents to be a far more significant factor influencing the careers of women than men in the university. Female interviewees were more likely to speak of experiences of sexism and prejudice, of struggles in being taken seriously while their male colleagues were more likely to note the improvement in opportunities that now existed for women in the university.

A related issue concerns the concentration of women in teaching and pastoral roles, as well as in disciplines traditionally defined as 'soft' within the university sector (Airini et al., 2010; Knights and Richards, 2003; Krofting, 2003; McTavish and Miller, 2009; White et al., 2011). The gendered nature of the research assessment exercise (RAE) in universities across the United Kingdom has been taken as a further example, with research pointing to the greater number of men who submit their work for assessment under the scheme and the difficulties that arise for women as they struggle to maintain 'valued' research output during their childbearing/rearing years (Harley, 2003; Knights and Richards, 2003; Lord and Preston, 2009; McTavish and Miller, 2009; Seay, 2010; Tomas et al., 2010; Wilson et al., 2011). While the process of assessment may be more transparent than under the traditional system, the value system underpinning the assessment itself is highly gendered. Given the increasing link that is now made between research funding, research output and university ranking, and the concentration of women in those disciplines where large research funds are not so readily available, this has major implications for embedding the masculinisation of senior management appointments in the university sector.

In the school sector, earlier work by Reay and Ball (2000) and Ball et al. (1995) in the United Kingdom illustrates how new managerialism steers head teachers, both male and female, into competitive ways of operating that may prove inimical to the appointment of women into these management positions. Similarly, Blackmore et al. (2006) outline the difficulty that ensues for female leaders, committed to collegial and open ways of working; they must alter their practice and exhibit 'strong' leadership and directed change to ensure their schools survive in a performance-driven environment. Moorosi (2010) highlights the impact of masculinist organizational cultures in secondary schools in South Africa, as well as sexist stereotypes over women's capacities in the management field. Other research points to the lack of an overt 'career' strategy by women in schools, as well as tensions in trying to balance care with professional responsibilities (Coleman, 2007; McLay, 2008; Oplatka and Tamir, 2009; Shapira et al., 2011; Smith, 2011; Thornton and Bricheno, 2000).

The remainder of the chapter explores the extent to which these issues arise similarly for senior appointees in education in Ireland. It considers how interviewees practiced their gendered identities and how/if this varied by educational sector.

## Practising gender across the education sectors – the 'doing' and 'undoing' of gender identities

Senior managers strategically managed their gender identities in line with the dominant gendered organizational cultures in their sectors. In the primary sector, especially, there was evidence that male principals, positioned as 'other', managed their maleness (Linstead and Thomas, 2002) in order to integrate into the more feminized cultures of primary school staff (Drudy et al., 2005). This is apparent not only in assumptions regarding the more feminized nature of men who enter primary teaching (Pullen and Simpson, 2009), but also in the comment of Andreas, a recently appointed principal, when he spoke of having to readjust his 'strong' management style:

> I would have come away with the impression that because it [staff] was so heavily female that a strong male may have presented a threat. I might be paranoid: it's a perception.
>
> (Andreas, male principal, Scoil Corrib primary-level school)

> I think men in education generally tend to be more [...] they tend to be more in touch with their female side, you know, because they're in a caring profession.
>
> (Niamh, female principal, Scoil Comeragh primary-level school)

In contrast, a more competitive masculinist culture was evident as one moved from primary to second level to higher education, not only in the significantly greater representation of men in management positions, but also in management styles that spoke of men in essentialist terms as being tough and competitive:

> [The] men that I have seen in Principal posts [are] a bit more rough and ready than women.
>
> (Fergal, education officer, Scoil Mourne second-level school)

> I would have many, many experiences of men taking on each other and it being a fight to the end [...] I don't think women have the same fighting instinct.
>
> (Siofra, female assessor, InisMeain higher education institution)

Just as Aindreas in Scoil Corrib felt he had to 'undo' his maleness in line with more feminized norms of identity performance at primary level, the same principle applied in reverse, at higher education for Andrew where managing a hierarchical culture (Kerfoot and Knights, 2004) was a challenge in making himself visible:

> I think the first time around I was the little guy, so we [in our centre] were not getting proper recognition for what we were doing. Once I became [a more senior manager] then I was visible.
>
> (Andrew, male senior post holder, Coláiste InisMeain higher education institution)

The belief that a 'softer' and more 'caring' non-hierarchical approach was a preferential mode of management for women or men was being challenged, even within the primary sector:

> Men can live their lives in separate boxes they will put their home and emotional life in one box and they will live their working life in another box, they can have a sporting life or whatever. Women do not tend to do that, you tend to apply emotional responses to a lot of areas and you tend to involve friendships and all of those relationships and I have learned that if you are to survive in the job you need the other approach, you have to be able to close the door.
>
> (Bridget, female principal, Scoil Allen primary-level school)

Three themes were identified that provide a connecting thread of analysis between organizational cultures and the simultaneous 'doing' and 'undoing' of gender and management in education. These themes raise questions about the additional elasticity work involved in extending oneself to meet new managerial demands. The first theme, *the experience of loneliness*, was expressed only by female interviewees; they were 'strangers' in a 'foreign land' (Leonard, 2002) due to the relative absence of other female colleagues at a similar level. The second theme was *'being taken seriously'*. This was expressed by both male and female colleagues in a manner which indicated an underlying competitive culture that pervaded higher education in particular. A final theme which emerged relates to how senior appointees positioned and presented themselves in this environment, the strategies they devised that involved *'being savvy'*, reading oneself accurately into the predefined 'rules' of the management 'game' and crafting one's 'self' accordingly.

### The experience of loneliness in the management role

Loneliness emerged in the comments of female senior appointees in the higher education sector. Implicit in such comments were feelings of isolation from a pre-existing network of colleagues who had shared interests. These important sources of support – and information – were clearly masculinist in form and perceived as difficult for the new appointees to 'tap' into:

> So initially when I came in first I was a bit lonely [...] I am the first female [senior post] and the others are all male [...] I felt a bit odd with the guys.
>
> (Una, female senior post holder Coláiste Rathlin)

> In our network [of schools], there are three or four women only so this is a very male culture. [...] It is difficult for a woman in this network, unfortunately.
>
> (Michael, male education officer, Scoil Speerin second-level school)

The toughness that was required in being a senior manager in the higher education sector often led to a loss of friends and the accompanying difficulty for women in securing themselves into a new professional collegial network:

> I suppose one of the difficulties is you have to be willing to take a lot of flak and to have people not like you and that is very hard for women. It is very hard for women not to be one of the gang so it is often quite lonely; the experience of it is quite lonely.
>
> (Siofra, female assessor, Coláiste InisMeain higher education institution)

Organizational culture was key here – and was also reflected in the comment of a female principal appointed to an all-boys' school:

> And I spoke to the Principal in my own School, he said, ah hem like its, you know, an all-male environment, it's going to be a difficult one, you'd be better going for a mixed school. So I thought, oh, well I'll put the application in and [...] I put it in and then I was called for an interview [...] it was all male [...] Board of [Assessors] [...] you know, when you go into a room, and I have to say, I walked into the room and I just saw the row, you know, the circle of people, and I just kind of looked at them all and my reaction was, I just want to run.
>
> (Muireann, female principal, Scoil Iveragh second-level school)

Clearly these female appointees were positioned as 'other', challenging traditional constructs of manager as 'male'. However, while they were aware of their 'otherness' within the male emporium of higher education especially, (Acker and Dillabough, 2007; Riordain et al., 2011) this did not imply that they felt they were discriminated against, overtly at any rate. Their responses to any experiences of sexism were in the main ambivalent reflecting an internalized acceptance of a paternalism that was excusable:

> Some older male comments have [expressed] a sort of humane sexism that is sort of understandable.
>
> (Neasa, female senior post holder, Saltees higher education institution)

But there was also evidence that gendered expectations were normalised:

> Women are at a later stage in their careers [when promoted] [...] and that is their decision and that probably makes sense to them and probably it is sensible.
>
> (Donal, male assessor, Scoil Derravaragh primary-level school)

> There is still a kind of acceptance in Irish society [...] that it is all right for a man to be at 7 o'clock, [...] there is a certain tolerance of that. But it is definitely not alright for a woman to be at work at that times and to have a man at home.
>
> (Macdara, male assessor, Scoil Neagh primary-level school)

Part of what women did to survive was to manage their isolation; they exercised agency and determination to overcome obstacles (Billing, 2011; Martin, 2006; Wilson et al., 2011). Neasa countered her relative isolation by strategically seeking out networks where other senior women met:

> I joined the [...] association and that brought me into contact with other women who were in senior management posts and they were fantastic.
>
> (Neasa, senior post holder, Saltees higher education institution)

Not all interviewees believed that organizational culture could be defined as 'masculinist' – arguing that gender differences arose for historical reasons rather than any undue bias in the system presently:

> It is probably partly historical[...] just there haven't been enough women in the system maybe wanting to go [for senior posts], I don't know. In times it was much more difficult, I think today it is maybe a bit easier.
>
> (Andrew, male senior post holder, Coláiste InisMeain higher education institution)

The female senior post holder in Coláiste Valentia, in referring to her earlier appointment in an all-male public service role, spoke of the collegiality she shared with her male colleagues:

> I worked almost all my life in a very male environment [...] I felt that there was a tremendous in some ways collegiality with my male colleagues, we were all in trouble together if you like [...] I was the first of a new generation of female [senior position] working in a very male environment, there would have been two much older women from a lot of the years past but I was the beginning of a different, the first married woman obviously.
>
> (Sorcha, female senior post holder, Coláiste Valentia higher education institution)

When asked had she experienced sexism at any point in her career, her response was ambivalent. She recognized the sexism and the discrimination but excused it:

> I have seen lots of it [sexism].When I was pregnant they made it absolutely clear that I was ruining the [organisation] [...]. And in fact

> they didn't pay me for that period of maternity leave [...].And when I came back the people were very kind but I was doing really stupid things, I was trying to breastfeed, I was coming in to a new job and because I felt under serious pressure from the maternity leave when I came back.[...]I didn't feel that I could tell them that I was breastfeeding and I needed a cup of tea or a glass of water or something. But they were very kind decent people, I'm not saying for a second, this wasn't bias or anything it's just that they had never faced this. They must have thought that they had got a mad woman, I mean I totally understand.
>
> (Sorcha, female senior post holder, Coláiste Valentia higher education institution)

Sorcha's acceptance of personal responsibility for these experiences demonstrates how she internalized her 'otherness'. And it shows that there is considerable ambiguity in how women manage their gender performances at work (Poggio, 2006; Pullen and Knights, 2007).

There was a belief that the culture of senior management was still unwelcoming for women, especially in higher education. However, the lack of women applying for top level posts in this sector was also excused, and seen as a personal choice rather than a structured lack of options even by senior women:

> I think the issues are such that I cannot see any immediate change in the balance between males and females in senior positions in education generally because women I think are more inclined (by and large, it is a generalisation) to look at the overall life situation [...]. Certainly on most of the boards I have been involved in for senior University positions there simply have been no female applicants. And that is another issue, some progress has been made in that regard in Primary Schools and Secondary Schools by encouraging women to apply and having networks of women and so on. But it hasn't come to that yet in the University sector.
>
> (Siofra, female assessor, Coláiste InisMeain higher education institution)

While being isolated is a challenge for all managers as detailed in Chapter 6, there is a gendered dynamic to the experience of isolation/loneliness that appears to be embedded in the organizational culture of the educational institutions themselves. It is worth noting, for example, that no interviewee at primary level mentioned the loneliness of their role in gendered terms, reflecting the more feminized culture of primary schools that is well documented in the literature (Drudy et al., 2005; Wilson et al., 2010; Skelton, 2009). While one of the interviewees at primary level was a male principal with an all-female staff (Aindreas, Scoil Corrib), experiences of loneliness/isolation/lack of connectedness to a gender-specific network did not emerge in his narratives.

### Being taken seriously in the senior management role

The second theme that emerged as significant in terms of gender related to being taken 'seriously' in the management role. Again this was an issue that emerged predominantly in the third-level sector, requiring interviewees to position and present themselves in a certain manner in order to make themselves 'heard' and 'seen' in the organization. Senior managers in higher education sectors, for example, spoke of the importance of status in being taken seriously. Status modes of self presentation are implicit, for example, in the comments of a senior post holder in Coláiste Rathlin over her efforts to secure a professorial title: 'I felt it made my job harder to do not having the title'. While 'title' conveyed prestige and status, there was also evidence of embodied modes of self-regulation that connected with being taken seriously. What Walkerdine (2004) speaks of as the 'looked-at-ness' of the feminine, has also been observed by other researchers in the field (Ross-Smith and Huppatz, 2010). This is reflected in the comment of Una regarding the difficulty for younger women and the interconnection between appearance and positioning:

> I have got a bit older my hair has gone a bit greyer! And somehow one of the benefits of being older and greyer is that you do get taken more seriously more easily than when you are younger and slimmer and attractive and all of that. You are either attractive or you are serious! And so if they decide if you are not among the attractive female potential candidates they are more inclined to listen to what you are saying, sadly that is my experience, it is a very cynical view. But one of the benefits of getting older and being more middle aged and moving up the senior ranks is that I do get listened to a bit more seriously, I think, at least that is what I feel.
>
> (Una, female senior post holder, Coláiste Rathlin higher education institution)

Issues of status modes of presentation did not apply to the same extent in the school sector, where, especially in primary schools, interviewees were more likely to identify themselves as 'equal' in status to their colleagues:

> I would prefer to be a colleague rather than principal [...] the term principal wouldn't sit comfortably with me but I would seek to empower people.
>
> (Conor, male principal, Scoil Derravaragh primary-level school)

Managing gender identities was a key part of 'doing' management. The more competitive and hierarchical culture in the third-level sector especially, and by implication the 'otherness' of the feminine in this field, created a tension for women in senior management positions both in 'doing' their role as well as deciding to go for these positions in the first place. The key issue here relates not only to dominant constructions of femininity, and by implication masculinity (Billing, 2011; Kerfoot and Knights, 2004; MacKenzie Davey, 2008), but the extent to which females in senior management positions have to tread a fine line in their social positioning in gendered terms. In asserting their visibility and voice, they both 'did' and 'undid' their femaleness. Masking femaleness (Linstead and Thomas, 2002) was reflected, for example, by distancing themselves from what was perceived as lower status caring work (Blackmore and Sachs, 2007) and the more typical nurturing 'mothering role':

> People have expectations of women in positions of power that they would never have of their males both in terms of how nice you are to them and how much time you must give to them and you sort of take on this motherly role and they wouldn't expect a man in that role to do it at all. You see the same thing in students and lecturers, you know, female lecturer is not there, she is just not available, the male lecturer is not there, he is busy. And the same thing carries on all the way up. But I have to be careful that I don't end up doing all the busy work, 'oh the sub-committee that is going to draft this that will bring it to the bigger group' you know, somehow the female will end up being drafted into that.
>
> (Sorcha, female senior post holder, Coláiste Valentia higher education institution)

The 'undoing' of gender (Pullen and Simpson, 2009; Butler, 2004) in terms of resisting a more service orientation in her positioning is also reflected in the comment by the principal of Scoil Iveragh with reference to her decision not to apply for deputy principal posts that were typically more service/administrative oriented:

> I just, I don't tend to apply for jobs that are assistants because I think a lot of women fall into that role of assistant and the female is often the assistant who does all the work, so I thought, well if I was going to put myself forward it would be the principal end of it.
>
> (Muireann, female principal, Scoil Iveragh second-level school)

Managing this double binary in terms of relations with female peers was an additional challenge, carrying with it ambiguities of what being a female, boss, manager and friend meant. This, it was felt, acted as a potential deterrent to women to go for promotion:

> Women are very afraid that if they take on a senior role that they will somehow lose their feminine qualifications as a female [...] a lot of females have that 'if I become the boss I won't be attractive, I won't be a good girlfriend, other women won't like me, senior women can be so mean'[...]. So I think there is a bit of an identity thing for women.
>
> (Una, female senior post holder, Coláiste Rathlin higher education institution)

> You get very tough in the game and I know from talking to my female colleagues they are quite determined they are not going there. I read Machiavelli's *Prince* and I'm utterly convinced by what it says.
>
> (Siofra, female assessor, Coláiste InisMeain higher education institution)

### 'Being savvy' and surviving the management 'game'

The reflexive managing of gender identities (Martin, 2006) was more pronounced among female interviewees in the study. A key element of this reflexivity derived from knowing and understanding the 'rules of the game' (Bourdieu, 1990).In this sense survival was a skill which had to be acquired, especially where the organizational culture did not fit so readily into one's own gendered norms. It was part of the skill of managing one's 'otherness'. In only one case was the management of gender identity mentioned specifically by a male interviewee who, as noted, worked as a principal in an all-female school. For female interviewees, survival was often expressed in terms of the need to be 'savvy' in how one positioned oneself with others. This was reflected, for example, in earlier comments in relation to not positioning oneself in stereotypically feminine ways – as caring, nurturing and motherly or as always putting oneself forward for the lesser status 'secretarial/administrative' type activities. It is reiterated by Una when she claims that it was her own lack of savvyness that precluded her from obtaining a professorship at the same time as some of her male colleagues:

> I did feel uncomfortable when I realized that I was the only female senior appointee [at this level] who wasn't professor [...] had I been more savvy I should have asked for it. I don't know that but I had the suspicion. So that is probably the only thing I think where my sex probably stood against me.
>
> (Una, female senior post holder, Coláiste Rathlin higher education institution)

> So you can still find this kind of slightly, not exactly secretarial but that kind of a role somehow can fall to you quite easily if you are not careful. And frankly if you refuse it you are often perceived as being difficult. And you just have to steer that, sometimes I fall into it, sometimes I say 'no' and sometimes I might say 'no' too strongly and maybe I am being difficult, I don't know. But that is a minefield that I still feel is there for us.
>
> (Una, female senior post holder, Coláiste Rathlin higher education institution)

> I don't go for the deferential 'yes Minister' kind of approach. I am a very political animal, you have to be to operate in this arena.
>
> (Neasa, female senior post holder, Saltees higher education institution)

'Being savvy' then was part of the strategies of resistance to dominant gendered norms. However, 'doing' gender is both a messy and ambiguous process (Pullen and Knights, 2007) and there was also evidence of female interviewees who practised their 'femaleness' (Martin, 2006) in a strategic way. They drew on female capital (Huppatz, 2009) that was also viewed as part of the savvyness of surviving the management role. This included, for example, drawing on the paternalism of older male colleagues to guide and mentor senior appointees in their new roles, accessing networks of senior women, or simply using their position as an 'outsider' to distance themselves from previous organizational norms:

> Some of the older men were slightly paternal a little bit, they went out of their way to see themselves as minding you but it was useful

> in some ways and I kind of exploited it a little bit. That was useful because you needed some guides and some mentors so that was useful.
>
> (Neasa, female senior post holder, Saltees higher education institution)

> So I really was quite an outsider coming in. That was a bit lonely in some ways but it was also an advantage probably as well because I couldn't be seen as having any particular bias or allegiance or whatever to any faction within the faculty.
>
> (Una, female senior post holder, Coláiste Rathlin higher education institution)

What was also clear in the narratives of these women was that they had a clear sense of their own competence and self confidence in their capacity to work in these senior management roles, irrespective of the more masculinized cultures within them. 'Being savvy' implied overcoming any gender stereotypes that may have existed and always putting oneself forward for a senior role:

> I still think there are an awful lot of problems with female self confidence and I would even see that in my students, right up to Post PhD and I think there is a responsibility on senior females like myself to encourage women of ability to continue on both at Undergraduate, Postgraduate. I encourage my administrative staff, I say 'why aren't you going for that grade 6 or whatever?' if I think they are able for it. [...] there are still an awful lot of crisis of confidence.
>
> (Una, female senior post holder, Colaiste Rathlin higher education institution)

## Concluding discussion

Organizational culture is a key factor governing the experience of senior management across the education sector. Organizational cultures are also gendered giving rise to different perceptions, experiences and demands on both male and female senior appointees. The analysis focused on gender as 'practise' – negotiated, sometimes messy and ambiguous, but always as a response and/or reaction to dominant organizational norms. This practising was more reflexive (Martin, 2006; Pullen and Knights, 2007) among female interviewees, who explicitly identified the impact of their gendered identities on how they 'did' management. Such reflexive practising derived from their need to 'manage' their otherness in their organizations. This was especially the case in the higher education sectors, where men traditionally managed and where a more performative, competitive and hierarchical culture prevailed. Contradictions were evident however in this 'doing' of femaleness as women struggled to manage more essentialist constructs of being nurturing and caring, with embodied status-driven forms of self presentation. Simultaneously there was evidence of using their femaleness strategically where this gave them access to important sources of knowledge and understanding about the management role. While men also clearly position themselves in gendered terms, in only one interview did a reflexive awareness of gender positioning emerge for a male principal appointed to an all-female primary school.

New managerialism requires a relentless practising of self among senior appointments. What this analysis highlights however is the additional gender work that is required of female senior appointees, especially in organizations where men predominate and where more overtly hegemomic forms of masculinity (Connell, 1995) dictate management practice. This gender work can be construed as an additional form of elasticity that is required in the management role. For women working in the higher education sector especially, it involved both 'doing' and 'undoing' the feminine (Linstead and Thomas, 2002; Knights, 2004; Ross-Smith and Huppatz, 2010); dealing with the loneliness of being on the 'outside' as well as learning to be savvy and playing the rules of the management game. Such patterns are becoming more rather than less embedded under new managerial reform. While men also struggled for recognition in masculinist organizational cultures as not all men subscribe to hegemonic forms of masculinity (Martin, 2006), only one male interviewee, a principal of a primary school with an all-female staff, identified his maleness in problematic terms.

A considerable challenge in the 'doing' of both management and gender relates to the binary of care work in both the professional and personal lives of those who apply for and are appointed to senior management positions. The construction of senior management positions as posts that require the deployment of unlimited resources of time and energy as a basic entry qualification serves to exclude those who aspire to integrate their professional and personal lives in a balanced manner. The increasing trend towards performativity across the education sector – coupled with the absence of clearly defined and sufficiently supported management roles in different levels of the school sector – will only serve to consolidate this pattern. This subject will be dealt with more explicitly in the next chapter.

In spite of recent legislative and policy provisions to promote gender equality and prevent overt discrimination in the allocation of senior management positions, the analysis suggests that indirect discrimination may be taking place as senior posts are defined in a care-free manner that strongly discourages those with primary care responsibilities from applying. The inevitable result is that many women (and some men) who are primary carers select themselves out from moving up to the senior ranks of educational management. While this can apply to both men and women, the experience of 'otherness' that was alluded to by women in the third-level sector especially suggests that having to manage their gender identity and their default care responsibilities serves as a strong deterrent to all but the most confident and exceptional women. The individualization of gendered experiences in the narratives of both senior appointees and assessors across the study, and the assumption that 'self-selection' out of management positions was not a matter of institutional concern and responsibility reflects the lack of understanding of how the gender-care nexus impacts on who becomes a senior manager. Given how homogenous senior management posts are (not only in gender terms, but also in terms of race, disability, care, sexuality etc.) in an increasingly pluralized society like Ireland, there is an urgent need to implement effective policies to promote diversity at management levels. In this sense adherence to anti-discrimination legislation as the sole mechanism for addressing gender and other inequalities in education can mask the more subtle forms of exclusion that operate in and through the institutionalized cultures of organizations.

# 8

# The Careless Rules of the Game: Pregnancy, Child Care and Management

As noted in Chapters 1 and 2, there has been a significant shift to corporatization and new managerialism in the Irish public service over the past two decades (Collins et al., 2007). While the pace and intensity of the managerialist movement in education is most visible in the higher education sector, it is operating at all levels and over a long period of time. Under the influence of the Organisation for Economic Co-operation and Development (OECD), human capital theory replaced the theocentric paradigm as the official ideology of Irish education in the late 1960s, mutating into what O'Sullivan has called 'mercantilism' in recent decades (2005: 180–223). This 'modernist' development was a global trend (Marginson, 2006). It was represented as egalitarian and gender inclusive, yet it was also a way of reshaping the power of capital and instituting new forms of male power within organizations (Bottomore and Sachs, 2007; Davies, et al., 2006; Whitehead, 2001). The focus on performativity, a core principle of new managerialism, not only created gender exclusions, it also marginalized people on disability, ethnicity, race and social class lines within organizations, something that has often been ignored by organizational studies (Holvino, 2010; Lumby, 2009).

There is another exclusionary dimension to the new management regimes of the corporatized state that is also significant. As new managerialism prizes performativity and requires mobile and flexible workers that are not tied by time or care responsibilities, the type of worker that is valued at senior level in particular is ideally detached, and, in the corporate sector, transnational (Connell, 1998). Although this corporate model is not fully institutionalized in education as yet, it is being introduced in European countries in a way that significantly disadvantages women who remain as primary carers within families even if they are school principals (Coronel et al., 2010). Moreover, new managerialism is fully operational in much of higher education with the growth of academic capitalism. There are expectations that universities not only service the economy directly, but that they alter their internal systems of operation along business lines (Metcalfe and Slaughter, 2008).

While care and gender are treated as being synonymous in much of the research literature, and they are very closely related, they are discrete identities. Women are the default carers globally (Folbre, 2004) and are therefore greatly constrained by care-free models of management; however, some men do primary care work (paid and unpaid) and not all women are carers. The class position of men frames their relations to caring, with upper middle class men being especially able to derogate hands-on primary care work to women, be they spouses or paid carers (Shows and Gerstel, 2009). This is not to suggest that poor or unemployed men take up primary caring in an equal way with women, and the evidence is that they do not (Legerski and Cornwall, 2010) nor do men do equal amounts of care work to women. However, men sometimes cannot avoid primary care work (Hanlon, 2009; Lynch et al., 2009). The class, migrant and nationality status of women also frames their care status, especially in the care economy where upper middle class men and women can hire poor, migrant women (mostly) to do primary care work within households (Ehrenreich and Hochschild, 2002). Marital status also impacts significantly on who does care work and under what conditions. Mothers who are sole carers have a profoundly different relationship to primary caring than women and men who are in couples (Dodson, 2007; Lynch and Lyons, 2009: 93–113). Care and gender are closely related but discrete categories of identity therefore; recognising how they overlap but are separate enables us to track the differential impact of affective relations on people's capacities to take up managerial positions.

In this study, while the differences between women and men senior managers followed traditional gender lines in care terms, there were differences *between* women in terms of how they managed schools or higher education institutions depending on whether or not they had dependent children[1] and/or were sole carers. Caring also impacted on men who had dependents, albeit in far less demanding ways than it did on women as almost all men were secondary rather than primary carers.

The way care interfaced with gender, and impacted on women's and men's ability to apply for or take up senior posts, also varied with the sector of education in which people worked. Primary schools were relatively care-friendly places in managerial terms with higher education being the least care-friendly. The more powerful the position, in terms of scale and scope of influence in managerial terms, the more likely it was to be defined as a care-less space, and the more likely it was to be occupied by men.

## Gender differences in the narratives

As noted in preceding chapters, women's narratives as to how care impacted on their management roles were different from those of men. Almost all female interviewees talked about care at some length; they were familiar with the language of caring and got emotionally engaged with the subject at interview. While some men also discussed caring and were actively engaged on the issue, they were the minority and all were principals in either primary or second-level schools.

Given that Irish schools are small by international standards, especially primary schools,[2] the role of school principal is very different in terms of the work it entails at management level compared with higher education (it often involves teaching as well as managing in smaller schools). These organizational differences are relevant when assessing the impact of new managerialism on education in the cultural context of Ireland; the scope for introducing advanced systems of control and regulation internally is constrained by the small size of many schools, with approximately 50 per cent having 100 or fewer children. School principals in small primary schools are also teachers; in smaller second-level schools, principals may also teach classes. The managerial-staff binary is fluid in a way that might not apply in bigger organizations like universities and institutes of technology.

The nature of managerial and teaching experience, and the culture of Irish schools, which have little internal competition and a relatively low emphasis on performativity especially at primary level (Drudy, 2005) may help explain why male principals (and assessors, many of whom were also principals) at primary and post-primary level were more care-friendly in their narratives than men in higher education.[3] While the lack of interest in care among higher education managers could be attributed to their age, as they were on average ten years older than school principals and had older (or adult) children in most cases, this is not a satisfactory explanation: women in higher education were quite interested in talking about the relationship between primary caring and management even though they too were some ten years older than school principals and had a similar profile in terms of the ages of their children.

Even allowing for gender differences, the 'biography of work' was very different across the various sectors of education: women and men in primary education especially, but also those in second level, had considerable experience of working with young children and teenagers for many years in classrooms before being appointed principals. This life experience tempered their discussions of management and made many (but not all) more child- and student-centred in their discussions of management. They had learned a care narrative 'on the job', as it were, while teaching. Women and men in higher education did not have similar experiences, as higher education is not led by a care narrative; as noted by one senior manager 'academic life is a very selfish one'.[4] However, female senior managers in higher education did employ a care narrative; they made it clear they could not ignore care work, especially in the private sphere, in a way senior men in academia could and did.

To document the experiences of women and men in relation to child care and management, the best place to start is the first phase of life, pregnancy, and prior to this the decision to have a child.

## Pregnancy and having children

While none of the female primary or post-primary principals said that their decisions whether or not to have children or when to have them or how many they would have were influenced by their management ambitions or interests, their experience of support for their pregnancy varied. One second-level principal (Maeve) told of two very different experiences in relation to her pregnancies.

Some time prior to her current appointment, Maeve worked in a relatively senior post (two-year secondment contract) with a male religious order. She realized she was pregnant as her contract was coming up for renewal at the end of her first year. Her account of how the male religious order handled her pregnancy shows how they tried to disengage from their statutory duties.

> I had been working with the [name of male religious order] and they had wanted me to stay on for another year until they discovered that I was pregnant. And it's interesting, not that they would, they couldn't have [done anything], but there was that sense that 'oh God' and there was a little bit of pressure. Would you not like to take a year off and then come back to us and the [former school

> employer] will take you back for a year, it was an interesting take, I suppose the male/female thing, maybe you know.
>
> (Maeve, female principal, Scoil Nephin second-level school)

However, her experience of how a second pregnancy was managed was different, and more supportive, although she did experience anxiety about telling the employer about the pregnancy.

When Maeve applied for the post of principal in her current school, she knew she was pregnant with her second child but this did not matter to her: 'It seemed like a good idea [to apply for this post] at that time'. After she was offered the principalship, the chairperson of the board rang her to ask her to sign the documents confirming her acceptance:

> So she [...] said 'Come up now and sign the forms', and I said 'Well I'd like the weekend to think about it'. I don't know whether she was a bit put out that you wouldn't say immediately you wanted it [...] and I mean John and I did have to sit down and look at the implications, I had also just discovered I was pregnant, so there was that other implication [...] of well, telling the nuns too, but you know once I told her it was like a weight lifted. She said 'you're still taking the job are you?' I said 'yeah fine'. I knew just the sense I got of her, yeah [she knew] we had to look at the implications for family life too.
>
> (Maeve, female principal, Scoil Nephin second-level school)

Being pregnant and being a primary school principal was acceptable and many of the women appointed as principals in primary schools were quite young. The principal of Scoil Sheelin had two young children, one aged three and a half years and one aged seven months. She explained how she became pregnant after accepting the post of principal and consequently missed much of the first year of the principalship. However, she was not worried by this:

> I kind of said well if they want me they will take my family wishes sort of thing. [...] it is funny because when I told _ [name of Chair BOM], you know I got on very well with [him] and I could tell him in a laughy-jokey sort of way. And he said 'well look when we interviewed you, you are young and you are female', [...] and he knew I had a young child, [...] 'but why would we think that you weren't going to have any more?'
>
> (Aoife, female principal, Scoil Sheelin primary-level school)

While pregnancy was acceptable for women who were married, one principal spoke of a close friend who was a teacher and was pregnant and not married. While nothing adverse happened to her, there was a 'ripple of fear' that it might, even though discrimination on pregnancy grounds had been illegal for many years:

> [Y]ou go back 10 years a friend of mine got pregnant as a teacher and wasn't married and it was kept quiet enough because the perception was that the bishop in question mightn't be too [pleased], the child is 8 now. [...] She kept her job, but, and of course she should keep her job, but there was a lot of ripple of fear.
>
> (Andreas, male principal, Corrib primary-level school)

Teachers in primary and post-primary schools in Ireland have working conditions that facilitate caring for children; not only do teachers have relatively long holidays[5] they can also take career breaks (for up to five years for child care or other work, while returning to their teaching posts). However, the situation in higher education is quite different. There is no guarantee if one takes leave that one will be assigned to one's original post; it depends on availability. Career breaks could also seriously impede chances of promotion (as could extended periods of maternity or care leave) as it is likely the person would lack the management and/or research profile that would be required to progress to senior lectureship, professorship or senior management positions. The differences between the sectors were highlighted in the experiences of senior women managers in relation to pregnancy.

Two of the women who were senior managers in the higher education sector stated that they limited the number of children they had (they had one and two, respectively – two of whom were in their late teens and the other in their early twenties at the time of interview) because of the difficulties of combining relatively senior posts of responsibility over the years with having children. In one case it was the experience of coming back to work with a team of people who did not approve of a relatively senior person taking maternity leave that instigated this decision.

As Sorcha, a female senior post holder in higher education, recounted, 'when I came back for the second time to the [former place of employment] [...] they made it absolutely clear that I was ruining the department [former place of employment] [...] I was coming in to a new job and I felt under serious pressure from the maternity leave when I came back'. Sorcha felt under so much pressure that she came back to work very early from maternity leave, when her baby was less than two months old, although she was entitled to 18 weeks paid leave at that time (20 years ago approximately):

> It broke my heart so that was the end and I determined, no more children I just couldn't cope with it, it was heartbreaking.
>
> (Sorcha, female senior post holder, Valentia higher education institution)

Although this senior post holder in Valentia higher education institution said that 'things are much easier now the maternity leave is much longer', she still felt she was treated badly when she had her second child. Not alone was she under pressure to return, her immediate boss tried to find ways of getting her previous department to pay for her maternity leave because of the time at which she joined the new department. She felt there was no recognition of her needs as a mother with a very young baby. Her internalized sense of having inconvenienced her employer and colleagues at the time remained with her. She continued to apologise for her pregnancy and mothering responsibilities and tried to excuse her colleagues for their negative attitudes.

> I didn't feel that I could tell them that I was breastfeeding and I needed a cup of tea or a glass of water or something. But they were very kind decent people, I'm not saying for a second, this wasn't bias or anything it's just that they had never faced this; they must have thought that they had got a mad woman I mean I totally understand.
>
> (Sorcha, female senior post holder, Valentia higher education institution)

For another current senior post holder at higher education level, the decision not to have a second child was made to ensure that she got a permanent tenured post. Una held that getting into a permanent post in higher education, a tenured track, would have been impossible with two young children.

> I mean it was a big influence in only having one, I never had another one and it wasn't because [...] [personal reasons given] but I made a conscious decision that I couldn't get tenure and be pregnant and have a second child, it was just not going to happen.
>
> (Una, female senior post holder, Rathlin higher education institution)

Una had worked in a number of countries before being appointed in Ireland. She believed that having children seriously disadvantaged women in terms of promotion, and even in terms of getting a permanent post in the university system.

> My experiences of women who get PhDs and then immediately have a baby and then look for a job and then suddenly find that they can't get it or their husband has got themselves a job and then they are tied into that city and there is no other University in that city so they can get temporary work. And in North America that is the death knell to a research career, temporary work, lecturing, all the hours that God sends at the low level courses that nobody else wants, massive amounts of grading, no time for research, any other time spent with the kids. And that can go on year in and year out and low and behold a position comes up in that department in your area and they will hire somebody else in over you and you will still have that temporary role. It is absolutely lethal and I have seen that over and over again. And I have seen that much more with females than males.
>
> (Una, female senior post holder, Rathlin higher education institution)

Having young children not only made it difficult to get a permanent post in higher education, it limited the time mothers had for intensive work. The time-intensive demands of research were in open conflict with the demands of being the primary carer for children:

> Also in universities, for women faculty members, the fact that most promotion now prioritises research means that it is very, very difficult for them at a particular stage in their career. It is very difficult for women to be able to devote the amount of time that seems to be necessitated by producing research and publications.
>
> (Sorcha, female senior post holder, Valentia higher education institution)

It was assumed by all the women that caring was likely to remain a women's job. Women were defined by care work in a way men were not.

Principals at primary and second level did not generally see pregnancy and child care as a barrier to getting full-time posts or promotions; care work and paid work were regarded as mutually accommodating for both teachers and principals after the early years of child care. As Fergal observed, 'you might have a teacher that is fully immersed in the life of the school, they might have a family or they might not I mean none of this is really relevant actually' (male education officer, Scoil Mourne second-level school). This was also the view of another male principal who was also an assessor:

> You have to assume that, as a Principal, no matter who it is, whether it's maternity leave, whether it's any sort of illness you have to find a replacement [...] I don't worry about that aspect, I honestly don't worry about that aspect at all.
>
> (Ronan, male assessor, Scoil Galtees second-level school)

Maeve, who was a principal in a girls' secondary school had maternity leave in her first year as principal in her current school. Although she did not think having a baby in her first year as principal was ideal; 'it wasn't a good start for trying to get a handle on things', she found the management in her school [a female religious order] very supportive. It contrasted with where she had worked previously with a male religious order:

> [The] Education Officer for all the [name of female religious order] in our area, again her first reaction, whatever her private reaction was, was to send me to card you know, delighted at the news, or whatever, so like it was a very different attitude.
>
> (Maeve, female principal, Scoil Nephin second-level school)

Moreover the management at Maeve's school was very accommodating of her needs as a parent, especially when she had child care issues. No one objected to her taking her young children to her office when there was a care problem:

> We have had days when they've [the children] been in the office because the baby-minder hasn't shown up, but that sort of adds to the community like you know.
>
> (Meabh, female principal, Scoil Nephin second-level school)

Primary, secondary and higher education were very different therefore in how they accommodated pregnancy and child care. Higher education was especially inhospitable while primary especially, and secondary to a lesser degree, were quite accommodating. However, conflict between paid work and caring was beginning to creep in as a gendered concern with rising performativity demands in all sectors. It exercised influence on women, who, at times, opted for career breaks as a way of managing caring and paid work.

## Career breaks

Taking time out for child rearing was a realisable option for women in primary education in particular; some women in second level also took career breaks for caring work although no male principals had taken career breaks for caring. Neither women nor men in higher education reported having career breaks when their children were young.

Two of the female principals interviewed had taken long career breaks when their children were small. Brigid, the principal of Scoil Allen primary school, had taken a five-year-career break from teaching to mind her three young children. Before she took leave she held a post of responsibility in her school. While she devoted her time to her children while on leave, she did start to re-engage in education towards the end of her time and planned to come back to teaching, and even to seek a management post where she could promote changes she believed were desirable in education:

> In that time [during the 5 year career break] I didn't study because my children were young, two of them are within a year of each other and never slept for various health reasons, but in the last two years I did do the teaching practice supervision. So I was in seeing other schools, seeing other situations and I suppose that gave me a feeling that it was possible to change and that there are a lot of different approaches to education.
>
> (Bridget, female principal, Scoil Allen primary-level school)

Niamh, the principal of a co-educational second-level school, had only worked for one year after qualifying and then taken over eight years out to rear her four children. She had not planned to come back full-time but did.

> Well you see when my four children were small I didn't work (*sic*) at all, I didn't go back to work until they were all kind of in school, so I didn't start work until then. Because I suppose that would have been a priority for me [...] I was out of work for 8 or 9 years and then I came back to work and I hadn't any intention of coming back to work full time even but you know, you get sucked in.
>
> (Niamh, female principal, Scoil Comeragh second-level school)

However, Niamh had studied over the years and successfully completed a Masters degree and qualified as a guidance counsellor. She had 'tried out different things' including doing private work but then came back to teaching. She did not think that having been out of teaching disadvantaged her in any way as she had been up-skilling herself through education. Like Brigid, Niamh assumed the role of primary carer was her responsibility and never assumed her husband would take that role, nor did she assume she 'worked' all those years she was caring.

The attitude to taking leave in higher education was very different. Una believed that taking part in job-sharing, or asking for extended care leave, would seriously disadvantage her promotion prospects in higher education. Speaking of job sharing which was not available when her child was a baby, she said that 'I'm not sure that I would have taken advantage of it because I would have been afraid that it might have negatively impacted on me, maybe I was just paranoid about it' (Una, female senior post holder, Rathlin higher education institution).

None of the men we interviewed had taken leave for care work. They had delayed applying for principalships, in some cases due to child care issues, but child care was not the only consideration in any case. One of the principals mentioned how his sporting commitments (and to a lesser degree, their care commitments) influenced his decision about the timing of his application for principalship:

> I mean the position came up here fifteen years ago. I didn't go for it then because, you know, really back then my family were younger, you know, and I felt that I wanted to give more time to sport. I'm very active in sport myself, playing. [...] So I felt at that stage I wasn't ready for it [...] I feel I could have gone (in the past) but I didn't want to go because I mean I was active in sport. I was playing, I'm still playing sport. [...] Well I feel I'm slowing down a little bit now so this [principalship] wasn't going to be a burden, you know.
>
> (Brendan, male principal, Scoil Errigal second-level school)

Having a background in sport was something a number of male school principals (at both primary and second level) mentioned as being in their favour when applying for posts. Conor, a primary school principal, claimed that he would have 'put his mortgage' on getting the principalship that he got as he had the right profile, and that included sport:

> I had a track record, a clean bill of health, I had a good CV going, [...] I had been post holder in my own school; I had been delivering

> in-service, living locally, I had a sporting background. [...] I don t care how many [applicants] there were, in this particular Principalship, I would have put my mortgage on it.
>
> (Conor, male principal, Scoil Derravaragh primary-level school)

Career breaks for child care were seen as options for women but not for men. None of the men had taken leave for child care although one principal (Conor in Derravaragh primary school) had changed his job (to avoid long commutes) due to his child care commitments. Interestingly, three of the senior men that we interviewed, two of whom were senior post holders in higher education, explained that their wives either took career breaks from work or worked part-time for child care reasons. And two of these three women were teachers.

While one of male principals (Aodhaigh in Scoil Derg primary school) had taken a five-year-career break, he did so to teach in another country where he worked for two years before moving to the UK, where he did a Master's in education before returning to Ireland to his original teaching post. His years abroad benefited him professionally as he was seconded to a more senior national post within five years, from which he moved after some time to being a school principal.

### Men's views: Child care as a woman's decision

When principals were asked about the impact of child care on applications for principalships and on the work of principals, there was considerable variation in the views expressed: some saw it as possible to combine the two jobs; others saw them as quite incompatible tasks, while still others displayed ambivalence. Senior men in higher education (and senior women, but to a lesser degree) did not regard senior management posts and child care as mutually compatible in that sector.

Andreas, the head of Corrib primary school, did not see the principal's job at primary level as either all-encompassing or incompatible with caring. However, he did think that it could be difficult for women because they were often assumed to be primary carers, a responsibility that he did not believe should be assigned to women:

> I disagree [with the idea that being a principal is an all-encompassing job], except when it comes to the gender issue again, where females are still perceived to be the chief childminder, it definitely would have an impact then. Because again it's a perception 'teaching is a

> great job for a working mum because they work around their children's hours', I don't agree with that.
>
> (Andreas, male principal, Scoil Corrib primary-level school)

Andreas was different from most other male principals and assessors however. Most believed that child care work was a woman's responsibility. Some even believed that being a principal was not compatible with child care and if there was a conflict then women would take leave, not men. Peadar, the principal in Scoil Galtees, epitomized this view. He had three young children, aged ten, seven and three years of age. He claimed his wife just could not go back to teach because she needed to be there for the children while he was a principal.

> She [...] was on a career break when I was in the previous school, and she intended going back teaching to her secondary school, but because of the time constraints and the commitment involved in this job, she simply couldn't [...] Because the kids are of an age, that she just couldn't go back.
>
> (Peadar, male principal, Scoil Galtees second-level school)

The decision to give up teaching was attributed to her as a personal decision, although it was clear that Peadar held traditional gendered views on child care:

> She made the decision anyway that she was giving up, to make sure that at least there would be somebody back home at the ranch [...] I mean, if we were both working, now we could have gone around to the family [for] support and all the rest of it, but the way it was, she felt that she wanted to be the child carer, *that it was her job* [our emphasis] and that they were brought into the world to be parented not farmed out [...] I know that probably sounds very unfeminist, but that was the feeling.
>
> (Peadar, male principal, Scoil Galtees second-level school)

The decision to take leave or to give up one's post for child care reasons was defined as 'a woman's choice' also by Tadhg, a senior post holder at Achill Higher Education College. He explained that his wife took a one-year-career break when their child was born. As the career break was not extended 'she retired from her job [...] she resigned [...] she made a choice and in ways it was a hard choice, but it wasn't

> hard at all, there was no choice, I mean [...] it's *her* [our emphasis] only child [...] she made the right decision'.
>
> (Tadhg, male senior post holder, Achill higher education institution)

It is interesting how, in his account of their child care arrangements, Tadgh described their daughter as 'her only child' although it was his only child too. He attributed 'ownership' of the child to his wife in a way that he did not attribute it to himself.

While some senior male managers claimed that the work of child care was negotiated between them and their spouses, the end of the negotiations followed a fairly predictable gendered pattern, with women taking primary responsibility for managing and doing child care. The senior men interviewed accepted that women would work part-time or take leave to do child care. A number of them saw this as an inevitable occurrence with very young children. They did not see this as a 'choice' for themselves.

**Juggling and managing: A women's issue**

While the women who had taken career breaks for care did not feel disadvantaged by this decision, this is not surprising given that they had now got senior posts. Indeed the language that women and men used about child care suggested that taking a career break to do mothering was an appropriate moral choice for women; it was part of being a good mother. No such moral imperative existed for fathers.

Both female principals and assessors in post-primary schools felt that managing a school when one's children were young was very demanding for women even if they achieved the balance successfully. One of the female principals who had a young child said that while she was able to manage, she found it difficult especially at holiday time. She compared her time as a very busy teacher with being a principal:

> But there were evenings that if you got a good bit of work done some evenings that you could take off a bit earlier but that hasn't been the case with this job. Even I suppose now having to work through holiday time and so on it is that little bit more difficult, it certainly is, and you do feel a major pull of trying to get that balance for all.
>
> (Fionnuala, female principal, Scoil Mourne second-level school)

Bridget, the principal of Scoil Allen primary school, had three children and was married. It was evident from the interview that she had primary care responsibility for hands-on care work and she too found it a challenge managing caring and managing the school:

> [A]s I said there is a huge responsibility in the principalship and then I take my responsibility with my children seriously. They are at an age where I am hugely involved with them: they need to be driven everywhere, they have a lot of interests, and they are pursuing some of them at a high level. I suppose yes. And I would make a point of leaving here, now I would stay for about an hour after school. The school closes at 2:25 and I would generally be gone by 4:00 at the latest but generally between 3:30 and 3:45. I would make a point of doing that because I have to be at home for my children.
>
> (Bridget, female principal, Scoil Allen primary-level school)

Niamh, the principal in the post-primary Scoil Comeragh, had a long career break when her children were young and only returned to teaching when her children were older. She did not think it was easy for women to manage child care with being a principal without a lot of support. Like male interviewees, she assumed that child care was a mother's responsibility and that the care of young children was not really compatible with being a second-level principal:

> There are loads of women who have children and who are principals and it works out fine [...] if I had small children, [...] I wouldn't do it.
>
> (Niamh, female principal, Scoil Comeragh second-level school)

Barra, the assessor in Comeragh held similar gendered views regarding care roles and responsibilities. He observed that the deputy principal in the school had not applied for the principalship (although she would have been well qualified for the post) as she had just had a baby; the deputy told him that her care responsibilities 'were just too demanding' at that time. Barra, accepted this as natural given women's 'nurturing responsibilities'.

The divide between women who had children and those who did not was very evident in the way women managed being a principal. Women who had no children were able to behave like traditional men as they did not have to juggle child care and being a principal. The principal in Scoil Foyle primary school spoke about how she did not have to bring work home as she stayed on as late as necessary to finish it. She was in her own words 'flexible'.

> I don't bring it home and I'll actually say 'no I'm not' [...] and having said that when, when I have stuff to do, like I don't mind going back

> out tonight, it'll be 11, half eleven by the time I come back, that's absolutely fine [...] Or if there's stuff to do I'll just keep going, keep going, keep going for the day until it stops.
>
> (Aisling, female principal, Scoil Foyle primary-level school)

Women principals with young children felt that women principals who had no children, and who could devote all their time to their school, put pressures (unintentionally) on other women to behave likewise. Brigid, a primary principal, assessed her functioning as a principal in terms of how single women without children managed similar roles. She did not compare herself to men with children, or to childless men; she felt that she would be judged in her role as principal as a mother in a way that men would not be judged as fathers.

> And I know of two principals who are friends of mine but they are both single ladies and they would be working late into the night which pressurises me sometimes when I consider the matter.
>
> (Bridget, female principal, Scoil Allen primary-level school)

## What makes a difference: Having support

Having a supportive partner was held to be of crucial importance for women who applied for and held senior posts in enabling them to succeed. While men did mention the supports they had (generally their wives who did not prioritize their jobs and/or careers in order to do child care), men assumed that they would have care supports, they did not cite it as something special or unexpected whereas women did. Care and support in their senior roles is not something women could take for granted.

Only men mentioned the importance of support prior to the interview stage when making the decision to apply and/or when managing at a senior level. Support was of practical importance if they had children and of emotional importance whether or not they had children. This finding is in accord with international research in the field in relation to what enables women to seek promotion (Pocock, 2005). Brigid, the principal in Scoil Allen, explained how she came to her decision to take the post:

> It was obviously going to have an effect on our family life and we discussed that but he [her husband] would be hugely supportive of anything that I wanted to do. He would never have presumed that

> he was the main breadwinner or anything like that so he was going to support anything that I wanted to do.
>
> (Bridget, female principal, Scoil Allen primary-level school)

Muireann, the principal in Scoil Iveragh, did not have children. She felt that most principals in her position did not have young children and was unsure if mothers could do the job unless they had 'back-up'.

> I think it would depend on the back-up that you have, and at what stage, I mean, there aren't many principals who, while they're in the post of principals, that they have children, like, that a child is born or whatever. There is one that I can think of, but I think it would depend on the network of support that you have.
>
> (Muireann, female principal, Scoil Iveragh second-level school)

What is interesting in this quote is the underlying assumption that it is problematic for women principals to give birth while being a principal. Clearly many men have children while being a principal but Muireann did not see that as being problematic for them.

Support also mattered for women in higher education. Sorcha, the senior post holder from Valentia higher education institution, said her partner was 'tremendously supportive' and they both supported each other in their responsibilities: 'I find it fantastic and he does too'. She claimed that most of the women she knew who were combining child care with holding senior posts had supportive partners.

> And most of the people I know, women who do it with all its difficulties, are doing it because for whatever reason perhaps their male partners are in a position to more significantly contribute. My sister is a principal in a very large school, the first lay principal in a very large secondary school and her husband works around her needs. He is the one who drops and collects and that sort of thing.
>
> (Sorcha, female senior post holder, Valentia higher education institution)

Una, the senior post holder in Rathlin higher education institution, also mentioned the importance of her partner: 'I mean it is actually helpful for me to have a partner because I bounce things off him and he is supportive' (Una, female senior post holder, Rathlin higher education institution).

Both men and women who had good care support were very much aware of it.

> [S]o I'm lucky in that sense, I suppose, I'm well supported, I know [my daughter] is very well cared for, so when I go home in the evening then I take over.
>
> (Tadgh, male senior post holder, Achill higher education institution)

Una was the only senior post holder who parented on her own for a considerable time. She contrasted her experience, now when she had a partner, with earlier in her life when she was parenting alone and without support 'I suppose there was a kind of loneliness about being female there. I was a single mother and I didn't find that very easy' (Una, female senior post holder, Rathlin higher education institution).

Regardless of where people worked in education, or even the age of their children, or if they had no children, having a supportive partner was of vital importance both in encouraging one to apply for a principalship or senior post and in fulfilling the job of principal or a senior manager in higher education. This was especially true for women.

Assessors also recognized the gender bind of care work for women and the importance of support:

> Well I think, well just take Caoimhe [principal of school] now [...] And I am amazed at the energy and the enthusiasm she brings to the school. And she is a good mother and she has a good husband. But maybe that is part of the answer too like, the other half, how supportive are they? How much of the load do they carry? You know, that varies.
>
> (MacDara, male assessor, Scoil Neagh primary-level school)

## Men as carers

There was only one male principal, Conor, who had engaged in seriously downsizing his workload to be involved in the care of his children. He had held a senior post at national level and changed to being a principal to have more time for his family:

> I pulled back from that because it was so national that it was just too much pressure [...] I had recently married and had young children

> and it was putting too much pressure on the home life, the wear and tear was too much being dragged across the four corners of Ireland.
>
> (Conor, male principal, Derravaragh primary-level school)

Conor claimed that you could manage caring and being a principal but only if you put a boundary on your availability for work which is what he did.

> I endeavour to be out of the school by 3:30 every day regardless. I have factored in two appointment evenings so if somebody looks for an appointment they know it is either Monday or Wednesday and you won't get [me] any other day other than Monday or Wednesday and even if it suited me, people are used to the notion and I am going to stick with that.
>
> (Conor, male principal, Derravaragh primary-level school)

Most men saw their role as parents as a care facilitator, being a secondary rather than a primary carer. They mentioned moving jobs or house to facilitate the caring of children with a spouse. However their reasons for not taking a post were not always to do with care alone; being seriously involved in sport influenced their decisions in a few cases. As noted above both Brendan, the principal in Scoil Errigal, and Gearóid, the principal in Scoil Sperrin, explained how, while child care responsibilities did play a part in their professional choices (especially in Gearóid's case) as to when to apply for principalships, child care alone did not determine them as sport and other considerations came in to play.

> No I wouldn't have done it [be a principal], no I enjoyed [the children] [...] That's one of the reasons I actually would have done it now is that is that they need me less, I was very involved with the sporting part of their life [...] and I also did a lot of the baby minding for them, my hours [as a classroom teacher] would have been more amenable to that.
>
> (Gearoid, male principal, Scoil Sperrin second-level school)

Tadhg, the head of Achill further education institution, explained that having a young child altered his work patterns also. While he still worked a long day (and his wife was at home full-time having given up her full-time post to be a carer), he devoted his evenings to playing with her from the time he came home after work until his young daughter went to bed.

> I leave at six and my three year old grabs me for the night, and that's it, I play dollies (laugh) [...] I switch off at ten o'clock at night when she's gone to bed. [...] If she wasn't there, I would be back here, I'd say three or four evenings a week, and it's probably a good thing, I, I'm forced by family commitments to down tools and go.
>
> (Tadhg, male senior post holder, Achill higher education institution)

However, Tadhg was not bound by care responsibilities as he explained that he came into work 'for a couple of hours every weekend' if he needed to; he was able to do this as his wife was the primary carer.

While no female principal stated any objections to engaging paid child care to support them in their position as principals, a couple of male principals were opposed to having paid care for their children, Conor being the person who held this view most strongly:

> The care and responsibilities they cannot be underestimated and sharing the workload and so on, is a major factor. But as regards providing childcare, parenting to me has to be done by parents not by carers and you put structures in that would facilitate teachers and principals during the integrity of the school day. Not after school caring service, not interested, I'll rear my own kids with my wife and that is the way I perceive it.
>
> (Conor, male principal, Derravaragh primary-level school)

## Women as primary carers

While our data show that men with children did make time accommodations to ensure their availability as carers, all the women with dependent children who held senior posts saw themselves as primary carers. The first way in which this manifested itself was in the fact that three of the female senior managers had taken career breaks to care for young children but no men had.

> Well you see when my four children were small I didn't work (*sic*) at all, I didn't go back to work until they were all kind of in school, so I didn't start work until then. Because I suppose that would have been

> a priority for me then you know and then I came back to work and was just, well I came to work.
>
> (Niamh, female principal, Scoil Comeragh second-level school)

While some men rescheduled their work times to help with child care, they did not organize their entire work lives around child care the way women principals did. In particular, women principals tried to be at home with their children after school. Leaving on time meant that they had to take work home to do it at night.

> I leave here at about fourish but I bring work home that I would start about 9:00pm [...] that's child minder logistics, it's the only reason I leave at 4:00. Before I had children I never left school, even though I'd go home for tea, now there are nights like last night when I said "sod the whole lot of them, I'm not doing anything", but I think you do have to [work at night] now and again.
>
> (Aoife, female principal, Scoil Sheelin primary-level school)

While coming in early to do administrative work or finishing late was a feature of male managers' lives generally, this was not a pattern for women with young children. Those principals who had younger children were tied by child minding arrangements. They took work home and tried to do it when the children were in bed or they worked at weekends.

> So the last couple of nights I've brought work home with me, and when the kids are gone to bed I can work on some of the paper work. I try not to bring it home, I mean whatever about, psychologically you do, but physically I try not to bring much work home with me because apart from anything else one of them is bound to either tear it up or you know! So I'm able to do some work on the laptop and if it's a busy time [...] I, you know, might come in on a Saturday or a Sunday only because there is stuff that has to go to the Department and it has to go on time or people don't get paid.
>
> (Maeve, female principal, Scoil Nephin second-level school)

This type of arrangement was not without its costs, including costs to family life.

> My husband works for himself as well so we don't see each other, he's in one end of the house [working] and I'm in the other. Sometimes

you just need to take reality checks. And I would spend the guts of the summer up here [in the school].

(Aoife, female principal, Scoil Sheelin primary-level school)

While none of the men interviewed spoke about having care dilemmas in relation to taking up their posts, a number of the women did, particularly in higher education. Although all the women (and most of the men) in higher education had older or adult children, care for their children was still a dilemma for women in a way it was not for men. One woman who had to move home to take up her new higher education post spoke about the difficulties this posed for her due to having teenage children.

As I say I was at a crossroads in life and I came here but with great difficulty in so far as I was very concerned about my children, my daughters and in fact I commuted [...] for most of the first year.

(Sorcha, female senior post holder, Valentia higher education institution)

Another female senior manager at higher education level claimed that not having children, and having a supportive partner, were crucial to her own ability to avail of promotional opportunities. Referring to her appointment, Sinead said:

Well, we don't have kids so that made it a lot easier. You wouldn't maybe make a decision as quickly if you had a family to move around but also the consequences would have been quite phenomenal.

(Sinead, female senior post holder, Tory higher education institution)

Care problems were time problems for women and time spent commuting exacerbated their time dilemmas. It lengthened the day and made meetings at night very difficult, especially where one was the primary carer of young children. One principal had moved to a new post to avoid the time spent commuting in her previous post (as principal in another school) as the 'juggling' was wearing her down.

This position came up and I suppose I knew the school, much closer to home, I know that it is just a very practical thing you know in terms of my own family and I found that in [name of other school], the school where [...] I found that I was going back at night for

> meetings maybe two to three nights a week. And I just found it was wearing me down [...] It's juggling.
>
> (Niamh, female principal, Scoil Comeragh second-level school)

While care responsibilities are gendered, not all women have such responsibilities. Aisling, the principal in Scoil Foyle primary school, did not have to bring work home as she stayed on as late as necessary to finish it. She was in her own words 'flexible':

> I don't bring it home and I'll actually say 'no I'm not' [...] And having said that when, when I have stuff to do, like I don't mind going back out tonight, it'll be 11, half eleven by the time I come back, that's absolutely fine [...] or if there's stuff to do I'll just keep going, keep going, keep going for the day until it stops.
>
> (Aisling, female principal, Scoil Foyle primary-level school)

Neither of the male principals in Scoil Derg (primary) nor Scoil Corrib (primary) had children and they were also free to orangize work schedules as they saw fit:

> I come in at 8 in the morning and do all my e-mails, you have to design your work schedule to suit you.
>
> (Andreas, male principal, Scoil Corrib primary-level school)

> I get in here at about 7:40 or 7:45 in the morning because I prefer to work early in the morning and then school starts at 8:50 so I would get a lot of the administration work done, any letters that I had to reply to first thing in the morning.
>
> (Aodhaigh, male principal, Scoil Derg primary-level school)

Being a lone parent poses serious care challenges for those combining paid and care work. Only one senior post holder had been a lone parent at some time in their careers, Una, the female senior post in Rathlin higher education institution. She had quite negative experiences around child care as well, but in her case as a more junior staff member.

> I didn't find that very easy and I didn't feel comfortable asking for any sort of accommodation to be made for it and indeed I didn't ask for accommodation to be made for it. But there would have been

> times when it would have been nice to manage things like my son being ill or this kind of stuff because he was quite young.
>
> (Una, female senior post holder, Rathlin higher education institution)

She was of the view that it was the fact of having children and having to devote time to caring for them that made it difficult for women to be promoted (or even made permanent) later on. She described being a mother as a 'killer' in terms of its career implications in higher education.

## Concluding remarks

While new managerialism is gendered in how it encodes attributes associated with hegemonic masculinity in management, including competitiveness and a focus on performance, it is also driven by a concept of care-lessness that is simultaneously gendered and separate from gender.

Those sectors of Irish education that have endorsed the new managerial ethic, notably higher educational institutions, have defined senior managerial posts as being ones that are largely care-free. Senior managers (and not just those who are at the very top) are expected to work long hours, to make work their life. While this model of management does allow women and men who are care-free to take up those posts, it precludes both women and men who have immediate care responsibilities. Given that women are still the primary carers in society, they are more likely to be excluded than men when a care-less model of management is in operation. The fact that none of the heads of Ireland's seven universities and only three of its institutes of technology have women directors, and that most senior posts in all higher education are male-dominated, including professorships, the care-less model of management precludes many women from senior positions.

What is notable from the data is that the care-less model of management does not hold to the same degree in primary education in particular, nor even in second level, although second level is located as a median point between primary and higher education in how management operates. The fact that the percentage of women as heads of schools/colleges falls from some 60 per cent at primary, to 37 per cent at second level, to less than 10 per cent (professors) or 18 per cent (all senior posts) in higher education (see Chapter 2) shows that the more prestigious, powerful and responsible the post, the more it is defined in care-less terms and the less likely women are to occupy it.

However, not all women or men are included or excluded automatically. Women and men who have no primary care responsibilities are both equally free to compete for senior posts that are effectively care-free. While men are more likely to be care-free, even if they have dependents, than women (Hanlon, 2009), women who have no children are also in this frame.[6] Men who have primary care responsibilities are also constrained by caring, but not to the same degree as women, because women are the default carers in most households.

Organizational research has focused on how the internal life of organizations constrains women in terms of promotion citing organizational norms, including the glass ceiling, and direct and indirect discrimination as major barriers. However, the wider cultural frame where women are located as default carers means that the *care ceiling* may be of equal or even greater significance in a new managerial age. Only women who divest themselves of care, either by not having children, or, if they have children, either waiting until they are grown up or ensuring they have a partner who supports them, are likely to make the cut to senior management, especially in higher education. Once there, however, women must still negotiate their way through a highly masculinised organisational culture.

# 9 New Managerialism, Carelessness and Gender

There is a new relationship between the education and the state in an age of educational capitalism. Education is no longer defined as a service or a right; it is regarded as an expensive investment that must deliver 'returns' to capital. The State, in the form of government, has the task of ensuring high productivity in these returns. But nation-states are no longer politically autonomous in a post-Westphalian phase of history (Fraser, 2008). Neither are they autonomous economically: the global financial crisis has made visible the way global capital frames national priorities, albeit mediated through nominally 'democratic' institutions like national parliaments. Governments, especially in small countries like Ireland, are situated at the nexus of powerful global institutions that not only influence their economic and political policies but also their educational policies. Multilateral agencies such as the (Organisation for Economic Co-operation and Development) OECD and the International Monetary Fund (IMF), political institutions such as the European Union (EU), and the compradors of global and local capital that operate within and without nation-state boundaries[1] all exercise degrees of influence over education. Business-oriented organizations are increasingly well placed within globalized networks to dictate the priorities of national education systems. Control and regulation is often indirect, as in the form of 'advice' from the OECD; the latter produces regular 'Country Reports' through its 'surveillance' procedures and promulgates a new market instrumentalism in education under the guise of 'independent' expertise (Henry et al., 2001).

At other times, business interests work more directly as when people with a business background are strategically placed in key positions on boards and bodies associated with education.[2] The diffusion of regulatory and governance mechanisms that are market-led is complex. It is mediated within states by institutions, legislative mechanisms and cultures that are unique to individual countries. New managerialism does not always have free reign as we have pointed out in Chapters 1 and 2. And, as we discuss below, teachers and teacher unions are powerful players in mediating the relationship of new managerialism to schools.

Neither are relations of control and regulation singular and unilateral; they are deeply gendered both nationally and internationally[3] (Blackmore, 2010; O'Connor, 2011) and they are disciplinary-led. Leadership and control is exercised disproportionately by men (and sometimes women) from particular fields of scholarship especially from selective fields in the sciences, technology and business.

## Two worlds of management

Although new managerialism is the reigning management discourse within the Irish public sector, it has been incorporated unevenly particularly in education. There are two paralleling worlds of incorporation. The first world is at primary and second level where new managerialism has been strongly contested, and is therefore constrained. The second world is at higher education where the incorporation of new managerialism has been relatively successful, especially in the university sector. To understand how new managerialism was and is resisted, it is important to locate it in the context of public governance in Ireland.

### The first world of primary and second level management

Ireland has operated unique forms of corporatist governance over many years. Initially, corporatism was guided by Catholic social teaching that 'sought to minimize state intervention in civil society so that people could express their Christianity through the voluntary organisation of their own economic and social lives' (Tovey and Share, 2000: 85). In later years, this corporatism took more secular forms: it found its most powerful expression in 'social partnership' agreements between the State, employers, trade unions, farmers and professional bodies from 1987 to 2008. Through social partnership, teaching unions,[4] as one of the largest single block of unions in the Irish Congress of Trade Unions, were deeply implicated in State policymaking. They could and did negotiate their relationship to new managerial practices.

One of the clearest manifestations of the power of the teachers and their unions was their incorporation as key decision-makers in framing education policy and practice in the Education Act (1998). While all the major parties to education are included in the partnership framework laid out for the governance of education, the naming of the teacher unions and associations as specific partners has ensured that policy changes could not be easily implemented without teacher consent:

> In carrying out his or her functions, the Minister [...] shall make all reasonable efforts to consult with patrons, national associations of parents, parents' associations in schools, recognised school management organisations, *recognised trade unions and staff associations representing teachers* [our emphasis] and such other persons who have a special interest in or knowledge of matters relating to education, including persons or groups of persons who have a special interest in, or experience of, the education of students with special educational needs.
>
> (Section 7, Education Act, 1998)

Teacher unions and associations are mentioned 19 times in the Education Act. All statutory agencies with a governance role in education are required to consult with them on management issues, be they school inspectors, patrons, boards of management or the minister. While other bodies, including national parent organizations and management organizations, must also be consulted, trade unions are among the most organized and best resourced given their high membership across all sectors of education. They were and are strategically located to resist changes that they do not wish to implement.

While principals and assessors recognized the role of religious and other management bodies in managing schools and in determining who was appointed, they alluded to the power of teacher unions in determining policies and practices in schools in particular:

> I would be very careful not to do something that would not be agreed by the Joint Managerial Body and the Union [name].
>
> (Sheila, female assessor, Scoil Nephin second-level school)

There was a belief that the unions exercised considerable power and influence especially when conflicts arose. In cases of appeals, Sheila, a very experienced assessor for senior posts claimed that

> [i]f you had a strong Union person and weak Management person then you have no hope.
>
> (Sheila, female assessor, Scoil Nephin second-level school)

Teachers exercised considerable control over new managerial demands on senior appointments through nominating staff to assessment boards. Influencing senior appointments was exercised in a variety of different ways depending on the type of school and the sector of education. In the Vocational Education Committee (VEC) sector, the unions had the right not only to nominate trade union members for panels of assessors for principalships, but also to raise objections to those nominated on panels from the management side. (The VEC could also raise questions regarding the union nominees.) Conleth, an assessor (and a former school principal) in the vocational sector, explained how it worked:

> The TUI puts forward a panel of people that are acceptable to them as being available for Interview Boards. And the VEC puts a panel to them [the Union] so they give a panel to the VEC and the VEC gives a panel to them and then there is an agreement – and that is the panel.
>
> (Conleth, assessor, Achill Further Education College)

When asked if the unions had 'the right to refuse' a nominee, Conleth said that it was possible, especially if someone had had a 'major problem with a union or something':

> They [the Union] have the right to refuse, that they don't want so-and-so on it because they feel there might be prejudices.
>
> (Conleth, assessor, Achill Further Education College)

It would be misleading however to present the division between management and teachers in schools in binary terms. All teachers at primary and second level are members of the same unions, whether they are in management or not. While there are two major professional associations for managers at primary level (the Irish Primary Principals' Network) and at second level, the National Association of Principals and Deputy Principals (NAPD), these are not representative bodies in industrial relations matters. There is therefore no major managerial/staff divide in the fields of primary and second-level education.[5] The fact that many primary school principals are teaching principals (owing to the small size of so many schools, see Chapter 2) and that some principals in second level also teach, especially deputy principals, this is a further factor consolidating teachers into a united professional body.

When teachers became school principals, they became keenly aware of the power of the unions. Tadgh, the principal of Coláiste Achill, a Further Education College, described them as 'terribly strong', while Fionnuala, principal Scoil Mourne secondary school, explained how at staff meetings 'the more vocal members of staff would be strong union [name] members' and this sometimes meant that other teachers would not volunteer to assist the principal if asked at a staff meeting. However, 'they will come very quietly and say I will do that but they don't want it to be known'.

While the teacher unions provided the main bulwark against new managerialism's demands, other management bodies, including the Catholic Church, religious orders and the VECs (that manage a large number of schools in the second-level sector) did not endorse managerialism for other reasons. They were a further bulwark against the new managerialism agenda in education, albeit more muted in their response.

Catholic schools in Ireland traditionally endorsed more humanist education with a focus on the arts and humanities (not the social sciences) to the detriment of physical and life sciences, and technological subjects (Clancy, 1995). As new mangerialism was emanating from a market-led system of values, as well as promoting further advancement of market-led sciences and technological subjects, the values underpinning it were not well aligned with the religious values underpinning Catholic education (O'Sullivan, 2006).[6]

Most principals we interviewed regardless of the religious ethos of the schools were strongly child-centred. A tradition of person-centred education was part of the discourse of both assessors and principals. And this person-centred perspective applied to managing staff and students:

> The door is literally always open, unless I'm talking to somebody and that is the way I like it. I would like to think that teachers and [...] pupils could come in to me if they had any kind of difficulty and I feel that they do. So [...] I would be conscious of not putting myself away from them and becoming the administrator.
>
> (Daithí, principal, Blackstairs secondary boys' school)

The strong religious influence on the traditions of Irish schools, with a focus on care ('pastoral care' being the term in Catholic schools) meant that new managerial values were perceived to be in tension with the traditional person-centred and child-centred values. And principals at both primary and second level were very clear as to where their priorities lay. As noted in Chapter 6, principals emphasized their personal commitment to their role, especially tending to the needs of teachers and students at a personal level. While they recognized the importance of 'excellence' in their management practices, they were strongly focused on the quality of student experience and fostering positive collegial relations with staff. Their commitment to students found expression in different ways, including continuing to teach even when very busy in the first year as principal due to their felt obligations to students:

> So I've decided for this year I'm teaching [...]. Yeah, well I had a Leaving Cert class year, so I wanted to continue on with them to Leaving Cert this year. [...] So probably next year I will also take on some teaching, maybe not the senior classes, I might take on the first years next year to get to know the children, you know, so at least you'll know them all the way up.
>
> (Brendan, principal, Scoil Errigal second-level school)

Managers in schools were not averse to some aspects of new managerialism, however, especially to its demand that teachers were more accountable for their performance. There was a very real sense of frustration among some principals about the inability of the education system to address incompetence among teachers when issues arose:

> There is very little you can do actually to deal with an incompetent teacher, even the Department of Education their hands are tied as to how to deal with it. We had a Whole School Evaluation here last year, We were one of the schools who had it. And I remember talking about this to the Inspector and saying, 'well there isn't a lot you can do and there isn't a lot we can do' [...]. This is one of the great complaints about the education system – how do you deal with the incompetent teachers? How do you weed them out? It is virtually impossible.
>
> (Daithi, principal, Blackstairs secondary boys' school)

But the culture of schools did vary and this impacted on how accountability worked. Not all schools had the type of problems that Daithi encountered in Blackstairs, even when they were fully unionized as was the case in Scoil Derg:

> We do have a union [name] representative, but we are a very open type school and consequently the staff, as I said, are a very good

> team. And they all work very well together. Ok, sometimes the team breaks down but you have to get on with the things then. Everybody rows in, but there is none of that rigidity and none of that saying well 'I don't have to do this because the Union says it'. There is none of that whatsoever.
>
> (Aodhaigh, principal, Scoil Derg primary-level school)

Even though most schools had good relations between unions and management, this was contingent on a range of factors over which principals exercised limited control, not least of which was the history of management-union relations in the school. Schools had cultures and traditions that impacted on how change was negotiated:

> We've a very [...] a nice spirit among our staff here and they would very seldom turn you down on anything. [...] It's the culture, it's the culture I think, yes.
>
> (Brendan, principal, Scoil Errigal second-level school)

The VECs manage a very large proportion of the most socially disadvantaged second-level schools in Ireland. The profile of VEC schools meant that they too had reasons to be concerned with the market-led appraisal systems of new managerialism. Systems of performance appraisal associated with new managerialism, such as league tables, could lead to the denigration (and potential closure) of the type of schools in socially and economically deprived areas that the VEC managed (no matter how unfair this might be). Principals and assessors were aware of the history of what happened in England to schools in poorer areas, and were not enthusiastic about certain new managerial practices for that reason. Furthermore, the top management posts in the VECs (the chief executive positions) were generally held by people who have been working at school principal level; it was highly unlikely they would be supportive of initiatives that would impact adversely on their own profession.

Concerns about new managerial practices did not mean that senior managers did not want change. Some principals and assessors did advert to the need to address the issue of staff underperformance, including that of school principals. Two of the principals, one in primary and the other at second level, claimed that principals should only be in the post for seven or eight years:

> At the end of the seven years your employers, your Board of Management [...] would have the right to re-employ you. In other

> words they could assess you and say 'yes' we are taking you or they could advertise.
>
> (Conleth, assessor, Coláiste Achill further education college)

However, he did not think that this would ever happen due to the power of the teacher unions:

> This was the proposal at one time. But I can guarantee you as long as the Union [name] are in power that's never going to happen – but there is a case for it, there is definitely a case for it.
>
> (Conleth, assessor, Coláiste Achill Further Education College)

New managerialism was not welcomed by most principals in schools as they claimed they lacked the resources and infrastructure to implement changes. The Department of Education demands for accountability (in seeking more and more information from schools) were perceived as time-wasting in the absence of resources; not only was there a lack of resources to do the accounting, there was also a lack of resources to implement changes even when they were desirable.

Principals spoke of being

> [b]ogged down by paper work, constantly under pressure because of issues like special ed, because of the, the current one is the NEWB, the National Education Welfare Board, we just seem to get forms after forms, putting in similar information and just not seeing a change.
>
> (Aindréas, male principal, Scoil Corrib primary-level school)

Principals had different ways of dealing with this increased accountability; in some cases carving out extra time in early mornings or late evenings to complete paperwork, in other cases working with school administrators and deputy principals to share the load, and in other contexts, taking a strategic decision to complete these administrative and tracking tasks reactively. Principals were unclear about the rationale behind much of increased paperwork; they felt that the administrative demands from the Department of Education and Science were underpinned by a surveillance approach that was financial rather than educational in focus.

> The attitude that seems to be coming from the Department in a lot of that form filling and bureaucracy is that, we're watching you, we're looking for mistakes [...] it's not very encouraging [...] extra work has

> been passed on to Principals it seems to be a policy of, anything new or anything that requires extra work, gets passed on [...] you get the impression that the main focus of the Department is financial rather than educational or welfare of the children.
>
> (Muiris, male principal, Scoil Erne primary-level school)

**Holding back the tide?**

Despite the lack of commitment to new managerialism, school principals could not hold back certain managerial practices that were being introduced throughout education. The challenges were expressed in different ways, depending on the character of the school. In schools that were not able to compete with others for new students, notably those in deprived areas of cities, prinicipals felt that they had to promote their school more although it was unlikely to entice those with 'social ambitions':

> I'm considering a leaflet campaign, going out there, making sure people know. Then there is a lot of things going on here, so at a local church service recently [...], our school choir performed, played instruments [...]. So it is to be seen out there and to make sure [...]. We need to move into publicising our school better.
>
> (Aindréas, principal, Scoil Corrib primary-level school)

However, in the case of Aindréas, the pressure to promote the school was not simply driven by market values but by professional allegiances, his desire to maintain the school in the neighbourhood and protect teachers' jobs:

> I'm going to start being more proactive about it. But it hasn't necessarily been done before apparently, but we're going to have to do it to keep our teacher numbers.
>
> (Aindréas, principal, Scoil Corrib primary-level school)

Other principals saw the marketing of the school as being part of the job; it was something the school always did as it was in competition with other schools:

> I mean I was the one that was doing the PR [before I was principal] so in other words I would be all the time, every, most weeks I would send something to local papers, [...] So I don't see that as an extra burden.
>
> (Brendan, principal, Scoil Errigal second-level school)

Pressure to promote the school was not an issue for schools where there was a consistent intake. However, there were pressures to be more business-like:

> One of the Members of the Board described the job that [...] I'm doing [as a business]. He is actually a CEO himself. You know, I think, it's not a business atmosphere in the sense that I do have an open door policy, and anyone who wants to come in. [...] It's not [...] rigid that you must have an appointment [...]. So in terms of the [...] business, in terms of trying to get the organisation and the structure, I mean, yes. But in terms of, you know, the human [aspect] the [human] face has to be there in education, because it's not [a business]. It's not clients only that you're dealing with, it's much more than that.
>
> (Muireann, principal, Scoil Iveragh secondary school)

Assessors did recognize that being a principal was a more demanding job than it had been previously. They identified the shift to more and more accountability (what was called 'bureaucracy' by both principals and assessors) by the Department of Education and Science as contributing to early retirements of senior staff, even though there was no particular financial incentive to do this at the time. Eibhlin, an assessor at Scoil Errigal second-level school, noted that '[t]he number of staff who have retired in recent times because of stress is enormous throughout the country'.

Those who were principals also recognized that there was a 'burn out' factor in being a principal for a long period. One principal who had been encouraged to apply some years previously for the post he then held had not done so because of the demands of being a principal made over time:

> I was asked would you ever think of going I'd said no, because at the time I thought the job was highly stressful, highly time-consuming, thankless, lonely.
>
> (Muiris, principal, Scoil Erne primary-level school)

Cathal only applied for the post after he had spent a year as acting principal when the previous principal got ill. Now that he was older, he would not have to spend too many years in the job. It was a position that was manageable, but only for a short time:

> I felt that I would cope with it, and because of my age, I reckoned I would be willing to do it for seven to ten years and, I think that's all anybody should be required to do it.
>
> (Muiris, principal, Scoil Erne primary-level school)

The post of principal was seen as stressful, even by those who felt they managed it well. The increasing 'paper work' (accountability) demands of the job were listed most as the reason for increasing stress:

> I have to say that there is an enormous amount of administration that I find myself challenged by that and I would have been a hugely organised person [...] I would have always prided myself on being very efficient. It is quite difficult to be very efficient with the Department of Education and with the amount of paperwork coming in, so certainly that is very stressful. But I am not surprised by it, and that doesn't stress me personally.
>
> (Bridget, principal, Scoil Allen primary-level school)

## Swimming with the tide: Higher education

As noted in Chapter 1, higher education was much more subject to new managerial regulation, not least because of the internationalized character of the work of universities. League tables and international performance indicators were governing the culture of academic management in higher education in ways that senior managers could not easily control. While institutes of technology were not subject to the same annual evaluations as universities in the global leagues tables, all higher education was subject to market scrutiny in a new way. Higher education was commanded to service the 'Smart Economy' and to 'strike a balance between the demands of the market and their academic mission' (Government of Ireland, National Strategy for Higher Education – Hunt Report, 2011: 92), in a way that did not apply to second level or primary schools. Higher education was also under surveillance by agencies that monitor labour market needs, particularly *The Expert Group on Future Skills Needs*. The *Skills Needs* group set an agenda for higher education and constantly directed educators to service the economy more effectively. Some senior managers were strongly convinced of the value of this system:

> Yes I mean [...] we can actually learn from business models. We have to have [them] in each university individually. And probably the university sector together has to have a corporate strategy. [...] there has to be commonality of purpose and that has to be expressed somewhere so people know what it is and can work with it.
>
> (Oisin, assessor, Coláiste Rathlin higher education institution)

This assessor denied there was even such a thing as 'managerialism' arguing that the changes in higher education were about efficiency:

> Managerial culture [...] I think that is a term that is loosely used by people who sometimes have a particular unhappiness with the changes, but I think it is actually a somewhat meaningless term because managerial culture means what? What I think we [...] needed to do as a sector is to create higher levels of strategic efficiency. [...] So we're going to have to create a greater sense of cohesion and strategic coordination [...]. I don't however call that a managerial culture, I think that is absurd.
>
> (Oisin, assessor, Coláiste Rathlin higher education institution)

Not all senior managers in higher education shared the view that new managerialism was unproblematic.

> I am very struck at the moment actually on the debate in Higher Education with regard to alternative styles of management, one of them being in a sense embodied in the [...] very centralised, very corporate-driven management approach as opposed to one which is predicated on academic departments having the highest levels of autonomy and self-directedness that is consistent with being accountable. I would be very clear in my preference to the second approaches of those to academic management and to management generally.
>
> (Tiernan, senior manager, Coláiste Inisbofin higher education institution)

Some did not endorse or reject market values explicitly. They were pragmatists believing market values were thrust upon people as 'the old notion of collegiality, where you all work together [...] has really gone because of legislation'. Universities were no longer 'loose collections of faculties' and people had to work and adapt to the new managerial order:

> In the Universities Act [1997] the Chief Officer who is the President has a whole range of responsibilities, legal responsibilities for which he is accountable and it is not of his doing, he doesn't have any choice about it. The funding is given to the Universities on that condition. And sometimes I feel what our colleagues...should...for a year or two, ...just take no funding, [and then] see what will happen.

> They would wake up quickly enough and realise, [...] leadership has responsibilities [...] to keep Universities running.
>
> (Siofra, senior manager, Inis Meain higher education institution)

The two worlds of management were different but they were enacted and lived out through the medium of identities and interests that were both gendered and disciplinary.

## Men, women, disciplines and new managerialism

In Chapter 4 we demonstrated how the practice of homosociability helps ensure that men of like mind hold a disproportionately high number of strategic roles in education. The areas of education that are most gender-balanced at management levels are primary and second-level education. The percentage of primary-school principals who are women increased from 50 per cent in 2004 to 60 per cent in 2010 (INTO, 2010: 138). The proportion of second-level principals who are women increased from just under 25 per cent in 2003–4 to 37 per cent in 2011 (Department of Education and Skills, 2011).[7] Given that primary teaching is overwhelmingly female (85 per cent are women) for over a generation, and that women comprise almost two thirds of teachers at second level, one could expect an even greater representation of women at school management levels. The number of women at management levels in Irish schools must also be read in the context of the size of many schools. The majority of primary schools have less than 200 children, with fewer than ten teachers, and a large minority would have four or fewer teachers. Being a primary school principal in Ireland is not a powerful managerial position. Even second-level schools are small by international standards, with many having fewer than 400 students. School principals do not exercise much influence individually in education policymaking, with the exception of those who are senior in trade unions, those who become active in other areas of public life such as party politics, or those working through the medium of their representative principals' associations.

The power and influence exercised by individuals who hold top rank positions in higher education is quite considerable. With only seven universities, fifteen institutes of technology and a small number of other state-aided higher education institutions, the scope for exercising influence is considerable for what is effectively a small pool of senior managers. Holding a top management position in higher education is therefore more important in policy terms in Ireland compared with having a similar post in a primary or second-level school. And women are seriously under-represented in senior posts at higher education levels: while 39 per cent of full-time academic staff in Irish universities were women in 2003–4, only 7.5 per cent of full professors and 12.5 per cent of associate professors were women (Department of Education, 2007: 343). No data was available on the proportion of women who held professorships in 2011. However, 80 per cent of the 78 top management posts that were occupied in the university sector in 2006 were held by men and all the heads of universities were men as were most of those who held vice-president or equivalent positions in 2011 (see Chapter 2).

**Not all men are in power**

Male dominance of senior posts in higher education persists despite the growing numbers of women in higher education, especially in universities (where students are disproportionately female). But not all men from all disciplines are in power; those who exercise most power are men in selective fields of science and technology and business both nationally and internationally (Blackmore, 2010; O'Connor, 2011). In 2011, all of the heads of Irish universities were from science, medicine, mathematics or engineering.[8] Both heads of the two largest teacher education colleges in Ireland were men while 12 of the 15 heads of the institutes of technology were men. Between them, these colleges educate most Irish students in higher education. Three quarters of the deputy/vice-presidents were also men as were 88 per cent of the deans in the Irish universities. (O'Connor, 2011: 141). The powerful position of vice-president/head of research is also a post that is most likely to be held by men, particularly men from science and technology disciplines.

The conflation of male power with business and scientific power, and between these and the academy, is not incidental. Women are disproportionately employed in both teaching and research in the arts, humanities and social sciences (AHSS) while men dominate the sciences, technology and engineering (DES, Sé Sí Report, 2007). But the areas in which women are concentrated have not been prioritized for funding in the research field over many years. The AHSS receive a very small share of direct and indirect research funding from the government in Ireland: in 2006, only 4.3 per cent of direct government higher education research and development funding went to the AHSS as did 14.2 per cent of indirect government funding. While the percentage of direct government funding represented a significant increase from 1998 (when it was only 2 per cent), this increase was undermined by the decline in indirect funding from 21 per cent in 1998 to 14.2 per cent in 2006 (IRCHSS, 2010: Table 2).

Given that science and technology are overwhelmingly male-led fields in Ireland, and that these are the areas that are prioritized for funding, it is no surprise that academic leadership is a men-of-science project, by default if not by design. In an era of academic capitalism (Slaughter and Leslie, 2001), men in the more commercialized areas of higher education are identified with the new 'success' stories of higher education in a way that is not possible for women or men in the non-commercial areas of the AHSS or the sciences. Moreover, the AHSS areas are also more closely aligned with the public sector and with non-governmental organizations that are voluntary and community-oriented. As the public sector has increasingly been demonized in the neo-liberal era (Harvey, 2005; Kirby and Murphy, 2011) and the community and voluntary sector remains vulnerable due to lack of supports (Carnegie Trust Report, 2010), the association of the AHSS with the declining public sector does and a weakened voluntary sector does not contribute to their standing. This pattern is not unique to Ireland as Blackmore has shown in the Australian case:

> Men dominate the high tech. and science knowledge networks that are more likely to attract private investment in public-private partnerships. Voluntary sectors collaborate around the public service sector, humanities and arts, all feminized fields.
>
> (Blackmore, 2010: 18)

Given their disproportionate associations with the low earning and non-profit sectors of research, scholarship and employment, women and men in the AHSS are defined as dependents in many respects. They lack the autonomy and power associated with the monied fields so their structural relationship to the academy is a subordinated one. Even though they may succeed within their disciplines, they are second-class citizens within a higher education sector that is increasingly both dependent on and integrated with the business world. While the same is likely to hold true for the less commercial areas of the sciences, this is an issue in which research is needed.

In the United States, there is evidence that there is a strong overlap between academic scientists and industry in particular fields, with 50 per cent of life sciences faculty staff in the United States being consultants to industry (Lieberwitz, 2007). Little is actually known about

Irish academics' private commercial interests and how these interface with their academic employment and scholarship. What is known is that a number of key academic leaders in Ireland have had strong links with business, either having business interests themselves or supporting a business model of management in higher education. The former president of UCC Professor Gerry Wrixon was a scientist who established a very successful company in the microelectronics field and later established the National Microelectronics Research Centre (NMRC) at UCC. After being appointed as president of UCC in 1999, he spoke out about the need for closer links between the university and industry.[9] Dr. Edward Walsh, president emeritus of UL, actively promoted a business model of education and research on campus throughout his long term as head of that university. He is a frequent commentator on the Irish media critiquing public sector institutions and extolling the virtue of commercial interests and values. The former president of Dublin City University Dr. Ferdinand Von Prondzynski was a non-executive director of the NASDAQ-listed e-learning company Skillsoft plc. and is also a strong supporter of links between business and universities.

All the Irish universities have specially designated units for campus companies. These provide opportunities for academics to develop commercially viable products from which they benefit financially especially when products are patented and sold. There is an elision of the difference between the public interest values and commercial values that is very serious in terms of failing to interrogate the interests at play in determining research priorities (Lieberwitz, 2007) although it has not been a matter of discussion or debate in Ireland to date (Lynch, 2006).

## The science and technology doxa – questions

On a first reading the power and influence of the 'men of science' appears justified in Ireland's case given the country's heavy reliance on Foreign Direct Investment as an economy, especially its reliance on a small number of (mainly US-based) firms for export-led growth in the science and technological fields (Forfás, the national agency responsible for monitoring the link between education and skills,[10] report on Competitiveness, 2010). Within this paradigm, the men (mostly) and women in the highly selective science-led disciplines are seen to be the ones that will prepare the work force for the high-skilled jobs in science and technology on which Ireland's economic future is believed to depend.

But this alignment of science and technology with the national interest is open to dispute (O'Connor, 2008). There is considerable evidence that the transnational companies that invest in Ireland do so because of the substantial tax concessions offered: Ireland has one of the lowest corporation profit tax rates in the EU at 12.5 per cent, while the use of transfer pricing reduces taxes on profits still further (Hearn, 2003; Allen, 2007).[11] Moreover, although foreign-owned technological companies dominate exports (notably pharmaceuticals, computer hardware and computing services), Forfás recognizes that the services-led area of economy has been growing in the new millennium and that merchandise trade has fallen:

> Between 2005 and 2008, Ireland's share of merchandise trade has fallen gradually, while our share of services (a smaller but growing component of world trade) continues to grow [...]. In 2008, services exports accounted for 44.5 per cent of total Irish exports compared to 21 per cent in 2000.
>
> (Forfás, 2010: 42, Bench Marking Ireland's Performance Report)

It also recognizes the importance of the indigenous sectors, much of which is not science- or technology-led, in terms of both employment and spending:

> The contribution of indigenous and foreign owned trading sectors to employment and direct expenditure on goods and services within the local economy is similar. Indigenous exporters employ 132,500 people while foreign owned exporting companies employ 139,500 people. Foreign owned exporting companies spent €21 billion on goods and services in the Irish economy in 2008 compared to €19 billion by indigenous exporters.
>
> (Forfás, 2010: 42, Bench Marking Ireland's Performance Report)

There have also been questions raised about the long-term viability and cost of high expenditure on particular fields of science, especially with the emergence of the economic crisis. The highly influential McCarthy Report in its review of public expenditure noted while 'there was a threefold increase in Government Budget Outlays & Appropriations for Research and Development' from 2000 to 2007, and the evidence adduced to date for the impact of State STI [Science, Technology and Innovation] investment on actual economic activity has not been compelling' (Government of Ireland, 2009: 14).

Whether Ireland's economic future being dependent on science and technology is justified or not, there is no doubt that the related industries benefit from this assumption as do the particular fields of science and technology: 95 per cent of direct government funding for research is granted to those sectors as is 85 per cent of indirect funding (IRCHSS, 2010: Table 2).

While the market relevance of higher education has been a constant theme in Irish public discourse since the early 2000s (see Chapter 10 on the Media in this book), the market relevance of second-level education is now increasingly being called into question. The impact of the market is symbolized by the claim that there is a 'crisis' in science and mathematics education at second level. There are increasing calls for incentivizing more students to study science, technology and mathematics. In 2010 all the universities agreed on a scheme to give bonus points to students undertaking higher level mathematics for the Leaving Certificate Examination at entry thereby increasing their chances of entry. This has been followed in 2011 with calls for granting greater value to science subjects at university entry.

Despite the 'crisis' that has been created about mathematics and science, Ireland has one of the highest proportions of science and technology graduates in the EU. In 2009, it had the sixth highest number of graduates (out of 27 countries) – with 17.2 per cent being science, mathematics or computing science (SMC) graduates per 1,000 – compared with just 13.5 per 1,000 in Germany and 13.0 per 1,000 in Sweden and 9.0 in Norway. A few countries had more SMC graduates, notably France at 20.2, Romania at 20.0, Finland at 19.0, Lithuania at 18.5 and the UK/Slovakia both at 17.5. While Ireland's graduate rates in science and technology have declined from a peak of 24.5 per 1,000 in 2005, this was quite an exceptional level of graduate output by international standards, as countries such as the United States has had only 9.2 to 10.9 graduates per year in science and technology over the 10 years (10.3 per 1,000 in 2009) while Japan has only varied from 12.3 to 14.3 per 1,000 over the same period (14.3 in 2009) (EUROSTAT, 2010).

The move to promote particular fields technology and science and, by default if not design, to neglect other fields in the sciences and all manner of research in the AHSS is a highly political act. The net outcome is that resources are concentrated in particular fields which are 'hailed' as commercially valuable, but without independent evaluation of the costs and benefits.

## Valuable women

To highlight the prioritization of certain disciplines and fields of study that are male-led is not to say that women are not valued in new managerial times as managers *per se*. They are valuable because they manage much of the messy work of bureaucracy, the emotional work that is required to mediate change, massage egos, and quell anger in the ruptured world of restructuring (Morley, 2003). Within an audit and accountability culture, women are aides-to-productivity through their social skills; they do the housework of the organization, often invisibly (Hey and Bradford, 2004). Their emotional work does not have a value in itself however as it is not care-led; it has a derivative value, that is performance and productivity-led (Blackmore, 2010: 206–12). This leads to internal contradictions and moral dilemmas as women (and men) manipulate and manage in the interests of the rank, the productivity goals, and the targets (Blackmore, 2010: 124). They have to manage their emotional insides (Chapter 7 above) and the moral contradictions of working hard for something to which they are not entirely committed.

While women are strongly socialized to be 'good' and to be 'caring', as indeed are teachers generally (including men) in their pre-service and in-service training, in new managerial times, teachers and educators adhering to the older ethics of caring education are emotionally and ethically challenged by the command to succeed, to be efficient at all costs, even though it may be at the cost of educational values that they believe should be prioritized (Blackmore, 2010: 210–12).

## Performativity and surveillance

Constant appraisal and measurement is core to the new managerial project. It encourages competitive, and at times aggressive, forms of social behaviour as each person feels he/she is under surveillance, so people are always measuring themselves comparatively with others. And they know they are measured by senior managers, as going up or down. What this does in many ways is to chill out forms of social interaction that are not assertive or self-congratulatory (Ball, 2003a). It breaks down solidarity as every person is required to engage in relentless competition. While the development of dispositions associated with constant 'measured worth' are most advanced in higher education (Davies, 2003), they are not confined to there (Blackmore, 2010; Hey and Bradford, 2004; Gleeson and Husbands, 2001). The task of managing self identity and 'hailing' one's own achievements becomes not just a personal choice but a necessity for all those who wish to succeed in senior management. While this study found that the values of new managerialism were most strongly endorsed in higher education, all sectors of education are increasingly subjected to the managerial gaze. The gaze is not always from the centre, it can be peripheral, and from parents in particular:

> I find that while the parents are great, there are a couple who have phoned the Department [of Education] and would go and check [my work] [...], nearly negating my professionalism, [...] I would dot my 'i's and cross my t's anyway but you are kind of going 'Oh I had better make sure [...] that I have got it so right and so water tight'. [...] And that doesn't do anything for your morale or your self esteem, they are chinking away [...] and they wouldn't come and complain to me, they go right to the top.
>
> (Aoife, principal, Scoil Sheelin primary-level school)

Not all surveillance is secretive; some parents were more overt in trying to control the school and the teachers, including by using threats:

> I would regularly have parents in threatening to go to the guards or Department of Education about simple things like having to hand over a mobile phone [used by children in class contrary to school policy] or whatever [...]
>
> (Niamh, principal, Comeragh second-level school)

However, principals had begun to manage these demands, even though they were a new phenomenon:

> I would say [parents] are very much more demanding than they were. There wouldn't be as much respect for the school system as there was previously [...] I get the pressure but it doesn't get to me because I deal with it, I am not afraid to say 'no'. I have learned to say 'no', I have learned to say [...] 'I will think about it or I will refer it to the Board' then I will take a decision and I will refer it back to them and that is it.
>
> (Conor, principal, Derravaragh primary-level school)

The fact that relatively few primary or secondary principals identified surveillance and external controls as over-riding concerns, by comparison with those in higher education, shows how powerful and significant the cultural differences are between the two worlds. While new mangerialism was knocking on the schools' doors, it had not fully entered as it had been resisted in many policy contexts within the wider machinery of the State.

## Carelessness in education

The principles of new managerialism are devised in a commercial context and manifest themselves in education through the promotion of forms of governance (measurement, surveillance, control, regulation) that are market-led. On first encounter, these principles seem laudable as they appear to give openness and accountability to the educational system. However, as education is not simply about 'products', prioritizing products over process undermines the very processes that created the products in the first instance.

New managerialism defines human relationships in transactional terms, as the means to achieving high performance and productivity within organizations. Educational managers are judged by what can be measured in their performances. While the socio-emotional aspects of human relations are valued in the new managerial normative order, they are valued for their productive dividends, not as ends in themselves. Only counting what is measureable focuses attention on outputs and subordinates process; it subordinates the life world of care to the systems world of measureable productivity, in both the life world of educators and those of students. The developmental work of teaching is subordinated to the countable product, and those for whom care and developmental work is costly (as they do not produce enough 'outputs' relative to 'inputs') are definitively second-class citizens; the ideology of the gifted is enhanced (Tomlinson, 2008).

While care and developmental work have an outcome dimension (Lynch et al., 2009), it is generally not measurable in a specifiable short time frame. The gains and losses from having or not having care are only seen over time. And caring is not open to measurement in terms of quality, substance and form within a metric measurement system. Even if caring could be monitored and measured through matrices, the very doing of this would force people into the calculation of other-centredness that would undermine the very principle of relatedness and mutuality that is at the heart of human solidarity. What is at issue here is a conflict of values regarding the governance and purposes of education, and the role of relational human beings within this process. If school leaders are simply treated as managers of performances, then they will inevitably value only those that contribute to the performance. The nurturance dimensions of education are undermined.

Most of the assessors interviewed, in this study, especially the male assessors in higher education, treated their care world as a private matter (see Chapter 5). They did not talk about how care relations impacted on getting into senior posts, or even into middle management, unless asked specifically about it. When appraising the relative merits of candidates, the relational lives of potential appointees were invisible. Given that equality legislation defines people's relational identities as private, for reasons of non-discrimination, this is understandable. However, the irony of this legal protection is that it has silenced the ways in which affective relations are deeply gendered and have profound implications for who is fully eligible to be a senior manager. Senior managements posts, especially in higher education, but increasingly at primary and second level, are assumed to be care-free; those appointed are assumed to be available to participate in a 'long-hours' work environment that precludes having responsibility for primary care work. If those who apply for senior posts get into those positions, it is presumed primary care will happen but it will be kept private and will not encroach on the world of senior management. This is a deeply gendered assumption but it does not work through direct or even indirect discrimination. Men (or women) do not set out to exclude women or carers. The normative order regulates it silently through the gendered doxas of care.

Both women and men in senior posts accepted the gendered inevitability of the care binary. With few exceptions, managers and assessors expected women to remain the default carers of society (both within and without organizations). While not all women were carers, their organizational identities were framed through a care lens in a way that did not apply to men. Women experienced anticipatory socialization to be followers rather than leaders through the moral imperative to care in contrast to the care-less narrative that is upheld for Irish men (Hanlon and Lynch, 2011). Even if they had no children or care responsibilities, women were assumed to be primary carers and to have the dispositions of carers that disabled them in some ways for senior posts (O'Connor, 2011). The emotionality that they embodied positioned them as the default carers of society and thereby as natural outsiders rather than insiders in competitive managerial regimes. But the exclusions were not only symbolic, they were real, as higher educational organizations especially were structured increasingly on a 24/7 hour work schedule that meant that care was assumed to be incidental to real life. Even female assessors, who were in senior positions, were quite fatalistic about the gendered order of caring. They generally expected women to manage it themselves, to 'juggle' things and to 'get through'. Most male and female assessors did not critique the gender implications of the intensification of work at senior managerial levels; a deeply anti-care mode of governance was in operation but was not known or named in care or gender terms. The signification of women as primary carers was important symbolically and organizationally. They did not fit the care-free citizenship model that was normalized in the senior appointments process.

## The backdrop

As the cultural context in which gender is being lived and practiced has changed radically in recent years, this may help explain the silences about how the care-free life of senior mangers has become normalized.

At the time of transition to new managerialist modes of governance, in the late 1990s and 2000s, there was strong pressure in Ireland for greater gender equality in senior appointments in the public sector. Equality cases were taken to the Equality Authority (EA) with positive effect and considerable publicity (Crowley, 2010).[12] The Higher Education Equality Unit in UCC was active in promoting analysis and discussion of gender issues (and on race and ethnicity, disability, mature students and minority rights issues generally) in higher education. However, the Higher Education Equality Unit (which monitored equality policies and practices in higher education) was closed in 2002. Its functions were amalgamated eventually in to the Higher Education Authority (HEA); there have been no major actions undertaken by the HEA to promote gender equality since its incorporation. The Gender Equality Unit in the Department of Education and Science was also closed in the mid-2000s (McGauran, 2005). The lack of interest in gender issues among academics and policymakers is reflected in the fact that no data is available from the HEA on the gender profile of academics since 2004. Just as seemed to have happened in Australia (Lingard, 2003: 34), the 1990s marked the endgame in Ireland in terms of the promotion of equality for women. The simple act of head-counting[13] limited though it may be in terms of only focusing on gender *per se* (without recognizing diversity among women and men in terms of race, ethnicity, disability, sexuality, age etc.), has ceased for the best part of ten years.

The reneging on gender equality was part of a wider backlash against equality principles and practices generally that merged with the advance of Ireland's Celtic Tiger form of neo-liberalism. Equality was associated with the 'nanny state', itself a sexist and ageist term so loved by neo-liberals. And women were associated with equality, with the caring state, with the public sector and with what was frequently labelled the 'poverty industry' in the community sector. Gender-based attacks took the form of bitter diatribes in the media on equality generally, and on gender equality in particular. It was exemplified in the work of two columnists in the *Irish Times* (Ireland's leading newspaper in policy terms) labelling feminists 'feminatzis' and 'cranks'. (It should be noted however that the attacks were not confined to women, they also included attacks on Travellers, ethnic minorities and other vulnerable groups.) At a system's level, there were deliberate actions to stymie the work of the Equality Authority (EA), culminating in a budget cut of 42 per cent in 2008. The cut to the EA was at a time when the average cuts in public sector budgets were in the order of no more than 9 per cent in most organizations (Crowley, 2010). The rationale behind the attack on the EA was not articulated but it was clear that it arose in part from its effectiveness in taking discrimination cases, especially cases in the public sector: roughly half the case files of the EA related to discrimination in the public sector at the time its budget was cut in 2008 (ibid.). In 2011 the EA was amalgamated with the Human Rights Commission, further limiting its powers and influence.

Although there are resistances and challenges to new managerialism in Ireland, these resistances are also facing counter-resistances from the powerful neo-liberal interests. The ways in which the media are party to neo-liberal interests in education are not the subject of much debate internationally in education. We devote the final chapter to this subject as we believe the media are strategic players in controlling and regulating the terms of the debate about new managerialism in Ireland.

# Part IV
# Framing Marketization

# 10 Framing Educational Agendas for Managers: The Role of the News Media

## Introduction

A continual thread that ran throughout the interviews conducted for this project concerned the influence of the media in shaping public perceptions and political pressures about education. Senior leaders in education spoke about the growing influence that media had on their work; both directly through increased pressures to market and publicize their schools, and indirectly through media-driven influence on parents and the wider community (such as league tables, media-generated moral panics about education and media analysis about the politics of education). Despite the persistent presence of media in their world, educators – and students – directly involved in the sphere often remained relatively powerless in the media sphere, lacking a means of direct access or participation in the news process. Those who worked within the education system were subject not only to the professional power and interests of those who represented them politically (such as statutory agencies and teacher unions), but also those who represented them culturally (the media).

The relationship between media and education has rarely been considered in-depth and 'discussion of the specific processes via which education news is structured remains minimal' (Warmington and Murphy, 2004: 287). Therefore, we decided to further explore the role of the print media in constructing and communicating educational issues as an addendum of the senior appointments in education research project. This analysis was completed after the case study research, drawing on these interviews and engaging in additional research conducted with news journalists and analysis of newspaper coverage.

This approach acknowledged that media are not just communicators and interpreters of education's politics, but they are active agents in framing the politics of education themselves. Lee (1997: 8) notes, 'the public nowadays absorbs far more information from the media [...] than from politicians. Indeed, many of the issues on the political agenda are set by the media. Government ministers regularly express more concern about the media response to issues than about the opposition's response in the Dáil [parliament]'. This analysis explores the processes by which education becomes news, analysing how it is shaped by the central actors of the media themselves, the state and interest groups like teacher trade unions. We review the characteristics of newspaper coverage of education in the context of this study on new managerialism and leadership in education, and explore the impact of media coverage for senior leaders. While the formative role of state and other education groups (such as trade unions and the Catholic Church) in Irish education has been examined in earlier chapters, the role of media as a profession in this dynamic has rarely been considered in-depth (McNamara, 2005). The background of newspaper correspondents seldom comes into view, let alone the impact of their practices on the creation of news (Corcoran, 2004) or how their engagement with news sources construct what becomes education discourse.

Media's communicative capacity and symbolic power to construct news and to mediate the voices of other actors gives them a prominent role in communicating policy, defining what is publically considered to be 'news' and mediating relations between other actors (Blackmore and Thorpe, 2003). Newspaper media do not act alone in this context, but are enmeshed in a complex communicative process that shapes the agenda of education. '[P]olitical parties, the business lobby and the trade unions are all powerful operators in the media marketplace, and are clearly at an advantage in pushing their agenda' (Corcoran, 2004: 32). The demands that a new managerial culture places on educators intersect with these mediated discourses about education to create powerful pressures on those working in this sector. This is particularly pertinent for educational leaders as they are stretched by the intensification of the management role explored in Chapter 7.

## Mediating the key actors in Irish education

As outlined in the opening chapters, the Irish education system has been shaped by a distinctive intersection of State, church and educational groups. A complex system of Catholic Church ownership and management of the majority of schools was balanced with substantial State funding and centralized control of the curriculum. As outlined in Chapters 1 and 2, this was combined with a history of conservative nationalism, a persistent pattern of emigration and a deep-seated anti-intellectualism in the socio-political sphere (Chubb, 1982), that resulted in Ireland being a fertile ground in which to breed neo-liberal policies in the 1990s (Phelan, 2007).

Statutory agencies, Vocational Education Committees, school management and leadership groups, teacher unions and to a lesser degree (middle class dominated) parents' groups are increasingly influential in the organization of Irish schools. Middle class interests dominate education (Lynch and Moran, 2006), coalescing with the influence of other key education actors (often from a similar middle class background) to mediate the dominant State and church influence on the Irish educational system. As outlined earlier, the teacher unions play a central role due to their numerical strength, their willingness to work collectively to protect pay and conditions and their consultative relationship with State and other statutory groups (Cunningham, 2009). Other groups including the media are also active players in framing the politics of education, exercising control over how education enters and is presented in public discourse. This chapter explores the dynamics of these relationships between the State, teacher trade unions and media for representations and public discourses of education in national newspapers.

## Researching media practices and discourses in Irish newspapers

This research addendum draws on the case study research with senior managers and assessors in education and specific research conducted about news representation of education. Qualitative interviews with education correspondents of national newspapers and key media personnel in teacher trade unions were combined with discourse analysis of newspaper and website coverage, to explore how educational issues were constructed in Irish media discourse. Combining interviews and discourse analysis enabled in-depth analysis of news representation and insights from key actors in the field 'to capture the diverse ways in which media interpenetrates in and through' educational policies and practices (Blackmore and Thorpe, 2003: 79). Two main broadsheet newspapers in Ireland were selected for analysis because of their key role in the exercise of symbolic power and shaping of popular opinion (Fairclough, 1995). They were high profile daily newspapers in Ireland with a daily readership of 539,000 people (15.3%) in the case of *The*

*Irish Independent* and 339,000 daily readers (10.5%) of *The Irish Times* in 2010.[1] Both newspapers played a central role in setting public opinion and were a reference point for national broadcast and local media as well as being an important source of advertising revenue (Farrell, 1984; Horgan, 2001). They were recognized by educators as a main source for education news, appointment vacancies and league tables.

These newspapers were searched through Lexis-Nexis database for dates between January 2005 and June 2006 based on keywords associated with education, leadership and new managerialism to give a purposive sampling method based on their centrality in current educational discourse.[2] While we acknowledge the limitations of this selection strategy in terms of the search capacity of computerized databases (Deacon, 2007), it gave a useful selection tool to identify the frequency of stories using topical keywords and was augmented by discourse analysis of website information and interviews with journalists and educators (see below). While educational leadership and management was only one theme in a wider complex of representations about education, it lay on a crucial juncture where political tensions about educational systems and rationales were evident. This time period represented a transitional time, where tensions with new managerialism and performativity came to the fore in Irish education and society. Asking respondents to reflect upon this time facilitated greater distance and reflectivity to absorb the features and challenges of this era.

The same keywords were used to analyse the websites of the Department of Education and Science (DES) and teacher trade unions during that time period, similar to the approach taken by Stack (2007). Material from these websites including press releases, campaign information, speeches and reports (also appearing in media stories) were analysed with a view to understanding how these agencies interacted with media to shape public discourses about education. The teacher unions represented educators' interests across the three sectors of primary, second level and higher education in Ireland. Press releases, speeches, conferences, reports and newsletters during that time were downloaded and entered into MAXqda qualitative software package for analysis.[3] We drew on Fairclough's critical discourse analysis (1995) to examine the analytical link between discourse and power dynamics. We explored how education was constructed and presented in news stories, acknowledging that discursive practices in the media 'functions to make that which is based in ideology appear neutral and commonsensical' (Stack, 2007: 1).

In-depth interviews with education correspondents from national newspapers and key personnel in teacher trade unions were conducted to explore their experiences of education news-making. These interviewees were purposively selected for their depth of involvement with Irish educational news reporting. This analysis was combined with the casestudies with recently appointed senior managers and assessors in Irish education to give insight into the experiences and voices of those working in this area. These interviews provided a counter-balance to the insights from discourse analysis of 126 newspaper articles, 400 DES press releases and 83 teacher union texts.

## The professional background and social configuration of journalism

Corcoran, in her analysis of the socio-economic background and political orientation of Irish journalists, notes that they are a highly educated group 'predominately drawn from the middle classes. They are entering an occupation that is increasingly professionalised and that is made up of a relatively homogeneous social grouping' (2004: 9). This class origin is similar to the class background of many of their readers, indicating how the newspaper media act as interlocutors for the class system. This class orientation is allied with close political ties and social networks with the political sphere (Foley, 2004), with strong 'occupational interlinkages between politicians and journalists [...] [where] joumalists moved on to careers in public relations in the private, governmental or public sectors' (Corcoran, 2004: 8). This is evident in the work of the education editor of the Irish Independent newspaper as OECD education consultant since the 1990s and his appointment in 2011 as special advisor for the Minister of Education and Skills.[4] The impact of this homogeneity of class background and social networks between the media, education and political spheres is significant.

The background context of journalists has to be located within the broader structures and processes of the newspaper industry. The translation of education issues into news is, in part, dependent on sources and processes that help to define the media agenda and tone. This is a heterodox process as government, education professionals and newspaper journalists intersect in the creation of news stories (Blackmore and Thomson, 2004). Newspapers work according to a rapid cycle of deadlines to provide a continual cycle of fresh news stories and angles (Bell and Garrett, 1998). Journalists' response to these rapid news cycles are guided by their sense of professional tradecraft[5] as they develop a 'sens pratique' or feel for the game (Bourdieu, 1998a). This enables news personnel to work in a habitual manner, automatically moulding material to the requirements of the news cycle and protects them from social questioning about the logic of their practices.

Baker (2000) acknowledges the complicit relationship between sources and journalists; as both parties accept these informal means of molding educational stories 'by custom and format'. Education correspondents identify good news sources as people possessing the values of objectivity, authenticity, availability and most importantly insight – 'what you really want is not so much information but the nuances, a read of the situation' (education correspondent, Irish national newspaper). This nuanced capacity of news sources is vital, with a journalist describing how a 'good' union press officer has

> an understanding of how the media operate. He [*sic*] knows what a story is. He knows how to time a story. He knows the nuances. He knows how we get things wrong, he knows how sub-editors work. Despite what teachers and the public believe, I don't write headlines. The headlines don't always bear a relationship to what I write. He knows all of that and he negotiates with his constituency and his executive and his members and mediates their views to us, and gets very good publicity for the union.
>
> (education correspondent, national newspaper)

## Creating education news: Production processes and media structures

As educational issues are picked up by the media from their sources, we see a translation process at work as content is filtered through the news production cycle. Issues are reframed in news templates, 'the structural, narrative, and technical formats that exist prior to the emergence of specific news events and which are drawn upon by news media in order to produce news 'issues' and 'debates' in readily consumable form' (Warmington and Murphy, 2004: 89). These templates are often based on the use of competing sources to give diverse viewpoints on a story. These competing voices further enhance the performativity and competitive spirit inherent in the new managerial ethos (Thrupp and Wilmott, 2003; Deem, 2004). The combination of these two rationales drives a strongly competitive logic between media sources, as State, trade unions and education organizations fight for media and public attention, as explored later.

Newspapers are located within a larger media web which includes national and local radio, television and other media, internet news sites, blogs and social networks. Blogging and discussion boards are becoming important communication fora for teachers, particularly younger teachers (acknowledging a generation gap as older teachers are sometimes slower to embrace new technologies). Consequently certain blogs are becoming influential and entering the news cycle as sources for education journalists to monitor. This has transformed the older linear image of a hierarchical news chain from editor downwards, as journalists can now pick stories from a multiplicity of different sources. Audiences also access stories in different ways as journalists transmit their stories in several media from newspaper print to on-line formats, podcasts, radio or TV interviews, and increasingly twitter, facebook and social networking sites. While this shift into new media for publication and reception of education news has diversified media practices, it has not radically transformed the way that journalists create news stories (Doran, 2011).

## Education as a media[ted] industry

News maintains a dominant profile in the media industry, with a noticeable market emerging for the general promotion of education services in the media, including education magazines for schools, supplements on science and other subjects, league tables, weekly education pages, exam helpline, marketing for schools, appointments, competitions and awards for schools. This diversity is also reflected in the variety of education themes that appear through these media in Irish public discourse. As Figure 10.1 below illustrates, national newspapers and the websites of the DES and the teacher unions contain material about a wide diversity of education themes. What is noticeable about these data is the larger scale of stories originating from the government department as compared to newspaper stories or trade union sources. These press releases celebrate the establishment and funding of different education initiatives (such as new school buildings, higher education funding, special education needs), framing these achievements in terms of their contribution to economic achievement and socio-cultural change, and emphasizing the need for continued reform.

The Irish newspapers highlight the themes of performance, leadership, and educational finances and funding respectively (see Figure 10.1 below), with proportionally more and lengthier stories about education featuring in *The Irish Times*. Stories about financing and economic themes are mixed in tone, with some welcoming or simply informing about new funding streams for schools and higher education, while the majority of stories are cautious or critical of the government's strategic attempt to introduce performance-related reforms of higher education for economic ends. The *Strategic Innovation Fund* is designed to 'incentivise and reward internal restructuring and reform efforts [...] [and] improve performance management systems' (*Irish Times*, 12 December 2005). While the teacher unions welcome the increased funding of education, they are quite critical or nuanced about the performativity tone of reforms, as explored below. This is more evident as we move across the sectors, with the primary level union broadly welcoming the funding, second level unions giving a mixed response and the higher education union being critical. Many of these unions co-opt the state's investment and knowledge economy discourse to support their own individual campaigns on special needs, class size or discipline. This re-interpretation of state discourses of funding and economic objectives aligns the teacher unions with the State's agenda, albeit to achieve different objectives as we explore in later sections.

News coverage of issues relating to performativity focuses primarily on the introduction of Whole School Evaluations (WSE) during this time. Different groups take clear positions – DES, news correspondents and others broadly supporting it, while many educational groups including teacher unions are nervous or critical about WSE implications for schools. Newspapers also focus on higher education reform in the context of new strategic funding requirements, including a critique of the relationship between reform, funding and performativity mentioned above. DES press releases on performance-related issues are mainly positive declarations about the introduction of the *Teaching Council*, higher education strategic funding and WSE with the latter providing the 'right type of information about schools at people's fingertips' (DES press release, 11 April 2006). The trade unions are overwhelmingly critical of the performativity turn in Irish education, especially of WSE which were publicly released for the first time during this era. This linking of funding and performativity requirements is a noteworthy theme given the impact on new managerial reforms in Irish education during this era.

The teacher union at primary level focuses on defining the increasingly complex role of school leadership, as 'those who manage the overall education system seem to make a virtue out of swamping school leaders in a rising tide of bureaucratic demands' (INTO Principal and Deputy Principals' conference, 7 October 2005). The unions at second level refract leadership issues through the lenses of their own lobbying issues such as gender equality, class size or discipline. DES press releases did not focus on leadership as a theme during this time, as Figure 10.1 below reveals. Newspapers covered many of the trade unions' press releases about leadership, in particular surveys of the declining numbers of applications of

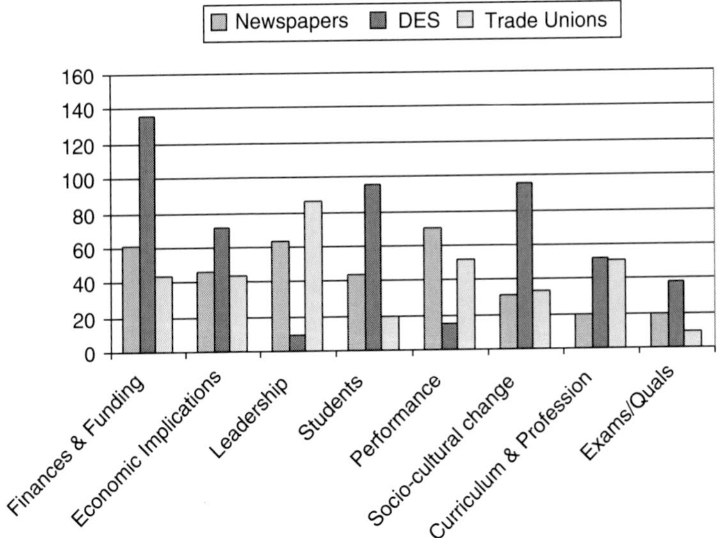


*Figure 10.1* Educational themes in Irish public discourses

school leadership and increased levels of stress. Newspapers also focused on specific leadership issues such as a high profile legal case during this time, implications of higher education reforms for leadership, impact of performativity on school leadership, with a broader range of stories on leadership covered by *The Irish Times* generally.

As reflected by the large scale of the DES press releases (see Figure 10.1 above), media correspondents internationally (Davis, 2000) and in Ireland note the vast increase in public relations agencies operating in the education sphere, as they receive

> a constant stream of press releases [...] they ring you up to say that they are sending you a press release, then they ring you up to say 'did you get the press release?' And then they ring you up to say 'do you need any more information?' and 'are you going to use it?'
>
> (education correspondent, national newspaper)

Education leaders likewise speak about the escalating public relations aspect of their role.

> I would see marketing becoming more and more prevalent and people are looking for PR opportunities and more or less running their

> schools using the media [...] I suppose you avail of opportunities of taking part in projects, inviting a photographer [...] just getting the message out there.
>
> (Conor, male principal, Scoil Derravaragh primary level school)

School principals are very conscious of the external economic implications of this publicity work and acknowledge its impact on school planning and resources.

> There's a marketing side in it in the sense that we are in competition with other schools and if you don't go out and market, then you don't get the pupils so you can't keep the teachers.
>
> (Niamh, female principal, Scoil Comeragh second level school)

Education interest groups also acknowledge that the media is an increasingly important tool in their efforts to influence government and public opinion (Baker, 2000), as we explore later in the case of trade unions. As McNamara notes, 'Media consultancy and grooming services extend beyond the political and financial elites. It [has] became common for the spokespersons of lobby and voluntary activist groups to take courses in handling the media' (2005: 4–5). Media researchers acknowledge the complexity of this media-politics intersection (Street, 2001), highlighting the need for a critical interrogation of media texts, the production processes and the media profession.

## Media and rising levels of performativity

In a time of intense media competition, the high circulation rates gained by education supplements, stories about school or college performance and league tables give a significant sales boost for newspapers. The publication of league tables causes enormous tensions for journalists, educators and parents as they balance criticisms of its crude performativity measures with demands for information and comparisons. Educational leaders describe how media and league tables impact on perceptions of schools as they fight to ensure that their school is not seen as 'dumping ground for children, you know [...]. The kids who come here get good results' (Brendan, male principal, Scoil Errigal second level school). Journalists admit culpability in this performativity drive as they have been central in promoting the publication of annual school listings and examination tables, acknowledging that 'anything which compares schools; league tables are huge for us in terms of readership, huge, anything that compares school is a big circulation builder' (education correspondent, national newspaper). They highlight the tensions inherent in league tables, acknowledging that

> [t]hey are inaccurate because you get the information from the colleges in different ways [...] I saw the downside of how they affect schools negatively and put pressure on schools to go higher up the league table and I think that is not a good idea for schools obviously. But having said all of that, there is a demand for it and when we do a supplement on league tables, they sell very well.
>
> (education correspondent, national newspaper)

Such coverage highlights the complexity of performativity for education, with fears that

> we have allowed the language of business and commerce to infiltrate all aspects of life with words such as inputs, outputs, products, strategic management initiatives. Everything nowadays has to be measured and if you don't measure up you are branded a failure. We have to get away from the use of such language in education.
>
> (*Irish Times*, 3 September 2005)

The tensions are evident in the newsroom negotiation between an education correspondent and news editors over the complex story of teachers' performance.

> News editors and subeditors don't like the phrase 'underperforming teachers', it's too bloody long [...] they prefer a nice catchy one like 'bad teachers'. I was told by one of my bosses that this [story] is not going to work, [he asked] 'how many teachers have been sacked over the last number of years?' and as it happens very few but that there has been a mechanism to get them out on early retirement. That mechanism has now been closed off, so this new arrangement is the only way to get rid of an underperforming teacher. So they [news editors] want to push the story and I say 'no you can't push it that far', and this is all done under time constraints and time pressure.
>
> (education correspondent, national newspaper)

This pressured atmosphere leaves very little space for deeper analysis or dialogic resolution of the issues. Media framing of stories fails to engage in structural analysis and offers 'quick fixes [...] as a panacea for society's ills' (Gerstl-Pepin, 2002: 50). Consequently, the impact of performativity in education is left unexplored by the tendency of media and government to 'oversimplify complex issues, the tendency to want to assign blame and the tendency to neglect what is important in the longer-term' (Levin, 2004: 77–8).

## Representation of teacher unions in Irish media

Teacher trade unions in Ireland are perceived as having 'solid institutional clout, insofar as they permeated every parish in Ireland, every political party in Ireland, every cultural, sporting and recreational body' (Mulvey cited in Cunningham, 2009: 217). They are seen as an active and well-organized power bloc, located in the decision-making nexus with a 'strong tradition of partnership between teacher unions, managerial bodies, parents and the Department of Education and Science' (Devine, 2010: 2). The unions offer a complex critique of state policies in their media and website publicity. They emphasize the public contribution of education and provide a sustained defense of the education profession. As discussed earlier, this has enabled Irish unions to offer a strong counter-voice to new managerialism that is aligned with opinions of school managers (many of whom are also union members). Teacher unions' role as a lobbying group for their members is clearly identified in their campaign objectives on issues such as curriculum reform, class size, teacher pay and conditions, special needs and disadvantage. Trade unions have maintained their powerful status in the Irish education field and have remained as consistent sources for media producers, in a long-established reciprocal relationship of trust.

Media play an important role in the public and political campaigns of the unions, but one that is embedded in a wider strategy that acknowledges

> the easiest thing to do is to get a headline, you know with a story, and the hardest thing is to make progress on the issues. I mean media is just one element that can be useful in bringing something forward but you have to keep your relationship with the Department of Education, both the permanent staff and the political officials as well so that you can actually make progress on it.
>
> (press officer, teacher union)

Media filter trade union stories and press releases through campaign coverage as State, trade unions and other interest groups engage in a battle for hearts and minds of the public. Much of this campaign coverage is dominated by the *Irish Times* newspaper that focuses on policy issues and the comparative status of different education groups as it is 'essentially a political paper, trying to find out what the background is to policy and policy generation' (education correspondent, national newspaper). As Bourdieu (1998b: 4) notes, journalists 'are more interested in the tactics of politics than in substance'.

While the general relationship between State and trade unions gains most media attention, teacher unions do differ from each other in terms of their media strategy and education objectives. At times, unions co-opt the State's knowledge economy discourse to support their objectives, arguing for the necessity of greater investment in the education system 'if we are serious about our ambitions to be successful in the knowledge era' (INTO press release, 14 May 2005). This re-interpretation of the knowledge economy discourse aligns teacher unions with the government's agenda, albeit to achieve very different objectives. It reveals their sense of the media – and policy – game, as they use State discourses to achieve their own ends (Bourdieu, 1998b).

There is a danger that this co-opting of the logic of performativity can have contradictory results, naturalizing inequality by aligning specific problems with schools, teachers or pedagogical approaches rather than critiquing underlying socio-economic issues (Stack, 2007: 107). It can reiterate the blame game rather than encouraging structural reform of the educational system. Many trade unions offer a strong critique of the growth of neo-liberal influences across education, highlighting the class inequalities that permeate the educational system which leave 'participation from lower socio-economic groups [as] the key challenge in the sector today' (*TUI News*, February 2006). They argue against oppositional framing where the 'dialectic of pitching private against public services is being fostered. That will only lead to an Ireland devoted to greed' (ASTI president's address to ASTI Congress, 2006: 13).

## Media representation of the relationship between State and trade unions

Newspapers compare the relative status of teacher unions with each other and the State during times of crisis ('flash' incidents such as the introduction of WSE) and 'colour pieces' that compare the performance of different trade unions. The seasonal calender of education events covered by Irish media includes the trade union conferences at Easter, school examination results (Junior and Leaving Certificate) and school openings in September. These events occur at quieter times in the media calender (when other key sources of news – political system and judicacy – are closed for holidays), guaranteeing widespread coverage for education issues. Many of these colour pieces analyse the relative status and influence of different education actors, identifying who holds 'respect from senior officials [...] and access to the corridors of power' to give unions considerable negotiating power with the DES (*Irish Times*, 29 March 2005).

The similar professional and class background between teachers and politicians is also noteworthy, given that 23 per cent of Irish parliamentary political representatives come from a teaching background.[6] While this homogeneity in background has not been explored in details in Ireland, preliminary 'data nevertheless suggest considerable informal ties between politics and the media' (Corcoran, 2004: 39). The State's dominant role is further consolidated by its position as a primary source of advertising and public relations in the Irish media (McNamara, 2005) that mirrors international patterns where government PR offices have become a dominant source of news (Davis, 2000).

This public relations machine is combined with the focus on personality politics which gives a leading position to the Minister of Education and Skills in media stories. This 'mediaization' of politics personalizes governance systems, focusing on political personalities and topical issues rather than systemic analysis of political structures (Fairclough, 2000: 3). An education news correspondent notes 'the person who can really generate education stories more than anybody else is the Minister for Education'. This focus on the personalities in politics reflects the general rise of personality politics and a celebrity culture (Dayan and Katz, 1992), as evidenced by a

> creeping tabloid mentality in newspapers in general. I mean the media in general have changed in that they have become more obsessed with celebrity and personalities than issues over the past few years and I think all the media, including our own, are guilty or certainly following that trend.
>
> (education correspondent, national newspaper)

The media's reproductive and disciplinary power is apparent in its capacity to define 'which knowledge (and audience) is of most worth, and in doing so sets up the conditions for certain 'truth claims' and 'regimes of truth' to circulate' (Stack, 2007: 102). Newspaper commentary illustrates the complex discourses that these 'regimes of truth' reveal. For example, the Irish teacher union campaigns against performativity and the publication of WSE in 2006. The unions argue that WSE reveal 'a focus on bureaucracy, on paperwork rather than the real business of engaging with our students is underway. I fail to see how this will serve the students' (ASTI president's address to Annual Convention, 2006). Other unions similarly reject government proposals for benchmarking and performance assessment of teaching staff, contending that it 'undermines collegiality and demotivates professionals [...] chang[ing] the governance of schools from the collegiate to the industrial/managerial model' (*TUI News*, May 2006). Tensions in the relationship between unions and government as filtered through the media highlight these key relations of discursive power, where State and trade unions use media to promote their 'truths'.

## Educators in the news: Bit players, local voices and managing news

The relative powerlessness of educators is clearly evident in their appearance 'in fairly arbitrary, non-purposive ways as 'bit players' in the combination of news, features, opinion, gossip and entertainment that constitutes the contemporary newspaper' (Rowe and Brass, 2008: 684). Educators are often located as named individuals – principals or teachers – to support or legitimate a general point made in the article.

> In a trembling voice 27-year-old <u>name of teacher</u> described 'hourly verbal abuse' and regular physical abuse 'or worse' in her school which she categorised as '100 per cent disadvantaged'. 'I put out fires, I break up fights and I handle irate students and parents on my own,' she told delegates. 'I spend hours writing incident reports and they are all filed. I don't want more reports. I want immediate change.'
>
> (*Irish Times*, 19 April 2006)

This evidence of 'footing' (Goffman, 1979) where journalists report another person's views rather than asserting their own enables them to 'present and endorse an opinion while at the same time create a distance from it' (Macmillan, 2002: 34). It disempowers educators into 'bit parts' as they illustrate commentary rather than being active participants in the co-creation of news. This positions educators and students as 'outside' voices within their own stories and reinforces the 'long-standing fatalism amongst [...] educationalists about the quality of education coverage in news media' (Warmington and Murphy, 2008: 286).

Specific issues arise for educators on a local level as they seek to manage media coverage. Demands from local newspapers and radio to schools for commentary about local issues have increased dramatically and 'every school, we'll say from Christmas onward, is looking to market themselves, everything they are doing to make sure it gets to the local papers, that there are photographs, all the reports, all this kind of thing gets in' (Macdara, male assessor, Scoil Neagh primary level school). Educational leaders struggle to manage these new tasks and turn to their unions for media training, especially in response to critical incidents in the school where they can support

> the principal teacher [...] to handle local media mainly but some in some cases national media [...] giving them an emergency plan, a statement to give to journalists, what to say and what not to say, and fielding some of the general questions around it. I mean basically what journalists want, I suppose it's understanding how the media works, I mean they all have deadlines and they all need some sort of a comment, and once they get that they're gone. But so many people, and it's perfectly understandable in a critical situation where a principal is trying to deal with twenty other things before the media.
>
> (press officer, teacher union)

## Impact on the working lives and identities of educational leaders

Educational leaders spoke about the impact of these media and publicity demands on their work practices. The growing consumerist ideology in Irish education is evident in competition for student enrolment, parents' attention, and funding. Principals acknowledged the 'marketing PR side to it [...] you're involved in this local community thing but that's also part of your marketing and keeping contacts with the local schools, networking' (Niamh, female principal, Scoil Comeragh second level school). These demands match the new managerialist discourse where 'education is regarded as a commodity; the school as a value-adding production unit; the headteacher as chief executive and managing director; the parents as consumers' (Grace, 1995: 21). Following a marketing logic, educational leaders emphasize the unique selling points of their institution, in some cases the academic achievement of their students, the caring ethos of the school or 'getting our team photos into the newspapers' (Maeve, female principal, Scoil Nephin second level school).

This can build an escalating sense of 'amorphous pressures and expectations of change' that is funnelled through the media from a myriad of sources including parental expectations, media representations and competition between schools (Blackmore and Thorpe, 2003: 579). This was not only between schools but also driven by demand from parents who are more proactive in seeking the best education possible for their children (Lynch and Moran, 2006; Ball, 2003b). Educators were concerned about the impact of marketization, league tables and ranking systems. They feared that these evaluative systems were not giving credit to the holistic aspects of education, especially the moral and caring aspects of education as compared to academic results or publication rates (Lynch, 2006; Devine et al., 2010). This was located within a sense of unbounded change and unrealistic expectations (Stack, 2007; Macmillan, 2002).

> Schools are regularly blamed for everything from littering to obesity to teenage pregnancy. In loco parentis they may be, but how much parenting can we really expect our schools to do? Some issues continually make the headlines – exam results, suicide, binge drinking, eating disorders, obesity – and each is attacked in isolation [...]. We never grapple with the deeper questions.
>
> (*Irish Times*, 11 October 2005)

Schools are caught in a performativity bind where the problems that they are expected to solve are beyond their remit and so they are 'always-already "failing"' (Blackmore and Thorpe, 2003: 587).

Consequently, image management and self-representation becomes an increasingly important part of educational leadership as leaders have to continually present a positive sense of identity for their school and their own leadership (Blackmore and Thorpe, 2003). School principals have 'to give over and above but unless they have it in themselves to give that, the whole thing will grind to a halt' (Lorcan, male assessor, Scoil Sperrin second level school). As explored earlier, this involves 'crafting an elastic self' capable of stretching to the multiple demands of the role. Part of this stretching is impelled by media, as their stories about education subtly impact on the way that educational leaders make sense of their professional lives and identities. The *Irish Times* report on how

> one of the greatest difficulties for principals and deputy principals is dealing with the growing notion of education as a commodity.

> Massive student support for the website ratemyteachers.ie suggests that many students view teachers in the same way as they view restaurants or film actors – as service providers who had better deliver the goods to their consumers or put up with public critique. Parents, in their own way, reflect the same attitude as they clamour for league tables and the publication of Whole School Evaluation reports.
>
> (*Irish Times*, 11 October 2005)

This sense of ceaseless demands results in schools being expected to solve societal woes, as public concerns about society and education are conflated. Educators become trapped in a 'failure' cycle of problems that is beyond their means to address (Blackmore and Thorpe, 2003; Levin, 2004). This elasticity of work expectations and the conflation of public/education concerns creates enormous strain as

> [e]motions of guilt and depression, feeling overburdened and swamped sat alongside the energy and buzz these senior appointees experienced in their roles as they 'managed their insides'.
>
> (Devine et al., 2010: 7)

It reveals the hegemonic tensions as demands for performativity and managerial efficiency impacts negatively on teachers' working lives. The 'long hours' culture and toughness of leadership roles in new managerial discourses parallels the media's taste for melodramatic imagery, as seen in Thomson et al. (2002) analysis of Australian media coverage of educational leadership as an extreme sport or Mockler's analysis of teachers as 'victim' (2004). This conflation of new managerialist and media imagery of educational leadership as an unendingly tough job results in the sense of hopelessness and fatalism on the part of educators and media audiences.

This sense of apathy and powerlessness is damaging, especially where the public relations forces of State, teacher unions and other groups are increasingly dominating media discourses and thereby quietening educators, parents and students' voices in this process (Blackmore and Thorpe, 2003: 584–5). There is a general silencing of the moral commitment to education and developmental rewards of working with learners that is evident throughout interviews with senior managers (Lynch et al., 2006; Grummell et al., 2009a; Devine et al., 2010). Educators spoke about the 'ethical and moral sense' to their work with students; 'this really strong vocational aspect to teaching [...] a sense of pride and a vocational aspect of what you do as a teacher that makes you want to do the best you can for the kids and for the school' (Muiris, male assessor, Scoil Derg, primary level school). There is an evident need to nurture this developmental and caring ethos of education in the face of this growing sense of powerlessness.

## Conclusion: Mediating impact of news discourses

This analysis of media coverage reveals the struggle over representations of education by the central actors (State, trade unions and educators) as they compete to define education in a rapidly changing Ireland. Ideological trends of performativity and competition intersect with media production practices to reinforce a dominant discourse of neo-liberalism that pervades media and public thinking about education. As Blackmore and Thorpe (2003: 580) remind us, the 'media in the privileging of some discourses and not others, media/tes policy'. This is evident in the groups that have remained silent throughout this analysis reflecting their lack of voice in the public sphere – children and young people's voices are rarely heard in public domains including education (Devine, 2003). Individual voices of students tend to remain unheard and invisible in the media aside from general stories about examination results, students awards or student misbehaviour.

A range of other education actors have also been neglected in this analysis including parents and community groups, educational management and leadership groups, school trusteeships, business and other public groups. This reflects their arbitrary and piecemeal coverage by the media whereas the State and unions, along with the Catholic Church, have consistently dominated education coverage in Irish media. Consequently, these former groups are rendered silent by the media; their concerns represented primarily through the dominant voices of State, unions and church. The implications of this marginalization require further analysis and research. Otherwise, the symbolic power of the media will continue to position its dominant representations as universal and self-evident truths (Wilkinson and Blackmore, 2008: 127). This neglects the agenda-setting power of the media production processes that locate certain powerful actors as news sources. It also highlights questions about the representative and democratic power of the media as it privileges the dominant voices of the State, media and education interest groups rather than the experiences of those active in the field.

This chapter has examined how the hegemonic power of the media operates as the rhythm of media production results in a complicit relationship between news sources and journalists. Both parties co-operate in the creation of educational stories in customary ways (based on media tradecraft) rather than explicit agenda and decision-making. This is allied with the tendency to translate complex education issues in 'readily consumable form' (Warmington and Murphy, 2004: 289), which the audience will recognize. The rapid publication cycle and consequent reliance on sources familiar with these processes results in control over media representations of education remaining outside of the scope of the students and educators at the heart of education. The pressured atmosphere of the pressroom leaves very little space for deeper analysis or dialogic resolution of the issues. Consequently, media coverage tends to 'oversimplify complex issues [...] assign blame and [...] neglect what is important in the longer-term' (Levin, 2004: 277–8). It reiterates a blame game rather than encouraging structural reform or critique.

Educators acknowledged the growing consumerism in Irish education, evident in competition for student enrolments, parents' attention and funding drives. Educational leaders spoke about increased marketing demands from their school and media requests for them to act as a local school spokesperson. Image management and self-representation becomes an increasingly important part of educational leadership as they have to continually present a sense of identity for their school and their own leadership, as explored in the earlier chapters. This creates enormous strain on school leaders and educators which is exasperated by the unbounded nature of media coverage and its conflation of societal and education concerns. There is a general silencing of the moral commitment to education and developmental rewards of working with learners, as apathy and powerlessness dominates. The public relations forces of government and managerial bodies are in danger of drowning out the educators, students and community that are at the heart of education.

# Notes

## 1 New Managerialism as a Political Project: The Irish Case

1. The term 'new managerialism' is sometimes referred to as 'new public service management' (NPM) in the literature.
2. 'We have labeled as a "spirit of capitalism" the ideology that justifies people's commitment to capitalism, and which renders this commitment attractive' (Boltanksi and Chiapello, 2005a: 162).
3. Farrell and Morris do observe however that professional occupations vary greatly in the power and control over their own occupational group within and between countries depending on the size and level of organizational bureaucracy, the strength of professional collectivization through associations and whether the professional is growing numerically.
4. Recent institutional changes in education have led to many, at least formally, similar new demands on teachers and schools across Europe (Johannessen et al., 2002; Rinne, 2000). For instance, head teachers have been given more responsibility for financial management, schools are obliged to develop their own curriculum and strategy within national frameworks, teachers are required to plan, document and evaluate their work and schools are urged to cooperate intensively with parents and other partners (Simola, 2005; Simola and Hakala, 2001; Webb et al., 2004a, 2004b).
5. Indebtedness in the 1980s was exacerbated by a number of interlocking factors, including declining growth, the global oil crisis, and a clientelist political system that was driven by populism. The removing of tax (rates) on land and most forms of property in 1977 by the Fianna Fáil Party in an attempt to win the general election (which they did win in a landslide victory) was the clearest example of how one of the most important forms of tax revenue for the state was removed with nothing to replace it.
6. See http://www.cpa.ie/publications/catalogue.htm for a list of publications from the Combat Poverty Agency, accessed 16 March 2012.
7. The website of Forfás (Ireland's policy advisory board for enterprise, trade, science, technology and innovation) has a long list of publications highlighting the government drive towards aligning education with the market. See http://www.forfas.ie/publication/, accessed 16 March 2012.
8. To say that the neo-liberal perspective glorifies the market and denigrates the State is not to deny the need that markets have for strong legislative and regulatory protections to protect commercial interests and legitimate market practices (Olssen, 1996; Apple, 2001). However, if international institutions (such as the European Union) and agreements (such as the General Agreement on Trade and Services) can override state actors in determining the regulatory environment for capitalist interests then the role of the nation-state is compromised in terms of its regulatory powers. While major capitalist states can and do exercise influence over the international regulatory environment for capitalism, the role of small states is severely limited.

The observation by economists that Ireland is one of the most 'open economies' in the world is merely a euphemism for stating that, as a nation-state, Ireland (and similarly small states) has very little control over the global trading environment in which it has to operate.

9. The actual adjusted wage share of the total economy, as a percentage of GDP, at factor cost per person employed, fell from 71.2 per cent in 1981–90 to 54 per cent in 2001–7 (Allen, 2010: Table 1).
10. The *Public Service Management Act,* 1997, Section 9 (1) makes it clear how responsibility could be devolved but power would remain centralized. The assignment of responsibility in respect of function 9 is as follows: (1) The assignment of the responsibility for the performance of functions to officers or to a grade or grades of officer of a Department or a Scheduled Office shall include a requirement, where deemed appropriate to the assignment, that the officer to whom the assignment is made shall (a) provide policy advice in relation to the subject-matter of the assignment and related matters; (b) achieve the outputs specified in the assignment; (c) assume responsibility for the statutory schemes or programmes specified in the assignment; (d) assume responsibility for the delivery of quality services in respect of the area of the assignment; (e) ensure that the expenditure made in respect of the area of the assignment accords with the purpose for which the expenditure was chargeable to the appropriation account of the Department or Scheduled Office and that value for money is obtained and (f) perform, on behalf of the Secretary General of the Department or Head of the Scheduled Office, functions in respect of appointments, performance and discipline of personnel in the area of the assignment, other than dismissals, that are the responsibility of the aforesaid Secretary General or Head pursuant to *section 4 (1)(h)*. (2) An officer of a Department or Scheduled Office to whom the responsibility for the performance of functions has been assigned shall be accountable for the performance of those functions to the Secretary General of the Department or Head of the Scheduled Office, as the case may be, and to such other officers (if any) as may be specified under the assignment.
11. Ireland's industrial relations framework was dominated by Social Partnership agreements between government, employers and trade unions for a 20-year period from 1987 to the financial banking crisis of 2008. In return for wage restraint across the public and private sector over a defined period of years, centralized bargaining on wage rates took place within the partnership framework. These agreements were strongly influenced by the public sector unions as the Irish Congress of Trade Unions is dominated by public sector unions and its sub-body, the Public Services Committee, plays a powerful role in determining working conditions and wages (Cradden, 2007: 176). Through this framework senior civil servants negotiated significant wage increases for themselves when public and private sector salaries were benchmarked by the PSBB (Public Service Benchmarking Body) which first reported in 2002.
12. There are many examples of teachers and educators who have used their educational backgrounds to enter business. Among the best known of these are the personnel involved in setting up the for-profit business sectors of education including Hibernia College of Education (Sean Rowland) and the Institute of Education (founder Raymond Kearns). In 2008 Sean Rowland who founded Hibernia was named Irish entrepreneur of the year.

13. Global wealth managers Merrill Lynch have recognized this and have defined education as a service that presented one of the major new opportunities for investors in profit terms (Moe et al., 1999). The rise of influential and financially endowed social movements in the United States to promote for-profit higher education (there are hundreds of for-profit colleges and universities in the United States) is a clear indication that for-profit trading in higher education is well underway (Morey, 2004). The largest of the for-profit universities, the University of Phoenix in Arizona, is trading for over 30 years and has 400,000 students. See http://www.phoenix.edu/students.html, accessed 16 March 2012.
14. Education may be defined as a marketable or tradable service but it remains also a basic human right enshrined in Article 24 of the *Universal Declaration of Human Rights*, Article 14 of the *International Covenant on Economic, Social and Cultural Rights* (ICESCR) and Article 42 of the *Irish Constitution*. Education is indispensable for realizing other rights, as well as enabling people to overcome social disadvantages. It plays a particularly important role in building the capacities of vulnerable people to defend and protect themselves from the abuse of power. It also has an intrinsic value for the development of the individuals, enhancing their capabilities, choices and freedoms. And it enables people to access employment and to develop their capacities as citizens in politics, culture and personal life. Apart from being a personal good, education is also a public good as it enriches cultural, social, political and economic life generally.
15. It now notes on its website that it is the largest single provider of primary school teachers annually. See http://hiberniacollege.com/schoolofeducation/h-dip-in-arts-in-primary-education/, accessed 20 September 2011. It exceeds the two large primary teacher education colleges, St. Patrick's College Drumcondra and Mary Immaculate College, Limerick, in annual output.
16. Changes to Whole School Evaluation (WSE) over time have led to the inclusion of parents' and students' evaluations as part of the WSE reports.
17. This had been a practice prior to political independence (under the Education Act, 1878, there was payment by results until it was abolished in 1924) and the memory of it was invoked to remind the public how detrimental it was not only for teachers but also for children.
18. Since 2003–4, WSE has been phased into primary and post-primary schools. It aims to improve schools and complements school inspections. The WSE has been developed using a partnership approach and it is designed to allow the whole school community to participate in the evaluation; affirm good practice in schools and provide advice and support; ensure school accountability by providing reliable data on the operation of the school; enable teachers and schools to use the evaluation criteria for school self-review and provide information to contribute to development of educational policies. The WSE evaluates schools under the headings of management, planning, curriculum provision, learning and teaching and support for students. The WSE process includes pre-evaluation meetings with staff and management, meeting with parents' association, school and classroom visits, preparation of a draft report, post-inspection meetings with staff and management, finalization of the WSE report and issue of report to school. For information, see website http://www.citizensinformation.ie/en/education/primary_and_post_primary_education/teachers_and_schools/schools_inspectorate.html, accessed 5 May 2011.

19. According to the Central Statistics Office, 61 per cent of teachers belonged to a trade union in 2009. CSO summary accessed through http://www.rte.ie/news/2010/0325/union.pdf, accessed 16 March 2012. However, as this 61 per cent figure would include many temporary and newly qualified teachers who would only have part-time hours, it does not reflect the actual union membership of permanently employed teachers, where almost all would be unionised.
20. See http://manyeyes.alphaworks.ibm.com/manyeyes/visualizations/occupations-of-tds-in-30th-dail/, accessed 16 March 2012.
21. See http://www.independent.ie/lifestyle/education/latest-news/teachers-still-top-of-class-for-31st-dail-representation-2560128.html, accessed 16 March 2012.
22. Academics in the 15 Institutes of Technology are represented generally by the Teachers Union of Ireland which is a powerful union (operating as one of the two big unions at second level as well), and this does place staff in these colleges in a strong negotiating position. IFUT (the Irish Federation of University Teachers) is the main union at third level for academics. However, academics in a number of universities and other colleges of higher education are part of SIPTU (the services, industrial and professional union) the largest union in the State. Library, technical, administrative and service staff in the various higher education colleges are also represented by different unions.
23. The joint conference of the Irish Universities Association (IUA) and the Irish Business and Employers Confederation (IBEC), 'Careering Towards the Knowledge Society: Are Business & Academia Geared Up to Provide a Future for High Level Researchers in Ireland?' Wednesday, 30 November 2005, DCU, is an example of the new kind of alliance the universities are developing with business interests. In the research field the links are well established: the Intel, 4th Level Ventures and the CRANN project are an example of this trend. Science Foundation Ireland (funded by the Irish taxpayer) has contributed €10 million to a new *Centre for Science, Engineering and Technology* (CSET) entitled the *Centre for Research on Adaptive Nanostructures and Nanodevices* (CRANN) in TCD, with partners in UCD and UCC (announced Jan. 2004). Intel Ireland is CRANN's main industry partner; it allocated four Intel staff members to CRANN where they have a five-year contract as researchers-in-residence at a cost of €2.9 million to Intel. While the collaboration was identified by TCD Provost John Hegarty as one which will help push TCD to the forefront of worldwide innovative research (Trinity Online Gazette), Intel is quite explicit about the corporate interests served by the partnership: 'By building technical leadership and research capability in Intel Ireland staff, CRANN allows Intel Ireland to add value to its existing operations while also demonstrating strategic value to Intel Corporation. CRANN enables Intel Ireland to explore niche scientific research in Ireland, which will allow the company to look towards Ireland for future Intel research initiatives' http://www.intel.com/ireland/about/pressroom/2004/january/011204ir.htm, accessed 17 May 2004.

## 2 The Culture of Governance in Irish Education

1. The Rules of National Schools were promulgated by the Department in 1965 and have been amended on a number of occasions since. The rules are

comprehensive in dealing with all aspects of the running of national schools, but do not have a legislative basis. Nonetheless, they are adhered by state-funded national school in the country. Rule 68 stipulates that'*[o]f all the parts of a school curriculum Religious Instruction is by far the most important, as its subject-matter, God's honour and service, includes the proper use of all man's faculties and affords the most powerful inducements to their proper use. Religious Instruction is, therefore, a fundamental part of the school course, and a religious spirit should inform and vivify the whole work of the school'*. The integrated curriculum is given statutory footing in section 15(2)(b) of the Education Act 1998 which states that'[a] *board shall perform the functions conferred on it and on a school by this Act and in carrying out its functions the board shall – do so in accordance with the policies determined by the Minister from time to time, uphold, and be accountable to the patron for so upholding, the characteristic spirit of the school as determined by the cultural, educational, moral, religious, social, linguistic and spiritual values and traditions which inform and are characteristic of the objectives and conduct of the school'*.

2. Section 37 of the Employment Equality Act, allows religious, medical or educational organizations to maintain their religious ethos, or prevent their religious ethos from being undermined. Discriminating in hiring a person(s) who could undermine this ethos is not illegal under Section 37. The Irish Congress of Trade Unions and other teacher unions oppose this clause.
3. New layers of school governance are now being developed at primary level to accommodate the increasing diversity that exists, to include Educate Together schools and most recently the community national schools under the patronage of the Vocational Education Committees. However, Devine (2011) notes that the increasing diversification of school 'choice' at primary level risks copper-fastening a segregated approach to education and especially the creation of 'immigrant' schools in large urban centres. An absence of debate over 'choice' is evident however with little public acknowledgement over the classed, raced and gendered dynamics which permeate the capacity to make and exercise such choice.
4. This did not hold true for primary (national) schools in most rural areas for a number of reasons. The most important reason was that most schools known as 'National' Schools were not planned by the Catholic Church but were set up as multidenominational co-educational institutions by the British government in 1831. They were set up for a variety of political (to control dissent and resistance) and cultural (Anglicization) reasons. They became denominational over time due to the staunch opposition of the Catholic Church in the late nineteenth century to the multi-denominational system (Coolahan, 1981: 3–38).
5. While relatively equal numbers of girls and boys are in single sex schools at primary level, significantly more girls are in single sex schools at second level, 33 per cent of boys and 43 per cent of girls.
6. Education Act 1998, Section 15(1).
7. In recent decades, bodies other than churches have been recognized as patrons. The patron of a multi-denominational school may be the board of trustees of the school or Educate Together, the limited company that acts as the representative organization of multi-denominational schools throughout Ireland. The patron of an Irish-language school may be Foras Pátrúnachtana Scoileanna Lán Ghaeilge, which is a limited company set up

for that purpose. More recently, the Minister for Education established a new model of patronage whereby the Vocational Education Committee (effectively a local authority body) can act as a patron for a new primary school in a situation where a traditional patron was not available. Two such schools were established by 2011.

8. Average net emigration was 43,000 per annum between 1956 and 1961 (Lee, 1989: 359). This amounted to more than half the birth rate for those years (see Walsh, 1968).
9. In 2006 the UK built approximately 200,000 housing units for a population of some 60 million. In Ireland, there were over 93,419 housing units built in 2006 for a population of 4.2 million (source: data provided by the Department of the Environment to K. Lynch for her lecture to Pobal for the Realising Equality and Inclusion: Building Better Policy and Practice. Conference Dublin Croke Park Conference Centre 22 November 2007).
10. A presentation given to the Combat Poverty Conference titled 'Who Cares about Educational Inequality in Neo-Liberal Ireland?' Dublin, 25 June 2008 by Kathleen Lynch elicited a very negative response from some senior civil servants. She was accused of not understanding how the economy worked and of being 'too negative'.
11. The DES does not exercise control over those colleges that are run as businesses.
12. The principal functions of the HEA are to develop higher education, to assist in the coordination of state investment in higher education and to prepare investment proposals, allocate state funding for teaching and research and promote equality of opportunity and democratization of higher education.
13. Information from the Higher Education Authority. Accessed through http://www.hea.ie/en/AboutHEA, accessed 16 March 2012.
14. Information from: http://www.education.ie/home/home.jsp?maincat=&pcategory=40196&ecategory=40272§ionpage=12251&language=EN&link=link001&page=20&doc=27920, accessed 25 April 2005.
15. Data for 1993–4 for primary- and second-level and higher education are from Lynch (1999). Data for 2001–4 for primary and second level are from the Department of Education and Science/Skills SéSí Report (2007). Data for 2009–10 and 2010–11 for primary level are from the INTO (Irish National Teachers' Organisation Central Executive Committee report to Congress in 2010). Second level data are from the Department of Education and Skills' and were published on their website in September 2011.
16. Higher Education Data for 2006 are from the Institute of Public Administration Diary, January 2006; this applies to data for the universities alone, Table 2 and the higher education sector overall, Table 3.
17. We analysed the top decimal of posts at senior management level across all higher education colleges in 2006 as identified in the Institute of Public Administration Diary in January of that year. This includes senior posts from president/director, vice-presidents, deans, heads of faculty and directors.
18. The Irish Human Rights Commission expressed concern to the *UN Committee on the Rights of the Child* in May 2006 on the issue of lack of fully multi-denominational and non-denominational education in the State.

## 3 The Case Studies of Senior Appointments

1. One of the case studies was of a national body involved in planning educational policy in Ireland.
2. Teaching principalships are appointed to schools under a particular size whereby principals retain a teaching role as well as their leadership duties. Administrative principals are appointed to schools above a particular size and do not have a teaching role.
3. The great majority of Irish second level schools do not charge fees. There are a small number (less than 10%) of secondary schools that do charge fees and these are the most socially selective schools. However, as the teachers in these schools are funded by the State, fees are not meeting full economic costs; fees are a means of subsidising the school to hire extra teachers, and pay for a wide variety of extracurricular activities and other services.

## 4 The Selection and Appointment of Senior Managers in Ireland

1. The board of management in primary and second level schools appointed the selection boards for principal appointments. It should consist of two nominees of the trustees, two nominees of the board of management and one external assessor agreed by the board of management, while VEC selection board should consist of one VEC nominee, one educator and one personnel expert. Some assessors come from a panel established by the diocesan office, trusteeships or education office of schools. Many external assessors are former principals with experience of selection boards. The selection committee must have gender representation. VEC schools must seek the approval of the VEC before appointing the board. Higher education selection boards usually consist of internal and external members with relevant managerial, academic or technical expertise. The director or president of the institution (or nominee) usually sits on senior management boards. There should be gender representation and all members should receive appropriate training.
2. See Department of Education and Science Circulars 02/02 and 19/05 for details about role and appointment of principals at primary school level and Circulars 04/98 and 20/98 for second level school principalships.
3. See VEC Board of Management Handbook Section 8 and appendices of relevant DES circulars at: http://www.ivea.ie/publications/bom/bom_handbook.pdf, accessed 19 October 2011.
4. See Department of Education and Science circular no. 19/05 for details.
5. See http://www.esri.ie/research/research_areas/education/Remc/working_papers/Ireland_Country_Report.pdfhttp://www.esri.ie/research/research_areas/education/Remc/working_papers/Ireland_Country_Report.pdf, accessed 19 October 2011.
6. This application process is now shifting to a more formalized online application system using the public procurement website: www.publicjobs.ie, with rules on procedure and sample advertisement given on Department of Education and Science circular no. 19/05. Agreement on standardized

application forms for teaching post was reached in 2010 (see Primary Circular 0062/2008).

7. Details of the Freedom of Information Acts is available at: http://foi.gov.ie/, accessed 19 October 2011.
8. Details about the Employment Equality Act 1998 and Equality Act 2004 are available at: http://www.equality.ie/en/Information/, accessed 19 October 2011.

## 5 Assessing Applicants: The Care Rules

1. In the Irish welfare system, people who were unemployed were defined as being on 'unemployment assistance' or 'unemployment benefit' over many decades. Since 2006 they are classified as being 'job seekers'. They are no longer permitted to be economically inactive, even though there are few employment opportunities due to the financial (banking) crisis.
2. Men do care work and emotional work too but it is not equated with masculinity in the way it is with femininity and womanhood.
3. *I think therefore I am.*
4. Yet an analysis of the etymological roots of the word 'education' shows that it originated in the Latin verb *educare* (which means to nurture and to develop through care), rather than from the verb *educere* (which means to lead out).
5. The Netherlands is one of the exceptions having an educational programme on how to care although it has its limitations (tenDam and Volman, 1998).
6. What the REA model ignores is that a significant proportion of humanity is dependent for survival on the work and care of others at a given time, and every individual is at some time dependent. The daily reproduction of the self, from the inner to the outer sphere, involves work, the simple work of maintaining and nourishing the body, and mind and the more elaborate nurturing work of producing quality of life for oneself and others physically, socially, and emotionally. Neither the market nor the polity could function effectively without the infrastructure of love, care and solidarity; yet public spheres are free riders on care work, in the sense that most care work is done without remuneration (Fineman, 2004). Moreover, there is often no dividend or gain from high dependency care work (Kittay, 1999; Lynch et al., 2009).
7. Despite the moral opprobrium accorded increasingly to the educated person as one who is not only autonomous and rational but also market-oriented, consuming and calculatingly self-interested, the fact remains that a large part of humanity at any given time are not self-financing consumers, notably children, people who are very frail, unpaid carers, people with work-constraining disabilities and people who are ill. Many people are in no position to make active consumer choices due to the poverty of their resources, time and/or capacities. Moreover, while people are undoubtedly rational economic actors and consumers, neither their rationality nor their economic and consumer choices can be presumed to be devoid of relationality (Gilligan, 1982; 1995). For most of humanity, much of life is lived in a state of profound and deep interdependency and for some prolonged dependency (Kittay, 1999).
8. For a more detailed discussion of this point, see Lynch (2007).

9. The Study was funded by the Gender Equality Unit of the Department of Education and Science.
10. The eight primary school principals who participated in the study (men and women) ranged in age from 37 to 49 years of age. Five principals had children (one had one child and the remaining four had two or more children) and three principals had no children. Of the five who had children, three had young children and two had older children (teenage or adults). Three of the principals with children were women.

    The eight second level principals (men and women who participated in the case studies ranged in age from 38 to 54 years of age. Six principals had children and two principals had no children (one was a Catholic priest, the other was a woman). Only two principals had young children under the age of four years (one male and one female).

    Three male and four female senior post holders in higher education institutions were interviewed. These included two senior post holders in institutes of technology, three from the universities, one from a further education college and one from the Department of Education and Science (a statutory agency). The post holders were at a senior management level, representing heads of faculties or departments and heads of institutions. They ranged in age from early 40s to late 50s. Four senior post holders had children and three did not have (two men, one of whom was just recently married, and two women). Aside from the one male post holder who had a young child, the remaining senior post holders who had children had older children (in their late teens and twenties).
11. Both the Employment Equality Act (1998) and the Equal Status Acts (2000, 2004) in the Republic of Ireland prohibit discrimination on nine grounds: family status (which is defined in terms of care responsibilities), marital status, sexual orientation, gender, traveller status, ethnicity and race, religion, disability and age.

## 6 Leading Educators: The Emotional Work of Managing Identities

1. The use of the term 'pastoral care' by school principals was widespread; it draws heavily from religious language, especially Catholic education where the prefix 'pastoral' is use to qualify discussions on care.

## 8 The Careless Rules of the Game: Pregnancy, Child Care and Management

1. The senior managers we interviewed did not state that they had primary care responsibilities for parents who had care needs. It was not an issue that arose in any of the conversations when we discussed care demands. As all those interviewed were new appointees, and that most of the primary principals ranged in age from their late thirties to late forties in age, their parents were most likely not at that stage of life where they were in need of care supports. Although higher education senior managers were, on average, ten years older

than those in primary or second level, they did not mention care of parents as a care issue. Most higher education managers had migrated (in some cases, a number of times, between countries, and also within Ireland) from their place of birth; even if their parents needed care they may not have been in a position to do primary care work due to their geographical location.

2. As the majority of Irish schools are small by international standards, primary schools being especially small (the great majority of primary schools would have less than eight teachers and there was a significant number with two to four teachers in rural areas, where principals would also be teaching classes as well as running the school). There would be very few schools at second level with more than 1,000 students, many having 600 or less (DES, Statistical Report, 2005, also see http://www.education.ie/home/home.jsp?pcategory=10917&ecategory=12016&language=EN/, accessed 10 April 2012.
3. Another factor that could be considered is that different types of men enter teaching compared to those that enter higher education. But this is not researched. Certainly primary teaching, and second level teaching to a considerable degree, have a strong collegial dimension – given that most primary and second level teachers in Ireland work closely together in small schools as they are not driven by targets at individual level, they can and do work cooperatively in school planning and other activities. All school evaluation is school-based. They also live in their own communities in most cases especially in rural schools and towns, and are frequently actively involved in sporting and community associations, music and the arts, indeed they are often leaders in these. This is not true of higher education. To succeed in higher education, one is compelled to be very self-centred in one's work, especially in terms of meeting publication targets, funding expectations etc. It could be that the more care-oriented men and women enter teaching although this would need to be researched. Given that men in teaching move very quickly up the ranks to management posts, relative to women, however, it could also be that men see teaching as a route to management rather than being care-friendly – they know they will benefit from the glass elevator potential of being in a female-dominated profession.
4. This quote is from a university head who asked to talk with us about the study in 2011 as he had read some of the papers published by the authors.
5. Irish primary teachers have two months holidays in summer (July and August) while most second level teachers have three months holidays (June, July and August). In addition, all teachers have two weeks holidays at Christmas and a further two weeks holidays at Easter. There is a mid-term break of one week, both in the pre-Christmas term as well (generally at Hallow'een) and a one-week Spring break, generally in February, for both primary and second level schools.
6. Although women can and do have care responsibilities for ageing parents that men are less likely to have (Lynch et al., 2009), it is not an issue raised in this study.

## 9 New Managerialism, Carelessness and Gender

1. The powerful international players include the World Trade Organisation, the G20 comprising finance ministers and central bank governors from 19

of the most powerful economies and the EU. According to the IMF they contribute to 84.1 per cent and 82.2 per cent of the world's economic growth. It also includes the G8 which are the United States, Japan, Russia, Canada, Germany, EU, France, Germany, UK and Italy. The European Roundtable of Industrialists are powerful players in determining priorities at the EU level, and, within Ireland, the Irish Business and Employers Confederation (IBEC), the Irish Small and Median Enterprises Association (ISME) are also market players exercising growing influence over education.

2. The chairperson of UCD's Governing Authority from 2005 until the late 2000s was Mr. Kieran McGowan, the former head of the Industrial Development Authority and Chairman of CRH plc; the Higher Education Authority is chaired since 2010 by Mr Hennessy, Chairman and former Chief Executive of Ericsson Ireland. Business interests are also represented on the Board of SFI that manages science funding in Ireland.
3. They are also raced as the principals and heads are overwhelmingly white and Western European.
4. There are three main teacher unions in Ireland, the INTO represents primary teachers and both the ASTI and the TUI represent second-level teachers. However, the TUI also represents most lecturers in the Institutes of Technology Sector of Higher Education. The Irish Federation of University Teachers (IFUT) is the union representing most academic staff in universities although SITPU and IMPACT also represent academic staff in various colleges. Technical, administrative and service staff in universities and other colleges are also represented by a range of different unions including SIPTU and IMPACT.
5. There had been a deep divide in Church-run Catholic schools as noted in Chapter 2.
6. The educational philosophy of the Conference of Religious of Ireland (CORI) was and is 'inspired by the teaching and practice of Jesus, which, it believes, offers a genuine path to human growth and maturity. In line with this philosophy, CORI Education, like the whole Conference, stands with poor people and evaluates its orientations and formulates its policies and strategies from that perspective. (Conference of Religious of Ireland, Education Vision Statement http://www.cori.ie/education/missionstatement/, downloaded 15 October 2011).
7. See http://www.education.ie/home/home.jsp?pcategory=10917&ecategory=12016&language=EN/, accessed 29 August 2011.
8. The heads in UCD, NUIM, UCC had backgrounds in medical science; the head of NUIG had an engineering background; the head of UL was a mathematician and the head of DCU a scientist (biomedical diagnostics).
9. See http://archives.tcm.ie/irishexaminer/1999/02/26/bhead.htm/, accessed 2 February 1999.
10. Forfás is the agency that monitors the production of graduates and its relationship to skills. The agency produces regular reports on the outputs of education, focusing especially on how education is servicing the economy. See http://www.forfas.ie/media/egfsn110803-Monitoring_Skills_Supply_2011.pdf, accessed 16 March 2012.
11. Although there is new legislation governing transfer pricing being applied since January 2011, there is also a let-out clause 'a grandfather clause' that means the new rules do not apply where agreements were already entered

into prior to 1 July 2010. See http://download.pwc.com/ie/pubs/finance_bill_2010_transfer_pricing_1.pdf, accessed 16 March 2012.

12. In 1998, a number of academic women had their discrimination case against UCD taken up by the Equality Authority. This led to an Equality Audit of the University. Other universities also had gender equality cases against them in the late 1990s and early 2000s including Dublin City University and the University of Limerick.
13. By head counting we mean compiling and publishing data on the number of professorships etc., held by women in the universities, publishing data on promotions and keeping a general record of what is happening to staffing in gender, disability, ethnicity, age terms etc.

## 10 Framing Educational Agendas for Managers: The Role of the News Media

1. http://www.jnrs.ie/survey.htm, accessed: 10 July 2011.
2. The keywords used to select newspaper articles about education were: education/ leaders/ principal/ performance/ management/ leadership. Material included news stories, editorials and opinions and letters to the editors, written mainly by education correspondents, but also other journalists, members of the public; and press releases, news wires and interviews with a wide array of other educational and political actors.
3. An open coding system of analysis was adopted building up a coding tree from keywords identified through inductive reading of the text, categorizing and cross-checking relationships and patterns between codes (Corbin, 2007).
4. See details at: http://www.education.ie/home/home.jsp?maincat=&pcategory=10861&ecategory=10876§ionpage=12251&language=EN&link=link001&page=3&doc=52596, accessed 10 July 2011.
5. Media tradecraft is the store of rules, conventions and ways of working that journalists have built up through their professional experiences (Wetzel et al., 1994: 111). Tradecraft and a fluent sense of what is 'newsworthy' are important elements in locating the media profession as part of the creative industries (Ellis, 1982).
6. See http://www-958.ibm.com/software/data/cognos/manyeyes/visualizations/occupations-of-tds-in-30th-dail, accessed 17 October 2011.

# Bibliography


Acker, J. (1990). 'Hierarchies, Jobs, Bodies: A Theory of Gendered Organizations'. *Gender and Society*, 4, 139–58.

Acker, J. (2000). 'Gendered Contradictions in Organizational Equity Projects'. *Organization* 7, 625–32.

Acker, S. (1995). 'Carry on Caring: The Work of Women Teachers'. *British Journal of Sociology of Education*, 16, 21–36.

Acker, S. and Dillabough, J. (2007). 'Women "learning to labour" in the "male emporium": Exploring Gendered Work in Teacher Education'. *Gender and Education*, 19(3), 297–316.

Alexander, J., Giesen, B. and Mast, J. (2006). *Social Performance.* Cambridge: Cambridge University Press.

Allen, K. (1997). *Fianna Fáil and Irish Labour: 1926 to the Present.* London: Pluto.

Allen, K. (2000). *The Celtic Tiger: The Myth of Social Partnership in Ireland.* Manchester: Manchester University Press.

Allen, K. (2003). 'Neither Boston nor Berlin: Class Polarization and Neo-Liberalism in the Irish Republic'. In: C. Coulter and S. Coleman (eds) *The End of Irish History?: Critical Reflections on the Celtic Tiger.* Manchester: Manchester University Press.

Allen, K. (2007). *The Corporate Takeover of Ireland.* Dublin: Irish Academic Press.

Allen, K. (2010). 'The Trade Unions: From Partnership to Crisis'. *Irish Journal of Sociology*, 18(2), 22–37.

Allis, N. (2000). 'Transformational Leadership – Democratic or Despotic?' *Educational Management and Administration*, 28, 7–20.

Alvesson, M. and Billing, Y. D. (2009). *Understanding Gender and Organizations.* London: Sage.

Alvesson, M. and Willmott, H. (2002). 'Identity Regulation as Organizational Control: Producing the Appropriate Individual'. *Journal of Management Studies. Special Issue: Micro Strategy and Strategizing: Towards An Activity-Based View*, 39, 619–44.

Apple, M. W. (2001). *Educating the "Right" way.* New York: RoutledgeFalmer.

Apple, M. (2004). 'Creating Difference: Neo-Liberalism, Neo-Conservatism and the Politics of Educational Reform'. *Educational Policy*, 18, 12–44.

Archer, L. (2008). 'The New Neoliberal Subjects? Younger Academics' Constructions of Professional Identity'. *Journal of Educational Policy*, 23(3), 265–85.

Australian Council for Educational Research (ACER) (2007). 'OECD Improving School Leadership Activity – Australia: Country Background Report'. Canberra: Department of Education, Employment and Workplace Relations.

Bailyn, L. (2003). 'Academic Careers and Gender Equity: Lessons Learned from MIT'. *Gender, Work and Organization*, 10, 137–53.

Baker, J., Lynch, K., Cantillon, S. and Walsh, J. (2004). *Equality: From Theory to Action.* Basingstoke: Palgrave Macmillan.

Ball, K. and Wicks, D. (2002). 'Editorial: Power, Representation and Voice'. *Gender, Work and Organization*, 9, 239–43.

Ball, S. J. (2001). 'Performativities and Fabrications in Education and Economy: Towards the Performative Society'. In: D. Gleeson and C. Husbands (eds) *The Performing School*. London: RoutledgeFalmer.

Ball, S. J. (2003a). 'The Teacher's Soul and the Terrors of Performativity'. *Journal of Education Policy*, 18, 215–28.

Ball, S. (2003b). *Class Strategies and the Education Market: The Middle Classes and Social Advantage*. London: RoutledgeFalmer.

Ball, S. J. (2007). *Education PLC*. London: Routledge.

Ball, S. J., Dworkin, A. G. and Vryonides, M. (2010). 'Globalization and Education: Introduction'. *Current Sociology*, 58, 523–29.

Barty, K., Thomson, P., Blackmore, J. and Sachs, J. (2005). 'Unpacking the Issues: Researching the Shortage of School Principals in Two States in Australia'. *The Australian Educational Researcher*, 32, 1–18.

Baumann, Z. (1991). *Modernity and Ambivalence*. Cambridge: Polity Press.

Beck, J. and Young, M. (2005). 'The Assault on the Professions and the Restructuring of Academic and Professional Identities: A Bernsteinian Analysis'. *British Journal of Sociology of Education*, 26, 183–97.

Beck, U. (1999). *World Risk Society*. Cambridge: Polity.

Beck, U. (2006). *The Cosmopolitan Vision*. Cambridge: Polity.

Beck, U. (2010). *Risk Society: Towards a New Modernity*. London: Sage.

Bell, A. and Garrett, P. (1998). *Approaches to Media Discourse*. Blackwell: Oxford.

Benhabib, S. (1992). *Situating the Self*. Cambridge: Polity Press.

Billing, Y. D. (2011). 'Are Women in Management Victims of the Phantom of the Male Norm?' *Gender, Work and Organization*, 18, 298–317.

Billing, Y. D. and Alvesson, M. (2000). 'Questioning the Notion of Feminine Leadership. A Critical Perspective on the Gender Labelling of Leadership'. *Gender, Work and Organization*, 7(3), 144–57.

Blackmore, J. (2010). 'Policy, Practice and Purpose in the Field of Education: A Critical Review'. *Critical Studies in Education*, 51, 101–11.

Blackmore, J. and Sachs, J. (2003). 'Zealotry or Nostalgic Regret? Women Leaders in Technical and Further Education in Australia: Agents of Change, Entrepreneurial Educators or Corporate Citizens?' *Gender Work and Organisation*, 10(4), 478–503.

Blackmore, J. and Sachs, J. (2007). *Performing and Reforming Leaders: Gender, Educational Restructuring and Organizational Change*. New York: State of New York Press.

Blackmore, J., Thomson, P. and Barty, K. (2006). 'Principal Selection: Homosociability, the Search for Security and the Production of Normalized Principal Identities'. *Educational Management Administration Leadership*, 34, 297–317.

Blackmore, J. and Thorpe, S. (2003). 'Media/ting Change: The Print Media's Role in Mediating Education Policy in a Period of Radical Reform in Victoria, Australia'. *Journal of Education Policy*, 18(6), 577–95.

Boltanski, L. and Chiapello, E. (2005a). 'The New Spirit of Capitalism'. *International Journal of Politics, Culture, and Society*, 18, 161–88.

Boltanski, L. and Chiapello, E. (2005b). *The New Spirit of Capitalism*. London: Verso.

Bolton, S. (2001). 'Changing Faces: Nurses as Emotional Jugglers'. *Sociology of Health and Illness*, 23(1), 85–100.

Bourdieu, P. (1998a). *Practical Reason: On the Theory of Action*. Cambridge: Polity.

Bourdieu, P. (1998b). *On Television and Journalism*. London: Pluto Press.
Bourdieu, P. (1990). *The Logic of Practice*. Cambridge: Polity.
Bourdieu, P. and Passeron, J-C. (1977). *Reproduction in Education, Society and Culture*. London: Sage.
Brooking, K. (2003). 'Boards of Trustees' Selection Practices of Principals in New Zealand Primary Schools: Will the Future be Female?'. Paper presented at BERA conference 11–13 September, Edinburgh, pp. 1–13.
Brooking, K., Collins, G., Court, M. and O'Neill, J. (2003). 'Getting Below the Surface of the Principal Recruitment "Crisis" in New Zealand Primary Schools'. *Australian Journal of Education*, 47, 146–59.
Bush, T. (2009). 'Leadership Development and School Improvement: Contemporary Issues in Leadership Development'. *Educational Review*, 61(4), 375–89.
Bush, T. (2010). 'Editorial: The Significance of Leadership Theory'. *Educational Management Administration & Leadership*, 38(3), 226–70.
Bush, T., Bell, L. and Middlewood, D. (2010). *The Principles of Educational Leadership and Management* (second Edition). New York: Sage.
Butler, J. (1990). *Gender Trouble: Feminism and the Subversion of Identity*. New York: Routledge.
Butler, J. (2004). *Undoing Gender*. London: Routledge.
Caldwell, B. and Spinks, J. (1992). *Leading the Self-Managing School*. London: Falmer.
Caldwell, B. J. (2008). 'Reconceptualizing the Self-Managing School'. *Educational Management Administration & Leadership*, 36, 235–52.
Caldwell, B., Calnin, G. and Cahill, W. (2003). 'Mission Impossible? An International Analysis of Head Teacher/Principal Training'. In: W. Bennett, M. Crawford and M. Cartwright (eds) *Effective Educational Leadership*. London: Open University in assoc. with Paul Chapman Publishing.
Cantillon, S. (2008). 'Equality: Distribution, Poverty and Social Welfare'. In: J. O Hagan and C. Newman (eds) *The Economy of Ireland*. Ireland: Gill & Macmillan.
Carnegie Trust (2010). *Ireland: Carnegie Trust Report*. Dublin: Carnegie Trust.
Central Statistics Office (CSO) (2006). *Religion*. Government Publications Office.
Chandler, J., Barry, J. and Clark, H. (2002). 'Stressing Academe: The Wear and Tear of New Public Management'. *Human Relations*, 55, 1051–69.
Cherniss, C., Extein, M., Goleman, D. and Weissberg, D. (2006). 'Emotional Intelligence: What Does the Research Really Indicate?' *Educational Psychologist*, 41, 239–45.
Chubb, B. (1982). *The Government and Politics of Ireland*. California: Stanford University Press.
Clancy, Patrick (1995). 'Education in the Republic of Ireland: The Project of Modernity'. In P. Clancy, S. Drudy, K. Lynch and L. O'Dowd (eds) *Irish Society: Sociological Perspectives*. Dublin: Gill and Macmillan.
Clancy, P., O'Connor, N. and Dillon, K. (2010). *Mapping the Golden Circle*. Dublin: TASC.
Clarke, D. (1984). *Church and State*. Cork: Cork University Press.
Clarke, J. and Newman, J. (1997). *The Managerial State*. London: Sage.
Clarke, J., Gewritz, S. and McLaughlin, E. (2000). *New Managerialism New Welfare?* London: Sage.
Clayton, S., Bambra, C., Gosling, R., Povall, S., Misso, K. and Whitehead, M. (2011). 'Assembling the Evidence Jigsaw: Insights from a Systematic Review of

UK Studies of Individual-Focused Return to Work Initiatives for Disabled and Long-Term Ill People'. *BMC Public Health*, 11, 170–81.

Clegg, S. (1990). *Modern Organizations: Organization Studies in the Postmodern World*. London: Sage.

Clegg, S. (2006). 'The Problem of Agency in Feminism: A Critical Realist Approach'. *Gender and Education*, 18(3), 309–24.

Cliffe, J. (2011). 'Emotional Intelligence: A Study of Female Secondary School Headteachers'. *Educational Management Administration & Leadership*, 39, 205–18.

Coates, J. (1995). 'Language, Gender and Career'. In: S. Mills (ed.) *Language and Gender: Interdisciplinary Perspectives*. Harlow: Longman.

Cockburn, C. (1991). *In the Way of Women: Men's Resistance to Sex Equality in Organizations*. Basingstoke: Palgrave Macmillan.

Cohen, J. (2006). 'Social, Emotional, Ethical, and Academic Education: Creating a Climate for Learning, Participation in Democracy, and Well-Being'. *Harvard Educational Review*, 76, 201–37.

Coleman, M. (2001). 'Achievement Against the Odds: The Female Secondary Headteachers in England and Wales'. *School Leadership and Management*, 21, 75–100.

Coleman, M. (2003). 'Gender and the Orthodoxies of Leadership'. *School Leadership and Management*, 23, 325–39.

Coleman, M. (2007). 'Gender and Educational Leadership in England: A Comparison of Secondary Headteachers' Views Over Time'. *School Leadership & Management*, 27, 383–99.

Colling, S., Conner, L., McPherson, K., Midson, B. and Wilson, C. (2010). 'Learning to Be Leaders in Higher Education: What Helps or Hinders Women's Advancement as Leaders in Universities'. *Educational Management Administration & Leadership, January 2011*, 39(1), 44–62, first published on 8 December 2010.

Collins, N. (2007). 'The Public Service and Regulatory Reform'. In: N. Collins, T. Cradden and P. Butler (eds) *Modernising Irish Government: The Politics of Administrative Reform*. Dublin: Gill & Macmillan.

Collins, N. and Cradden, T. (2004). *Political Issues in Ireland Today*. Manchester: Manchester University Press.

Collins, N., Cradden, T. and Butler, P. (2007). *Modernising Irish Government: The Politics of Administrative Reform*. Dublin: Gill & Macmillan.

Collinson, D. L. (2003). 'Identities and Insecurities: Selves at Work'. *Organization*, 10, 527–47.

Collison, D. and Hearn, J. (eds) (2003). *Critical Studies on Men, Masculinities and Management*. London: Sage Publications.

Coltrane, S. and Galt, J. (2000). 'The History of Men's Caring'. In M. Harrington Meyer (ed.) *Care Work: Gender, Class and the Welfare State*. New York, London: Routledge.

Conference of Religious of Ireland (24 July 2009). Submission to the Review of the Process for Recognising Primary Schools. Available at: http://www.cori.ie/education/389-education (accessed 10 October 2011).

Connell, R. (1995). *Masculinities*. Cambridge, UK: Polity Press.

Connell, R. (1998). 'Masculinities and Globalization'. *Men and Masculinities*, 1(1), 3–23.

Connell, R. W. (2000). *The Men and the Boys*. Sydney: Allen & Unwin.

Connell, R. W. (2006). 'The Experience of Gender Change in Public Sector Organizations'. *Gender, Work and Organization*, 13(5), 435–52.

Connell, R. W. and Wood, J. (2005). 'Globalization and Business Masculinities'. *Men and Masculinities*, 7(4), 347–64.

Coolahan, J. (1981). *Irish Education: History and Structure*. Dublin: Institute of Public Administration.

Cooley, C. (1902). *Human Nature and the Social Order*. New York: Scribner.

Corbin, J. (2007). *Basics of Qualitative Research: Techniques and Procedures for Developing Grounded Theory* (third edition). Thousand Oaks: Sage.

Corcoran, M. (2004). 'The Political Preferences and Value Orientations of Irish Journalists'. *Irish Journal of Sociology*, 13(2), 23–42.

Coronel, J. M., Moreno, E. and Carrasco, M. J. (2010). 'Work-Family Conflicts and the Organizational Work Culture as Barriers to Women Educational Managers'. *Gender, Work and Organization*, 17, 219–39.

Corsun, D. and Costen, W. (2001). 'Is the Glass Ceiling Unbreakable? Habitus, Fields, and the Stalling of Women and Minorities in Management'. *Journal of Management Inquiry*, 10, 16–25.

Coulter, C. and Coleman, S. (eds) (2003). *The End of Irish History?: Critical Reflections on the Celtic Tiger*. Manchester: Manchester University Press.

Court, M. (2004). 'Talking Back to New Public Management Versions of Accountability in Education'. *Educational Management Administration & Leadership*, 32, 171–94.

Cradden, T. (2007). 'People Management: HRM in the Public Service'. In N. Collins, T. Cradden and P. Butler (2007). *Modernising Irish Government: The Politics of Administrative Reform*. Dublin: Gill & Macmillan.

Crawford, M. (2007). 'Rationality and Emotion in Primary School Leadership: An Exploration of Key Themes'. *Educational Review*, 59, 87–98.

Creemers, B. P. M. and Kyriakides, L. (2010). 'Using the Dynamic Model to Develop an Evidenced Based Theory Driven Approach to School Improvement'. *Irish Educational Studies*, 29(1), 5–25.

Crow, G. and Weindling, D. (2010). 'Learning to be Political: New English Headteachers' Roles'. *Educational Policy*, 24, 137–58.

Cunningham, J. (2009). *Unlikely Radicals: Irish Post Primary Teachers and the ASTI, 1909–2009*. Cork: Cork University Press.

Currie, J., Thiele, B. and Harris, P. (2000). Sacrifices in Greedy Universities: Are They Gendered?' *Gender and Education*, 12, 269–91.

Davies, B., Gottsche, M. and Bansel, P. (2006). 'The Rise and Fall of the Neo-Liberal University'. *European Journal of Education: Research, Development and Policies*, 41, 305.

Davies-Netzley, S. A. (1998). 'Women above the Glass Ceiling: Perceptions on Corporate Mobility and Strategies for Success'. *Gender and Society*, 12, 339–55.

Davis, A. (2000). 'Public Relations, News Production and Changing Patterns of Source Access in the British National Media'. *Media Culture Society*, 22(1), 39–59.

Day, C. (2005). 'Principals Who Sustain Success: Making a Difference in Schools in Challenging Circumstances'. *International Journal of Leadership in Education*, 8(4), 273–90.

Day, C., Kington, A., Stobart, G. and Sammons, P. (2006). 'The Personal and Professional Selves of Teachers: Stable and Unstable Identities'. *British Educational Research Journal*, 32, 601–16.

Day, C., Harris, A., Hadfield, M., Tolley, H. and Beresford, J. (2000). *Leading Schools in Times of Change*. Philadelphia: Open University Press Philadelphia.

Dayan, D. and Katz, E. (1992). *Media Events: The Live Broadcasting of History*. Massachusetts: Harvard University Press.

Deacon, D. (2007). 'Yesterday's Papers and Today's Technology: Digital Newspaper Archives and "Push Button" Content Analysis'. *European Journal of Communication*, 22(1), 5–25.

Deem, R. (2002). 'New Managerialism and the Management of UK Universities: The Manager-Academic'. In: S. Ketteridge, S. Marshall and F. Heather (eds) *The Effective Academic: A Handbook for Enhanced Academic Practice*. London: Kogan Page.

Deem, R. (2003). 'Gender, Organisational Cultures and the Practices of Manager Academics in UK Universities'. *Gender, Work and Organization*, 10, 239–59.

Deem, R. (2004). 'The Knowledge Worker, the Manager-Academic and the Contemporary UK University: New and Old Forms of Public Management?' *Financial Accountability & Management*, 20, 107–28.

Deem, R. (2007). 'Managing a Meritocracy or an Equitable Organisation? Senior Managers and Employees Views about Equal Opportunities Policies in UK Universities'. *Journal of Education Policy*, 22, 615–36.

Deem, R. and Johnson, R. (2003). 'Risking the University? Learning to be a Manager-Academic in UK Universities'. *Sociological Research Online*, 8(3). Available at: http://www.socresonline.org.uk/8/3/deem.html.

Deem, R. and Ozga, J. (2000). 'Transforming Post-Compulsory Education? Femocrats at Work in the Academy'. *Women's Studies International Forum*, 23, 153–66.

Deem, R., Ozga, J. T. and Prichard, C. (2000). 'Managing Further Education: Is It Still Men's Work Too?' *Journal of Further and Higher Education*, 11, 231–51.

Department of Education and Science (1995). 'Charting our Education Future'. White Paper on Education. Dublin: Stationery Office.

Department of Education and Science (2003). 'Appointments to Posts of Responsibility (circular 07/03)'. 1–33, Available at: http://www.education.ie/servlet/blobservlet/pc07_03.pdf (accessed 19 March 2012).

Department of Education and Science (2004a). 'Seniority of Primary Teachers (circular 02/04)'. Available at: http://www.gaelscoileanna.ie/assets/seniority-of-primary-teachers.pdf (accessed 19 March 2012).

Department of Education and Science (2004b). 'Regulations Governing the Appointment and Retention of Teachers in Primary Schools for the School Year 2004/05 (circular 15/05)'. Available at: www.into.ie/ROI/PrincipalTeachers/pc15_05.doc (accessed 19 March 2012).

Department of Education and Science (2004c). A Brief Description of the Irish Education System. Available at: http://www.most.ie/webreports/Fatima%20reports/School/dept_education_system04.pdf (accessed 19 March 2012).

Department of Education and Skills (DES) (2007). 'SéSí: Gender in Irish Education'. Dublin: Government Publications Office.

Department of Education and Skills (DES) (2009). 'Customer Service Action Plan 2009–2011 Revised'. Available at: http://www.education.ie/servlet/blobservlet/cs_action_plan_2009_2011.pdf (accessed 5 May 2011).

Department of Education and Skills (DES) (2010). 'Investing in Global Relationships: Ireland's International Education Strategy 2010–15'. Report of the High-Level Group on International Education to the Tánaiste and Minister for Education and Skills. Dublin: Government Publications. Available

at: http://www.merrionstreet.ie/wp-content/uploads/2010/09/GLOBAL-REPORT-Sept-20101.pdf (accessed 19 March 2012).
Department of Education and Skills (DES) (2011). 'National Strategy for Higher Education to 2030 – Report of the Strategy Group'. Report to Minister for Education and Science. Dublin: Department of Education and Skills.
Deutsch, F. M. (2007). 'Undoing Gender'. *Gender & Society*, 21, 106–27.
Devereux, E. (1998). *Devils and Angels: Television, Ideology and the Coverage of Poverty*. Luton: John Libbey Media/University of Luton Press.
Devine, D. (2003). *Children Power and Schooling: How Childhood is Structured in the Primary School*. Stoke -on-trent: Trentham.
Devine, D. (2011). *Immigration and Schooling in the Republic of Ireland – Making a Difference?* Manchester: Manchester University Press.
Devine, D., Grummell, B. and Lynch, K. (2011). 'Crafting the Elastic Self? Gender and Identities in Senior Appointments in Irish Education'. *Gender, Work and Organization*, 18, doi: 10.1111/j.1468-0432.2009.00513.x.
Dillabough, J.-A. and Acker, S. (2002). 'Globalisation, Women's Work and Teacher Education: A Cross-National Analysis'. *International Studies in the Sociology of Education*, 12, 227–60.
Dinham, S., Anderson, M., Caldwell, B. and Weldon, P. (2011). 'Breakthroughs in School Leadership Development in Australia'. *School Leadership and Development*, 31(2), 139–54.
Docking, J. (2000). *New Labour's Policies for Schools: Raising the Standard?* London: David Fulton.
Dodson, L. (2007). 'Wage-Poor Mothers and Moral Economy'. *Social Politics: International Studies in Gender, State & Society*, 14, 258–80.
Doran, M. (2010). 'Media Literacy and Social Activism: Participatory Research with St Michael's Estate Regeneration Team'. Ph.D. Thesis. School of Social Justice, University College Dublin.
Doring, A. (2002). 'Challenges to the Academic Role of Change Agent'. *Journal of Further and Higher Education*, 26, 139–48.
Drudy, S. (2006). 'Gender Differences in Entrance Patterns and Awards in Initial Teacher Education'. *Irish Educational Studies*, 25, 259–73.
Drudy, S. (2008). 'Gender Balance/Gender Bias: The Teaching Profession and the Impact of Feminisation'. *Gender and Education*, 20, 309–23.
Drudy, S. and Lynch, K. (1993). *Schools and Society in Ireland*. Dublin: Gill & Macmillan.
Drudy, S., Martin, M., Woods, M. and O'Flynn, J. (2005). *Men and the Classroom: Gender Imbalances in Teaching*. London: Routledge.
Eagly, A. and Carli, L. (2007). 'Women and the Labyrinth of Leadership'. *Harvard Business Review*, 65, 62–71.
Earley, P., Evans, J., Collarbone, P., Gold, A. and Halpin, D. (2002). *Establishing the Current State of School Leadership in England*. HMSO: DFES.
Ehrenreich, B. and Hochschild, A. R. (eds) (2002). *Global Women: Nannies, Maid and Sex Workers in the New Economy*. New York: Holt.
Esping-Andersen, G. (1990). *The Three Worlds of Welfare Capitalism*. Cambridge, UK: Polity/Princeton.
EUROSTAT (2010). *Science and Technology Graduates by Gender*. Available at: http://epp.eurostat.ec.europa.eu/tgm/table.do?tab=table&init=1&language=en&pcode=tsiir050&plugin=1 (accessed 19 March 2012).

Everett, J. (2002). 'Organisational Research and the Praxeology Of Pierre Bourdieu'. *Organisational Research Methods*, 5, 56–80.

Expert Group on Future Skills Needs (EGFSN) (2011). Statement of Activity 2010. Available at: http://www.skillsireland.ie/media/egfsn2110504-Statement_of_Activity_2010.pdf (accessed 5 May 2011).

Ezzy, D. (2002). *Qualitative Analysis – Practice and Innovation*. London: Routledge.

Fahey, T. (ed.) (1999). *Social Housing in Ireland: A Study of Success, Failure and Lessons Learned*. Dublin: Oak Press.

Fahey, T., Russell, H. and Whelan, C. (eds) (2007). *Best of Times? The Social Impact of the Celtic Tiger*. Dublin: Institute of Public Administration.

Fairclough, N. (1995). *Media Discourse*. London: Edward Arnold.

Fairclough, N. (2000). *New Labour, New Language*. London: Routledge.

Farrell, B. (ed.) (1984). *Communications and Community in Ireland*. Dublin: Mercier.

Farrell, B. (ed.) (1998). *Issues in Education: Changing Education, Changing Society*. Dublin: ASTI.

Farrell, C. M. and Morris, J. (2003). 'The Neo-Bureaucratic State: Professionals, Managers and Professional Managers in Schools, General Practices and Social Work'. *Organization-Interdisciplinary Journal of Organization Theory and Society*, 10, 129.

Fine, P., Sawahel, W. and Jarjour, M. (2009). 'Women No Longer the Second Sex'. *University World News* [Online]. Available at: http://www.universityworldnews.com/article.php?story=20091023110831548 (accessed 1 December 2010).

Fineman, M. (2004). *The Autonomy Myth: A Theory of Dependency*. New York: New Press.

Fineman, M. (2008). 'The Vulnerable Subject'. *Yale Journal of Law and Feminism*, 20, 1–24.

Finch, J. and Groves, D. (1983). *A Labour of Love: Women, Work, and Caring*. UK: Routledge & Kegan Paul.

Fink D. and Brayman, C. (2006). 'School Leadership Succession and the Challenges of Change'. *Educational Administration Quarterly*, 42, 62–89.

Fitzgerald, T. and Gunter, H. (2006). 'Teacher Leadership: A New Form of Managerialism?' *New Zealand Journal of Educational Leadership*, 21, 44–57.

Fleming, P. and Sewell, G. (2002). 'Looking for "The Good Soldier, Švejk": Alternative Modalities of Resistance in the Contemporary Workplace'. *Sociology*, 36(4), 857–73.

Fletcher, C., Boden, R., Kent, J. and Tinson, J. (2007). 'Performing Women: The Gendered Dimensions of the UK New Research Economy'. *Gender Work and Organisation*, 14(5), 433–53.

Fletcher, J. (2004). 'The Paradox of Postheroic Leadership: An Essay on Gender, Power and Transformational Change'. *The Leadership Quarterly*, 15, 647–61.

Fletcher-Campbell, F. (2003). 'Promotion to Middle Management: Some Practitioners' Perceptions'. *Educational Research*, 45, 1–15.

Folbre, N. (1994). *Who Pays for the Kids?: Gender and the Structures of Constraint*. London: Routledge.

Folbre, N. (2004). 'A Theory of the Misallocation of Time'. In: N. Folbre and M. E. Bittman (eds) *Family Time: The Social Organization of Care*. London: Routledge.

Folbre, N. and Bittman, M. (eds) (2004). *Family Time: The Social Organization of Care*. New York: Routledge.

Forfas (2004). 'Building Ireland's Knowledge Economy – The Irish Action Plan for Promoting Investment in R&D to 2010'. Report to the Interdepartmental Committee on Science, Technology and Innovation. Dublin: Forfas.

Forfás (2009). *Monitoring Ireland's Skills Supply – Trends in Education and Training Outputs 2009*. Available at: http://www.forfas.ie/publication/search.jsp?ft=/publications/2009/Title,4779,en.php (accessed 10 April 2012).

Forfás (2010). 'Bench Marking Ireland's Performance Report'. Dublin: Forfás.

Foucault. M. (1979). *Discipline and Punish: The Birth of the Prison.* New York: Vintage Books.

Foucault, M. (1980). *Michel Foucault: Power Knowledge.* Hertfordshire: Harvester Wheatsheaf.

Fraser, N. (2008). *Scales of Justice.* Cambridge: Polity Press.

Fraser, N. and Gordon, L. (1997). 'A Genealogy of "Dependency"'. In: N. Fraser, *Justice Interruptus: Critical Reflections on the 'Postsocialist' Condition.* New York: Routledge.

Frowe, I. (2005). 'Professional Trust'. *British Journal of Educational Studies*, 53, 34–53.

Furtner, M. R., Rauthmann, J. F. and Sachse, P. (2010). 'The Socio-Emotionally Intelligent Self-Leader: Examining Relations between Self-Leadership and Socio-Emotional Intelligence'. *Social Behavior & Personality: An International Journal*, 38, 1191–6.

Garfinkel, H. (1987). *Studies in Ethnomethodology.* Cambridge: Polity.

Garrett, P. M. (2008). 'How to Be Modern: New Labour's Neoliberal Modernity and the Change for Children Programme'. *British Journal of Social Work*, 38, 270–89.

Garvin, T. (2004). *Preventing the Future: Why was Ireland So Poor for So Long?* Dublin: Gill and Macmillan.

Gerstl-Pepin, C. (2002). 'Media (Mis)Representations of Education in the 2000 Presidential Election'. *Educational Policy*, 16 (37), 37–55.

Giddens, A. (1984). *The Constitution of Society – Outline of the Theory of Structuration.* Los Angeles: University of California Press.

Gilligan, C. (1982). *In a Different Voice: Psychological Theory and Women's Development.* Cambridge, MA: Harvard University Press.

Gilligan, C. (1995). 'Hearing the Difference: Theorizing Connection', *Hypatia*, 10, 120–7.

Giroux, H. A. (2002). 'Neoliberalism, Corporate Culture, and the Promise of Higher Education: The University as a Democratic Public Sphere'. *Harvard Educational Review*, 72, 1–31.

Gleeson, D. and Husbands, C. (eds) (2001). *The Performing School: Managing, Teaching and Learning in a Performance Culture.* London: RoutledgeFalmer.

Gleeson, D. and Knights, D. (2008). 'Reluctant Leaders: An Analysis of Middle Managers' Perceptions of Leadership in Further Education in England'. *Leadership*, 4, 49–72.

Gleeson, D. and Shain, F. (2003). 'Managing Ambiguity in Further Education'. In: W. Bennett, M. Crawford and M. Cartwright (eds) *Effective Educational Leadership.* London: Sage Publications.

Gleeson, J. (2010). *Curriculum in Context; Power, Partnership and Praxis in Ireland.* Bern: Peter Lang.

Gleeson, J. and ÓDonnabhain, D. (2009). 'Strategic Planning and Accountability in Irish Education'. *Irish Educational Studies*, 28, 27–46.

Goffman, E. (1961). *Encounters: Two Studies in the Sociology of Interaction.* Indianapolis: Bobbs-Merrill.

Goffman, E. (1971). *The Presentation of Self in Everyday Life*. Harmondsworth: Penguin.

Goffman, E. (1979). *Gender Advertisements*. London: Macmillan.

Goleman, D. (1995). *Emotional Intelligence*. London: Bloomsbury.

Goodley, D. (2011). 'Problematising Policy: Conceptions of 'Child', 'Disabled' and 'Parents' in Social Policy in England'. *International Journal of Inclusive Education*, 15, 71–85.

Gornick, J. and Meyers, M. (2003). *Families That Work*. New York: Russell Sage.

Government of Ireland (2009). *Report of the Special Group on Public Service Numbers and Expenditure Programmes* (McCarthy Report). Dublin: Government Publications Office.

Grace, G. (1995). *School Leadership: Beyond Education Management*. London: Falmer.

Grace, G. (2002). *Catholic Schools: Missions, Markets and Morality*. London: RoutledgeFalmer.

Grewal, D. and Salovey, P. (2005). 'Feeling Smart: The Science of Emotional Intelligence'. *American Scientist*, 93, 330–9.

Gronn, P. (2003). *The New Work of Educational Leaders: Changing Leadership Practice in an Era of School Reform*. London: Paul Chapman.

Gronn, P. and Lucey, K. (2006). 'Cloning Their Own: Aspirant Principals and the School-Based Selection Game'. *Australian Journal of Education*, 50, 102–21.

Gronn, P. and Rawlings-Sanaei, F. (2003). 'Principal Recruitment in a Climate of Leadership Disengagement'. *Australian Journal of Education*, 47, 172–85.

Grummell, B., Devine, D. and Lynch, K. (2009a). 'Appointing Senior Managers in Education: Homosociability, Local Logics and Authenticity in the Selection Process'. *Educational Management Administration and Leadership*, 37(3), 329–49.

Grummell, B., Devine, D. and Lynch, K. (2009b). 'The Care-Less Manager: Gender, Care and New Managerialism in Higher Education'. *Gender & Education*, 21, 191–208.

Guillaume, C. and Pochic, S. (2009). 'What Would You Sacrifice? Access to Top Management and the Work–Life Balance'. *Gender, Work and Organisation*, 16(1), 14–36.

Gunter, H. (2001). *Leaders and Leadership in Education*. London: Paul Chapman.

Gunter, H. and Fitztgerald, T. (2008). 'The Future of Leadership Research'. *School Leadership and Management*, 28(3), 261–79.

Habermas, J. (1987). *The Theory of Communicative Action, Vol 2: Lifeworld and System: A Critique of Functional Reason*. Boston: Beacon Press.

Hakim, C. (2000). *Work-Lifestyle Choices in the 21st Century*. New York: Oxford University Press.

Halford, S. and Leonard, P. (2001). *Gender, Power and Organisations*. New York: Palgrave Macmillan.

Hanlon, N. (2008). 'Masculinities and Affective Equality: Love Labour and Care Labour in Men's Lives'. Ph.D. Thesis, University College Dublin.

Hanlon, N. (2009). 'Masculine Caregiving Identities: An Exploratory Analysis'. In: K. Lynch, M. Lyons and J. Baker (eds) *Affective Equality: Who Cares?* London: Palgrave Macmillan.

Hanlon, N. and Lynch, K. (2011). 'Care-Free Masculinities in Ireland'. In: E. Ruspini, J. Hearn, B. Pease and K. Pringle (eds) *Men and Masculinities around the World: Transforming Men's Practices*. New York: Palgrave Macmillan.

Harley, S. (2003). 'Research Selectivity and Female Academics in the UK Universities: From Gentleman's Club and Barrack Yard to Smart Macho?' *Gender and Education*, 15(4): 377–92.

Hartley, D. (1999). 'Marketing and the Re-Enchantment of School Management'. *British Journal of Sociology of Education*, 20, 309.

Harvey, D. (2005). *A Brief History of Neoliberalism*. Oxford: Oxford University Press.

Hatcher, C. (2003). 'Refashioning a Passionate Manager: Gender at Work'. *Gender, Work and Organization*, 10, 391–411.

Held, V. (1995). 'The Meshing of Care and Justice'. *Hypatia: A Journal of Feminist Philosophy*, 10, 128–32.

Henry, M., Lingard, B., Rizvi, F. and Taylor, S. (2001). *The OECD: Globalisation and Education Policy*. Pergamon: Amsterdam and London.

Hey, V. and Bradford, S. (2004). 'The Return of the Repressed?: The Gender Politics of Emergent Forms of Professionalism in Education'. *Journal of Education Policy*, 19, 691–713.

Hill, D. (2005). 'Globalisation and Its Educational Discontents: Neoliberalisation and Its Impacts on Education Workers' Rights, Pay and Conditions'. *International Studies in Sociology of Education*, 15, 257–88.

Hobson, B. (ed.) (2000). *Gender and Citizenship in Transition*. London: Macmillan.

Hochschild, A. (1989). *The Second Shift: Working Parents and the Revolution at Home*. Harmondsworth, UK: Penguin.

Hojgaard, L. (2002). 'Tracing Differentiation in Gendered Leadership: An Analysis of Differences in Gender Composition in Top Management in Business, Politics and the Civil Service'. *Gender, Work and Organization*, 9, 15–37.

Holvino, E. (2010). 'Intersections: The Simultaneity of Race, Gender and Class in Organization Studies'. *Gender, Work and Organization*, 17, 248–77.

Horgan, J. (2001). *Irish Media: A Critical History since 1922*. London: Routledge.

Houtsonen, J., Czaplicka, M., Lindblad, S., Sohlberg, P. and Sugrue, C. (2010). 'Welfare State Restructuring in Education and Its National Refractions'. *Current Sociology*, 58, 597–622.

Huppatz, K. (2009). 'Reworking Bourdieu's "Capital": Feminine and Female Capitals in the Field of Paid Caring Work'. *Sociology*, 43, 45–66.

Inglis, T. (1987). *Moral Monopoly: Catholic Church in Modern Irish Society*. Dublin: Gill and Macmillan.

Inglis, T. (2008). *Global Ireland*. New York: Routledge.

INTO (Irish National Teacher's Organisation). 'Central Executive Committee Report 2009/10'. Dublin: INTO.

IRCHSS (Irish Research Council for the Humanities and Social Sciences) (2010). *Playing to Our Strengths: The Role of the Arts, Humanities and Social Sciences and Implications for Public Policy*. Dublin: Higher Education Authority and IRCHSS.

Irish Bishops Conference (2007). *Catholic Primary Schools*. Dublin: Veritas.

Irish Government (1965). 'Investment in Education'. Dublin: Stationery Office.

Jenkins, R. (2004). *Social Identity.* London: Routledge Taylor Francis.

Jennings, K. and Lomas, L. (2003). 'Implementing Performance Management for Headteachers in English Secondary Schools: A Case Study'. *Educational Management Administration and Leadership*, 31, 369.

Johannesson, I. A., Lindblad, S. and Simola, H. (2002). 'An Inevitable Progress? Educational Restructuring in Finland, Iceland and Sweden at the Turn of the Millennium'. *Scandinavian Journal of Educational Research*, 46(3), 325–39.

Jonasdottir, A. G. (1994). *Why Women are Oppressed.* Philadelphia: Temple University Press.

Kanter, R. (1977). *Men and Women of the Corporation.* New York: Basic Books.

Kennedy, K. Giblin, T. and McHugh, D. (1988). *The Economic Development of Ireland in the Twentieth Century.* London: Routledge.

Keogh, H. (2004). 'Adult Education in Ireland: The Implications of Developments at European Union level'. *The Adult Learner.* Dublin: AONTAS, 18–26.

Kirby, P. (2002). *The Celtic Tiger in Distress: Growth with Inequality in Ireland.* Basingstoke: Palgrave Macmillan.

Kirby, P., Gibbons, L. and M. Cronin (eds) (2002). *Reinventing Ireland: Culture, Society and the Global Economy.* London: Pluto Press.

Kirby, P. and Murphy, M. (2011). 'Globalisation and Models of State: Debates and Evidence from Ireland'. *New Political Economy*, 16(1), 19–39.

Kittay, E. F. (1999). *Love's Labor: Essays on Women, Equality, and Dependency.* New York: Routledge.

Knights, D. and Kerfoot, D. (2004). 'Between Representations and Subjectivity: Gender Binaries and the Politics of Organisational Transformation'. *Gender Work and Organisation*, 11(4), 430–54.

Knights, D. and Richards, W. (2003). 'Sex Discrimination in UK Academia'. *Gender, Work and Organization*, 10, 213–38.

Kondo, D. (1990). *Crafting Selves: Power, Gender and Discourse of Identity in a Japanese Workplace.* Chicago: University of Chicago Press.

Korpi, W. and Palme, J. (1998). 'The Paradox of Redistribution and Strategies of Equality: Welfare State Institutions, Inequality, and Poverty in the Western Countries'. *American Sociological Review*, 63, 661–87.

Lafferty, G. and Fleming, J. (2000). 'The Restructuring of Academic Work in Australia: Power, Management and Gender'. *British Journal of Sociology of Education*, 21, 257–67.

Lee, J. J. (1989). *Ireland, 1912–1985: Politics and Society.* Cambridge: Cambridge University Press.

Legerski, E. M. and Cornwall, M. (2010). 'Working-Class Job Loss, Gender, and the Negotiation of Household Labor'. *Gender and Society*, 24, 447–74.

Leonard, P. (2002). 'Organizing Gender? Looking at Metaphors as Frames of Meaning in Gender/Organizational Texts'. *Gender, Work and Organization*, 9, 60–80.

Levin, B. (2004). 'Media-Government Relations in Education'. *Journal of Education Policy*, 19(3), 271–83.

Lieberwitz, Risa (2007). 'University Science Research Funding: Privatizing Policy and Practice'. In: Paula E. Stephan and Ronald G. Ehrenberg (eds) *Science and the University.* Madison: University of Wisconsin Press.

Lingard, B., Hayes, D., Mills, M. and Christie, P. (2003). *Leading Learning: Making Hope Practical in Schools.* Maidenhead: Open University Press.

Lingard, B. (2003). 'Where to in Gender Policy in Education After Recuperative Masculinity Politics'. *International Journal of Inclusive Education*, 7(1), 33–56.

Linstead, A. and Thomas, R. T. (2002). '"What Do You Want from Me?" A Poststructuralist Feminist Reading of Middle Managers' Identities'. *Culture and Organization*, 8(1), 1–20.

Lister, R. (1997). *Citizenship: Feminist Perspectives*. Basingstoke: Palgrave Macmillan.

Lopes, P. N., Grewal, D., Kadis, J., Gall, M. and Salovey, P. (2006). 'Evidence that Emotional Intelligence is Related to Job Performance and Affect and Attitudes at Work'. *Psicothema*,18, 132–8.

Lord, L. A. and Preston, A. (2009). 'Understanding Leadership Experiences: The Need for Story Sharing and Feminist Literature as a Survival Manual for Leadership'. Available at: http://espace.library.curtin.edu.au:80/R?func=dbin-jump-full&local_base=gen01-era02&object_id=131410 (accessed 19 March 2012).

Lumby, J. (2009). 'Performativity and Identity: Mechanisms of Exclusion'. *Journal of Education Policy*, 24, 353–69.

Lynch, K. (1987). 'Dominant Ideologies in Irish Educational Thought: Consensualism, Essentialism and Meritocratic Individualism'. *Economic and Social Review*, 18, 101–22.

Lynch, K. (2006). 'Neo-Liberalism and Marketisation: The Implications for Higher Education'. *European Educational Research Journal*, 5(1), 1–17.

Lynch, K. (2007). 'Love Labour as a Distinct and Non-Commodifiable Form of Care Labour'. *The Sociological Review*, 55, 550–70.

Lynch, K. (2010). 'Carelessness: A Hidden Doxa of Higher Education'. *Arts and Humanities in Higher Education*, 9, 54–67.

Lynch, K. and Baker, J. (2005). 'Equality in Education: An Equality of Condition Perspective'. *Theory and Research in Education*, 3, 131–64.

Lynch, K., Baker, J. and Lyons, M. (2009). *Affective Equality: Love, Care and Injustice*. London: Palgrave Macmillan.

Lynch, K., Crean, M. and Moran, M. (2010). 'Equality and Social Justice: The University as a Site of Struggle'. In: M. Apple, S. J. Ball, and L. A. Gandin (ed.) *International Handbook of Sociology of Education*. New York: Routledge.

Lynch, K., Grummell, B., Devine, D. and Lyons, M. (2006). *Senior Appointments in Education: A Study of Management Culture and Its Gender Implications*. Dublin: Gender Equality Unit, Department of Education and Science.

Lynch, K., Lyons, M. and Cantillon, S. (2007). 'Breaking Silence: Educating Citizens for Love, Care and Solidarity'. *International Studies in Sociology of Education*, 17, 1–19.

Lynch, K. and Moran, M. (2006). 'Markets, Schools and the Convertibility of Economic Capital: The Complex Dynamics of Class Choice'. *British Journal of Sociology of Education*, 27, 221–35.

Lynch, K. and O'Riordan, C. (1998). 'Inequality in Higher Education: A Study of Class Barriers'. *British Journal of Sociology of Education*, 19, 445–78.

Lyon, D. and Woodward, A. E. (2004). 'Gender and Time at the Top: Cultural Constructions of Time in High-Level Careers and Homes'. *The European Journal of Women's Studies*, 11, 205–21.

Mackenzie Davey, K. (2008). 'Women's Accounts of Organizational Politics as a Gendering Process'. *Gender, Work and Organization*, 15, 650–71.

MacMillan, K. (2002). 'Narratives of Social Disruption: Education News in the British Tabloid Press'. *Discourse: Studies in the Cultural Politics of Education*, 23(1), 27–38.

Mahony, P., Hextall, I. and Menter, I. (2002). 'Threshold Assessment: Another Peculiarity of the English or More McDonaldization?' *International Studies in the Sociology of Education*, 12(2), 145–67.

Marginson, S. (2006). 'Dynamics of Global Competition in Higher Education'. *Higher Education*, 52, 1–39.

Martin, P. Y. (2006). 'Practising Gender at Work: Further Thoughts on Reflexivity'. *Gender, Work and Organization*, 13(3), 254–76.

Masschelein, J. and Simons, M. (2002). 'An Adequate Education in a Globalised World? A Note on Immunisation Against Being-Together'. *Journal of Philosophy of Education*, 36(4), 589–608.

Mawhinney, A. (2007). 'Freedom of Religion in the Irish Primary School System: A Failure to Protect Human Rights?' *Legal Studies*, 27, 379–403.

Mawhinney, A. (2009). *Freedom of Religion and Schools: The Case of Ireland.* Saarbrücken: VDM Verlag.

McDonnell, O. and O'Donovan, O. (2009). 'Private Health Insurance as a Technology of Solidarity? The Myth of 'Community' in Irish Healthcare Policy'. *Irish Journal of Sociology*, 17, 6–23.

McGauran, Anne Marie (2005). *Plus ca Change? The Gender Mainstreaming of the Irish National Development Plan.* Dublin: Trinity College, Policy Institute.

McGuinness, S. (2005). 'The Recruitment and Retention of School Principals: The View from Research'. The Challenge of Recruiting and Retaining School Leaders Conference, March 2005. Cork, Ireland.

Mclay, M. (2008). 'Headteacher Career Paths in UK Independent Secondary Coeducational Schools: Gender Issues'. *Educational Management Administration & Leadership*, 36, 353–72.

McNair, S. (1997). 'Is There a Crisis? Does It Matter?' In: R. Barnett and A. Griffin (eds) *The End of Knowledge in Higher Education.* London: Cassell.

McNamara, P. (2005). *The Case of Ireland: Adequate Information Management in Europe Project Report.* Available at: http://www.aim-project.net/uploads/media/Ireland.pdf (accessed 19 March 2012).

McNay, L. (1999). 'Subject, Psyche and Agency: The Work of Judith Butler'. *Theory Culture Society*, 16, 175.

McNay, L. (2007). *Against Recognition.* Cambridge: Polity Press.

McTavish, D and Miller, K.. (2009). 'Gender Balance in Leadership?: Reform and Modernization in the UK Further Education Sector'. *Educational Management Administration & Leadership*, 37, 350–65.

McSharry, R. and White, P. (2000). *The Making of the Celtic Tiger: The Inside Story of Ireland's Booming Economy.* Dublin: Mercier Press.

Mead, G. (1934). *Mind, Self, and Society*. Chicago: University of Chicago Press.

Meade, R. (2005). 'We Hate It Here, Please Let Us Stay! Irish Social Partnership and the Community/Voluntary Sector's Conflicted Experiences of Recognition'. *Critical Social Policy*, 25, 349–73.

Metcalfe, A. and Slaughter, S. (2008). 'The Differential Effects of Academic Capitalism on Women in the Academy'. In: J. Glazer-Raymo (ed.) *Unfinished Agendas: New and Continuing Gender Challenges in Higher Education*. Baltimore, NJ: John Hopkins' Press.

Metcalfe, B. and Linstead, A. (2003). 'Gendering Teamwork: Re-Writing the Feminine'. *Gender, Work and Organization*, 10, 94–119.

Moe, M., Bailey, K. and Lau, R. (1999). *The Book of Knowledge: Investing in the Growing Education and Training Industry*. Delaware: Merrill Lynch.

Moller, J. (2009). 'Learning to Share: A Vision of Leadership Practice'. *International Journal of Leadership in Education*, 12(3), 253–67.

Moorosi, P. (2010). 'South African Female Principals' Career Paths: Understanding the Gender Gap in Secondary School Management'. *Educational Management Administration & Leadership*, 38, 547–62.

Moreau, M. P., Osgood, J. and Halsall, A. (2007). 'Making Sense of the Glass Ceiling in Schools: An Exploration of Women Teachers' Discourses'. *Gender and Education*, 19, 237–53.

Morley, L. (2003). *Quality and Power in Higher Education*. Buckingham: Open University Press.

Morley, L. (2005). 'Opportunity or Exploitation? Women and Quality Assurance in Higher Education'. *Gender and Education*, 17, 411–29.

Mulcahy, D. G. (1981). *Curriculum & Policy in Irish Post-Primary Education*. Dublin: Institute of Public Administration.

Murphy, M. (2002). 'Social Partnership – Is It "The Only Game in Town"?' *Community Development Journal*, 37, 80–90.

Murphy, M. and Kirby, P. (2011). *Towards the Second Republic; Irish Capitalism in Crisis*. London: Pluto.

Neale, J. and Özkanli, O. (2010). 'Organisational Barriers for Women in Senior Management: A Comparison of Turkish and New Zealand Universities'. *Gender and Education*, 22, 547–63.

Newman, J. (1995). 'Gender and Cultural Change'. In: C. Itzin and J. Newman (eds) *Gender, Culture and Organizational Change: Putting Theory into Practice*. London: Routledge.

Newman, J. H. (1875). *The Idea of a University*. London: Longmans.

Ní Murchú, N. (1995). 'Newspaper Coverage of Industrial Relations in Irish Education: Teachers on Strike, 1918–1986'. Ph.D. thesis (unpublished). University College Dublin.

Noddings, N. (1984). *Caring: A Feminine Approach to Ethics & Moral Education*. London/Berkeley, CA: University of California Press.

Noddings, N. (2003). *Happiness and Education*. Cambridge: Cambridge University Press.

Nowotny, Helga, Scott, Peter and Gibbons, Michael (2003). '"Mode 2" Revisited: The New Production of Knowledge'. *Minerva*, 41, 179–94.

Nussbaum, M. C. (1995). 'Emotions and Women's Capabilities'. In: M. C. Nussbaum and J. Glover (eds) *Women, Culture, and Development: A Study of Human Capabilities*. Oxford: Oxford University Press.

Nussbaum, M. C. (2001). *Upheavals of Thought: The Intelligence of Emotions*. Cambridge: Cambridge University Press.

O'Brien, M. (2005). 'Mothers as Educational Workers: Mothers' Emotional Work at their Children's Transfer to Second-Level Schooling'. *Irish Educational Studies*, 24(2–3), 223–43.

O'Brien, M. (2007). 'Mothers' Emotional Care Work in Education and Its Moral Imperative'. *Gender and Education*, 19, 159–77.

O'Connor, P. (2006). 'Private Troubles, Public Issues: The Irish Sociological Imagination'. *Irish Journal of Sociology*, 15, 5–22.

O'Connor, P. (2007a). 'The Challenge of Gender in an Irish University Context' (paper accessed from author).

O'Connor, P. (2007b). 'The Elephant in the Corner: Gender and Policies related to Higher Education'. Conference on Women in Higher Education. Queens University Belfast, April 19th–20th 2007.

O'Connor, P. (2010a). 'Is Senior Management in Irish Universities Male-Dominated? What are the Implications?' *Irish Journal of Sociology*, 18, 1–21.

O'Connor, P. (2010b). 'Gender and Organisational Culture at Senior Management Level: Limits and Possibilities for Change?' In: J. Harford and C. Rush (eds) *Women and Higher Education in Ireland 1850–2010. Have Women Made a Difference?* Oxford: Peter Lang.

O'Connor, S. (1968). 'Post-Primary Education Now and in the Future'. *Studies*, 57, 233–49.

O'Hearn, D. (2003). 'Macroeconomic Policy in the Celtic Tiger: A Critical Assessment'. In: C. Coulter and S. Coleman (eds) *The End of Irish History*. Manchester: Manchester University Press.

O'Gorman, E. and Sugrue, C. (2007). 'Intercultural Education: Primary Challenges in Dublin 15'. Dublin: A report funded by the Social Inclusion Unit of the Department of Education and Science.

Ó Riain, S. (2006). 'Social Partnership as a Mode of Governance: Introduction to the Special Issue'. *Economic and Social Review*, 37, 3, 311–18.

O'Riain, S. and O'Connell, P. (2000). 'The Role of the State in Growth and Welfare'. In: B. Nolan, with P. O'Connell and C. T. Whelan (eds) *Bust to Boom? The Irish Experience of Growth and Inequality*. Dublin: Institute of Public Administration.

O'Sullivan, D. (1992). 'Shaping Educational Debate: A Case Study and an Interpretation'. *The Economic and Social Review*, 23, 423–38.

O'Sullivan, D. (2006). *Cultural Politics and Irish Education since the 1950s: Policy Paradigms and Power*. Dublin: Institute of Public Administration.

O'Toole, F. (2009). *Ship of Fools: How Stupidity and Corruption Sank the Celtic Tiger*. London: Faber & Faber.

OECD (1991). 'Reviews of National Policies for Education: Ireland'. Paris: OECD.

OECD (2004). *Review of National Policies for Education: Review of Higher Education in Ireland*. Paris: OECD.

OECD (2008). *Improving School Leadership: Volume 1 Policy and Practice*. Paris: OECD.

Olssen, M. (1996). 'In Defence of the Welfare State and Publicly Provided Education'. *Journal of Education Policy*, 11, 337–62.

Olssen, M. and Peters, M. A. (2005). 'Neoliberalism, Higher Education and the Knowledge Economy: From the Free Market to Knowledge Capitalism'. *Journal of Education Policy*, 20, 313–45.

Oplatka, I. and Tamir, V. (2009). '"I Don't Want to Be a School Head": Women Deputy Heads' Insightful Constructions of Career Advancement and Retention'. *Educational Management Administration & Leadership*, 37, 216–38.

Ozga, J. and Deem, R. (2000). 'Carrying the Burden of Transformation: The Experiences of Women Managers in UK Higher and Further Education'. *Discourse: Studies in the Cultural Politics of Education*, 12, 141–53.

Peters, M. (2005). 'The New Prudentialism in Education: Actuarial Rationality and the Entrepreneurial Self'. *Educational Theory*, 55, 123–37.

Peters, T. and Waterman, R. H. (1982). *In Search of Excellence.* New York: Harper Row.

Pettinger, L., Parry, J., Taylor, R. and Gluckmann, M. (eds) (2006). *A New Sociology of Work?* Oxford: Basil Blackwell.

Phelan, S. (2007). 'The Discourses of Neoliberal Hegemony: The Case of the Irish Republic'. *Critical Discourse Studies*, 4, 29–48.

Poggio, B. (2006). 'Editorial: Outline of a Theory of Gender Practices'. *Gender, Work and Organization*, 13(3), 225–32.

Pollitt, C. (2003). *The Essential Public Manager.* Buckingham and Philadelphia: Open University Press.

Power, M. (1999). *The Audit Society: Rituals of Verification.* Oxford: Oxford University Press.

Probert, B. (2005). 'I Just Didn't Fit in: Gender and Unequal Outcomes in Academic Careers'. *Gender, Work and Organization*, 12(1), 50–72.

Pullen, A. and Knights, D. (2007). 'Editorial: Undoing Gender: Organizing and Disorganizing Performance'. *Gender, Work and Organization*, 14(6), 504–11.

Pullen, A. and Simpson, R. (2009). 'Managing Difference in Feminized Work: Men, Otherness and Social Practice'. *Human Relations*, 62(4), 561–87.

Reason, P. (ed.) (1981). *Human Inquiry in Action: Developments in New Paradigm Research.* London: Sage.

Reay, D. and Ball, S. (2000). 'Essentials of Female Management: Women's Ways of Working in the Education Market-Place?' *Educational Administration Abstracts*, 28(2), 145–59.

Rinne, R. (2000). 'The Globalisation of Education: Finnish Education on the Doorstep of the New EU Millennium'. *Educational Review*, 52(2), 131–42.

Robertson, S. L., Bonal, X. and Dale, R. (2002). 'GATS and the Education Service Industry: The Politics of Scale and Global Reterritorialization'. *Comparative Education Review*, 46, 472–96.

Rose, N. (1989). *Governing the Soul: The Shaping of the Private Self.* London: Routledge.

Rose, N. (2001). *Governing the Soul.* Cambridge: Cambridge University Press.

Ross-Smith, A. and Huppatz, K. (2010). 'Management, Women and Gender Capital'. *Gender, Work and Organization*, 17(5), 547–66.

Rowe, D. and Brass, K. (2008). 'The Uses of Academic Knowledge: The University in the Media'. *Media Culture Society*, 30(5), 677–98.

Russell, H., O'Connell, P. and McGinty, F. (2009). 'The Impact of Flexible Working Arrangements on Work–Life Conflict and Work Pressure in Ireland'. *Gender, Work and Organisation*, 16(1), 73–97.

Rutherford, J. (2005). 'Cultural Studies in the Corporate University'. *Cultural Studies*, 19, 297–317.

Sachs, J. and Blackmore, J. (1998). 'You Never Show You Can't Cope: women in school leadership roles managing their emotions'. *Gender & Education*, 10(3), 265–79.

Savage, M. and Witz, A. (1992). *Gender and Bureaucracy.* Oxford: Blackwell.

Sayer, A. (2005). *The Moral Significance of Class.* Cambridge: Cambridge University Press.

Seay, S. E. (2010). 'A Comparison of Family Care Responsibilities of First-Generation and Non-First-Generation Female Administrators in the Academy'. *Educational Management Administration & Leadership*, 38, 563–77.

Sevenhuijsen, S. (1998). *Citizenship and the Ethics of Care: Feminist Considerations on Justice, Morality and Politics*. London: Routledge.

Shakeshaft, C. (2006). 'Gender and Educational Management'. In: C. Skelton, B. Francis and L. Smulyan (eds) *The SAGE Handbook of Gender and Education*. London: SAGE.

Shapira, T., Arar, K. and Azaiza, F. (2011). '"They Didn't Consider Me and No-One Even Took Me into Account": Female School Principals in the Arab Education System in Israel'. *Educational Management Administration & Leadership*, 39, 25–43.

Shows, C. and Gerstel, N. (2009). 'Fathering, Class and Gender'. *Gender and Society*, 23, 161–87.

Simkins, T. (2005). 'Leadership in Education: "What Works" or "What Makes Sense"?' *Educational Management Administration Leadership*, 33, 9–26.

Simola, H. (2005). 'The Finnish Miracle of PISA: Historical and Sociological Remarks on Teaching and Teacher Education'. *Comparative Education*, 41, 455–70.

Simola, H. and Hakala, K. (2001). 'Finnish School Professionals Talk about Educational Change'. In: S. Lindblad and T. S. Popkewitz (eds) *Listening to Education Actors on Governance and Social Integration and Exclusion, A Report from the EGSIE project, Uppsala Reports on Education 37*. Uppsala University.

Sinclair, A. (2009). 'Seducing Leadership: Stories of Leadership Development'. *Gender, Work and Organization*, 16, 266–84.

Skeggs, B. (1997). *Formations of Class and Gender: Becoming Respectable*. London: Sage.

Skelton, C. (2009). 'Failing to Get Men into Primary Teaching: A Feminist Critique'. *Journal of Education Policy*, 24, 39–54.

Sklair, L. (2001). *The Transnational Capitalist Class*. Oxford: Blackwell.

Slaughter, S. and Leslie, L. L. (2001). 'Expanding and Elaborating the Concept of Academic Capitalism'. *Organization*, 8(2), 154–61.

Sloan, M. M. (2010). 'Controlling Anger and Happiness at Work: An Examination of Gender Differences'. *Gender, Work and Organization*. DOI: 10.1111/j.1468-0432.2010.00518.x.

Smith, J. (2011). 'Agency and Female Teachers' Career Decisions: A Life History Study of 40 Women'. *Educational Management Administration & Leadership*, 39, 7–24.

Spillane, J. P. and Diamond, J. B. (2007). *Distributed Leadership in Practice*. New York: Teachers College Press.

Stack, M. (2007). 'Constructing "Common Sense" Policies for Schools: The Role of Journalists'. *International Journal of Leadership in Education*, 10(3), 247–64.

St. Aubyn, M., Pina, A., Garcia, F. and Pais, J. (2009). 'Study on the Efficiency and Effectiveness of Public Spending on Tertiary Education'. Available at: http://ec.europa.eu/economy_finance/publications/publication16267_en.pdf (accessed 10 May 2011).

Stefkovich, J. and Begley, P. T. (2007). 'Ethical School Leadership'. *Educational Management Administration and Leadership*, 35(2), 205–24.

Sternberg, R. J. (1998). 'Abilities as Forms of Developing Expertise'. *Educational Researcher*, 27(3), 11–20.

Sternberg, R. J. (2005). 'A Model of Educational Leadership: Wisdom, Intelligence, and Creativity, Synthesized'. *International Journal of Leadership in Education*, 8, 347–64.

Strain, M. (2009). 'Some Ethical and Cultural Implications of the Leadership "Turn" in Education: On the Distinction between Performance and Performativity'. *Educational Management Administration & Leadership*, 37, 67–84.

Street, J. (2001). *Mass Media, Politics and Democracy*. Hampshire: Palgrave Macmillan.

Sugrue, C. and Furlong, C. (2002). 'The Cosmologies of Irish Primary Principals' Identities: Between the Modern and the Postmodern?' *International Journal of Leadership in Education*, 5, 189–210.

Sugrue, C. (2004). *Curriculum and Ideology: Irish Experiences, International Perspectives*. Dublin: Liffey Press.

Sugrue, C. (2005). *Passionate Principalship: Learning from Life Histories of School Leaders*. London: RoutledgeFalmer.

Swan, E. (2008). 'You Make Me Feel like a Woman: Therapeutic Cultures and the Contagion of Femininity'. *Gender, Work and Organization*, 15, 88–107.

Teddlie, C. and Reynolds, D. (2002). *International Handbook of School Effectiveness Research*. London: Routledge.

Tett, L. and Riddell, S. (2009). 'Educators Responses to Policy Concerns about the Gender Balance of the Teaching Profession in Scotland'. *Journal of Education Policy*, 24, 477–93.

Thomas, R., Mills, A. J. and Helms Mills, J. (eds) (2004). *Identity Politics at Work: Resisting Gender, Gendering Resistance*. London: Routledge.

Thompson, B. (2007). 'Working Beyond the Glass Ceiling: Women Managers in Initial Teacher Training in England'. *Gender and Education*, 19, 339–52.

Thomson, P., Blackmore, J., Sachs, J. and Tregenza, K. (2002). 'High Stakes Principalship–Sleepness Nights, Heart Attacks and Sudden Death Accountabilities: Reading Media Representations of the US Principal Shortage'. Paper presented at Australian Association for Research in Education Conference, 1–5 December, Queensland.

Thornton, M. and Bricheno, P. (2000). 'Primary School Teachers' Careers in England and Wales: The Relationship between Gender, Role, Position and Promotion Aspirations'. *Pedagogy, Culture and Society*, 8, 187–206.

Thrupp, M. (2005). 'The National College for School Leadership: A Critique'. *Management in Education (Education Publishing Worldwide Ltd)*, 19(2), 13–19.

Thrupp, M. and Lupton, R. (2006). 'Taking School Contexts More Seriously: The Social Justice Challenge'. *British Journal of Educational Studies*, 54, 308–28.

Thrupp, M. and Lupton, R. (2011). 'Variations on a Middle Class Theme: English Primary Schools in Socially Advantaged Contexts'. *Journal of Education Policy*, 26, 289–312.

Thrupp, M. and Willmott, R. (2003). *Education Management in Managerialist Times: Beyond the Textual Apologists*. Buckingham: Open University Press.

Tilly, C. (1998). *Durable Inequality*. Berkeley, CA: University of California Press.

Titley, G. (2010). 'Ireland, Media and Civil Society'. In: N. Fenton, D. Freedman and T. Witschge (eds) *Protecting the News: Civil Society and the Media*. London: Leverhulme Media Research Centre, Carnegie UK Trust.

Tomas, M., Manuel Lavie, J., Del Mar Duran, M. and Guillamon, C. (2010). 'Women in Academic Administration at the University'. *Educational Management Administration & Leadership*, 38, 487–98.

Tomlinson, Sally (2008). 'Gifted, Talented and High Ability: Selection for Education in a One-Dimensional World'. *Oxford Review of Education*, 34(1), 59–74.

Tovey, Hilary and Share, Perry (2000). *A Sociology of Ireland.* Dublin: Gill and Macmillan.

Townsend, T. (2011). 'Changing Times: New Issues for School Leaders'. *School Leadership & Management,* 31(2), 91–2.

Toynbee, P. (2007). 'Re-Thinking Humanity in Care Work'. In: S. Bolton and M. Houlihan (eds) *Searching for the Human in Human Resource Management.* Basingstoke: Palgrave Macmillan.

Tronto, J. C. (1993). *Moral Boundaries: A Political Argument for an Ethic of Care.* New York: Routledge, Chapman and Hall.

UNESCO (19–20 July 2007). 2nd Regional Research Seminar for Latin America and the Caribbean. The UNESCO Forum on Higher Education, Research and Knowledge in collaboration with The Trinidad and Tobago National Commission for UNESCO and The Ministry of Science, Technology and Tertiary Education. Ballroom, Hilton Trinidad Conference Centre. Available at: http://portal.unesco.org/education/fr/files/53768/11841637425Paper-Neves.pdf/Paper-Neves.pdf (accessed 19 March 2012).

United Nations (1948). Universal Declaration of Human Rights. UNG Assembly http://www.un.org/en/documents/udhr/ (accessed 19 March 2012).

United States Government Accountability Office (GAO). (2010). 'For-Profit Colleges: Undercover Testing Finds Colleges Encouraged Fraud and Engaged in Deceptive and Questionable Marketing Practices'. Available at: http://www.gao.gov/new.items/d10948t.pdf (accessed June 2011).

Vandervoort, D. J. (2006). 'The Importance of Emotional Intelligence in Higher Education'. *Current Psychology,* 25, 4–7.

Walker, A. and Shuangye, C. (2007). 'Leader Authenticity in Intercultural School Contexts'. *Educational Management Administration and Leadership,* 35(2), 185–204.

Walkerdine, V. (2004). 'Neo Liberalism, Femininity and Choice'. Paper presented to the London School of Economics ESRC seminar series. Available at: www.lse.edu\collections\newfemininities\firstseminar.htm (accessed February 2009).

Walsh, B. M. (1968). 'Another Look at the Concept of Overpopulation2'. *Economic Development and Cultural Change,* 17(1), 95–8.

Warmington, P. and Murphy, R. (2004). 'Could Do Better? Media Depictions of UK Educational Assessment Results'. *Journal of Education Policy,* 19(3), 285–99.

Wang, T. (2005). 'Exploring Chinese Educators' Learning Experiences and Transnational Pedagogies'. *International Journal of Pedagogies and Learning,* 1(3), 44–69.

Webb, R. (2005). 'Leading Teaching and Learning in the Primary School: From "Educative Leadership" to "Pedagogical Leadership"'. *Educational Management Administration Leadership,* 33, 69–91.

Webb, R., Vulliamy, G., Hamalainen, S., Sarja, A., Kimonen, E. and Nevalainen, R. (2004). 'A Comparative Analysis of Primary Teacher Professionalism in England and Finland'. *Comparative Education,* 40, 83–107.

Weiner, G. (2008). 'Fast Policies, Fast Theories and Fast Lives: When Everything Becomes Performance'. *Discourse: Studies in the Cultural Politics of Education,* 29, 289–95.

West, C. and Zimmerman, D. (1987). 'Doing Gender'. *Gender and Society,* 1(2), 125–51.

Wetzel, D. C., Radtke, P. H. and Stern, H. W. (1994). *Instructional Effectiveness of Video Media.* New Jersey: Lawrence Erlbaum.

White, K., Carvalho, T. and Riordan, S. (2011). 'Gender, Power and Managerialism in Universities'. *Journal of Higher Education Policy & Management*, 33, 179–88.

Whitehead, S. ( 2001). 'Woman as Manager: A Seductive Ontology'. *Gender, Work and Organization*, 8, 84–107.

Whyte, J. H. (1984). *Church and State in Modern Ireland 1923–1979*. Dublin: Gill and Macmillan.

Wilkinson, J. and Blackmore, J. (2008). 'Re-Presenting Women and Leadership: A Methodological Journey'. *International Journal of Qualitative Studies in Education*, 21(2), 123–36.

Wilson, J., Marks, G., Noone, L. and Hamilton MacKenzie, J. (2010). 'Retaining a Foothold on the Slippery Paths of Academia: University Women, Indirect Discrimination, and the Academic Marketplace'. *Gender and Education*, 22, 535–45.

Wilson, V., Powney, J., Hall, S. and Davidson, J. (2011). 'Agency and Female Teachers' Career Decisions: A Life History Study of 40 Women'. *Educational Management Administration & Leadership*, 39, 7–24.

Wright, E. O. (2010). *Envisioning Real Utopias*. London: Verso.

Ybema, Y., Keenoy, R., Oswick, C., Bevergungen, A., Ellis, N. and Sabelis, I. (2009). 'Articulating Identities'. *Human Relations*, 62, 299.

Yuval-Davis, N. (1997). 'Women, Citizenship and Difference'. *Feminist Review*, 57, 4–27.

Zorn, D. and Boler, M. (2007). 'Rethinking Emotions and Educational Leadership'. *International Journal of Leadership in Education*, 10, 137–51.

# Index

Note: Page numbers followed by "*n*" refer to notes.